THE BRITISH
SHELL SHORTAGE
OF THE FIRST WORLD WAR

THE BRITISH
SHELL SHORTAGE
OF THE FIRST WORLD WAR

PHILLIP HARDING

FONTHILL

Fonthill Media Language Policy

Fonthill Media publishes in the international English language market. One language edition is published worldwide. As there are minor differences in spelling and presentation, especially with regard to American English and British English, a policy is necessary to define which form of English to use. The Fonthill Policy is to use the form of English used by the author. Phillip Harding was born and educated in England and now lives in Esssex, therefore British English has been adopted in this publication.

Fonthill Media Limited
Fonthill Media LLC
www.fonthillmedia.com
office@fonthillmedia.com

First published in the United Kingdom
And the United States of America 2015

British Library Cataloguing in Publication Data:
A catalogue record for this book is available from the British Library

ISBN: 978-1-78155-453-1

Printed and bound in Great Britain by CPI Group (UK) Ltd, Croydon, CR0 4YY

CONTENTS

Acknowledgements

My thanks to the staff at the Royal Green Jackets Museum for their help and to the members of The Rifles Living History Society. Both institutions do a wonderful job in ensuring that the riflemen of past times are remembered by the public.

Without the assistance of Tony Eden of Riflemen Tours I would never have found the battlefields. He has a wonderful ability of looking at a modern landscape and pointing out exactly where the trenches, emplacements, etc., were. He is a real mine of information and a man I would not hesitate to recommend to anyone who wishes to view the Flanders battlefields.

My thanks to Jennifer Brown of the Braintree District Museum (which holds the Crittall archive) who gave me access to the archive and arranged permission for me to include the photograph of the munition workers at the Crittall Factory.

I must thank my family who have put up with my single-mindedness in respect to my research and seemingly—to me anyway—never tire of listening to my interesting facts. I have lost count of the war cemeteries that I have dragged my long-suffering wife around, but without her support I would not have been able to produce this book.

We must remember those that fought, were wounded, and died in the First World War. As a nation, we must continue to show our respect, especially on Remembrance Sunday.

Thank you for reading this book.

Preface

The shortage of shells in the First World War became a scandal that rocked the British Government. It would be simple to attribute the cause of the 'shell scandal' to a mundane explanation such as a lack of munitions, but it was so much more than this.

The causes of the scandal are many and varied, but are rooted in the following: the Government's misunderstanding of the international conflict that would result in the First World War; the nation's unwillingness to become fully committed to the war until it had raged for almost three years; the control and over-regulation of industry by Civil Service mandarins; the censorship of the national media which was forced to portray success, despite the huge casualty lists that told the true story; and the political manoeuvrings in both Government and military circles, bordering upon the Machiavellian. All these factors were intricately linked to the shell scandal, and this book aims to examine them.

The shell shortage led to a battle of wills between the senior military figures of the day, with a catastrophic outcome being played out on the battlefield. I have used the battles of Neuve Chapelle and Aubers Ridge, and specifically the actions undertaken by the Rifle Brigade in those battles, to highlight what the munitions shortage meant to the soldiers on the ground. As John Buchan writes in *Nelson's History of the War*, 'The lesson was writ too plain to be missed. We must pay in shells or in human lives'.[1]

1

Guns, Shells, and Britain's Pre-War Munitions Industry

Since man first began propelling objects through the air in order to bring harm to an enemy, he has sought ever more inventive ways in which to send them quicker, farther, and more accurately. The First World War was the first war fought with modern weapons of mass destruction like high-explosive shells; such weapons were improved during the course of the war, purely to kill and injure more of the enemy. But it should also be remembered that September 1914 saw the 16th (The Queen's) Lancers of the 3rd Cavalry Brigade ride into battle carrying lances, much as they had done when the regiment was established in 1759.[2]

The main mechanized weapons at the beginning of the war were machine guns and artillery guns; it is these that caused the majority of the injuries and deaths, with rifle and machine-gun fire accounting for 35 per cent, and artillery fire accounting for in excess of 60 per cent of the casualties.[4]

Machine guns had been around for some time, but they were revolutionised by the mechanism that used the force of the recoil to extract the empty cartridge case while pushing a new round into the firing chamber. This mechanism had been designed between 1883 and 1885 in Hatton Garden, London, by Hiram Maxim, an American who had emigrated to Britain. Maxim formed a partnership with the steel entrepreneur Edward Vickers, and their joint-venture company was ultimately absorbed by the Vickers Company, which then created the British Vickers machine gun. The Germans created the *Maschinengewehr* (MG) 01, based on the Maxim and under licence to Vickers. This was developed into the MG08 in 1908, which became the German Army standard machine gun for the First World War.

Machine guns like the Vickers and MG08 are still often referred to as 'Maxims'. They could fire between 450 and 600 rounds per minute, and were accurately described as 'the concentrated essence of infantry', where a 3-second burst fired 15 rounds—enough to cut a man in half.[5]

Artillery is a class of weapons designed to launch projectiles beyond the range of small-arms fire and with higher destructive power. During the First World War, artillery pieces were divided into two types: field guns and howitzers. A field gun was intended for direct fire, with the target usually visible to the gunner. The howitzer, conversely, was intended to fire the projectile at a high angle at a target that was often not in the clear sight of the gunner. This needed a forward observation officer (FOO) to relay the target's coordinates and where the shell fell. The shell would be propelled along a trajectory at an angle dependent upon the distance to the target. For example, a 9.2-inch howitzer shell could have an apex of up to 8,000 feet.[5]

Shell Construction

The projectiles fired by the lighter field guns used an innovation called 'quick firing' or QF. This projectile contained within a single cartridge both the shell and the propellant in one unit. The design enabled a much higher rate of fire but was only suitable for lighter guns.

Similar to a bullet in a rifle, the brass cartridge contained within its base a primer that upon being struck by a firing pin exploded, sending a jet of flame into the cartridge case. Inside the cartridge case the propellant was ignited, and as the pressure built up, the shell was forced out of the neck of the cartridge and along the barrel towards the target, the rear of the cartridge would be expelled to be reused later.

The heavier breech-loading guns and howitzers required a separate shell which would be loaded first into the breech, followed by the propellant in combustible silk or shalloon bags; the cloth contained the explosive propellant and reduced the chance of the cordite being ignited from the heat of a previous charge.[6]

The shell is the aggressive part of the weapon that was fired from the barrel and designed to inflict damage to the enemy or to their defences. The two basic types of shell that are detailed here are those containing high-explosives, which detonated on contact or at a pre-set distance, and those containing shrapnel bullets, which were designed to explode above the heads of troops, scything them with their destructive lead balls. It was against the latter that the 'tin' or 'shrapnel' helmets were designed and issued in 1916 with an angled lip to protect the head from the projectiles falling from above. Previous to this, British troops wore cloth hats and the German's wore leather *pickelhelms,* each providing very limited protection from modern weapons.

The making of the shells was very technical; just the fuze[7] had over fifty parts that had to fit and work as accurately as a clock. The overall construction of shells involved the following:

> ...the metal trades, blast furnaces, steel works, iron and steel foundries, forges, stamps, drops and dyes, rolling mills, drawn rod and wireworks, and behind them, the colliery and the iron ore quarry. It required factories and these in turn require machinery—covered electrical plant, factory equipment and machine tools, engines, pumps, turbines, road and rail transport, boiler making and constructional engineering works.[8]

The 18-pdr field gun was the most common piece of artillery in the British Army and therefore the majority of shells manufactured were made for these guns. The following is taken from a document provided by the Government to The Crittall Manufacturing Company Limited, describing the various parts of the shell:

Cartridge Case: This is made of Copper or Brass and on the 18-Pdr is ten inches in length, approximately doubling the length of the projectile. Fitted to the shell by being pressed into a groove on the band, its use is to contain and mechanically preserve the propelling charge.

Shell Body: This is the aggressive portion of the projectile. It is designed to convey its contents of either Shrapnel or High Explosive to its target.

Fuze: This is the final part of the projectile, forming the nose of the shell and is a contrivance for exploding the bursting charge either on impact or at any given period after leaving the gun.

Copper Band: The Copper Band, otherwise known as the 'Driving Band' has two functions a) to act with the rifling of the gun to spin the shell, and; b) to seal the pressure from the exploding propelling charge behind the shell, thereby obtaining the maximum power to propel the shell from the gun. It should be positioned as near to the base of the projectile as possible, as this allows for more accurate shooting, whereas in fixed or quick-firing ordnance, it should be as far forward so that the shell is firmly secured in its case.

Base Plate: This is a small piece of bar-steel set in the bottom of the shell with its grain running opposite to the shell base. This prevents the expanding gas from the propelling charge entering the shell and thereby causing the bursting charge to ignite; destroying the gun and most likely killing or seriously wounding the gun crew.[9]

The shell body was made from steel, which is an alloy of iron containing carbon to increase its hardness. It was cast in the fluid state into a malleable ingot; the composition of the ingot could be altered, but in general terms the ratio for shells was between 35 per cent to 7 per cent carbon, together with small percentages of nickel, manganese, and silicon.[10] Both cast and forged steel were used in the manufacture of shells, although cast steel could not be made as thin as forged. To produce the outside of the shell, the solid ingot was re-heated and then punched with a die to form the cavity. The cavity and shape of the shell was then extended using successive dies.

It should be borne in mind that a gun fires the shells in a long curve, and it was therefore absolutely essential that the weight of the shell was exact, as any difference would affect the flight and possibly prevent the shell from hitting the desired target.[11] In order to make the shell fly straight, it is made to spin by the 'rifling' of the barrel of the gun. This is similar to that of a screw thread biting into the medium that it is being driven into; the copper-band of the shell bites into the rifling, therefore providing the gyroscopic effect that makes the shell spin. The 'Crittall' document provides a cautionary note on the subject:

…it must be pointed out that any failure of the band to withstand the stripping action of the rifling will alter the flight and therefore the range of the shell; the effect of a faulty band being that the base of the shell wobbles, and in extreme cases the shell even turns over endwise.[12]

During the process of manufacture and the packing for transport, the shell could be easily damaged, and workers were warned to handle them with care, not to place shells on top of one-another, and not to drop them into their packing cases, especially as the latter could damage the driving-bands. Faulty ammunition would result in 'short shells', where the shells exploded short of the target, often on or over 'friendly' trenches. This could be caused by damage during transportation, worn-barrels, and differences in the quality and uniformity of the propellant, to name a few. The shell not reaching the target resulted in enemy defences remaining undamaged and barbed-wire entanglements uncut.

Without explosives, the guns could not fire the shell and the shell could not explode. These explosives were created by combining various chemicals to react with each other to produce an expanding gas with different properties.

Explosives

The combination of combustible and oxygen-supplying substances, or the addition of oxygen to a chemical combination of elements such as nitrogen, hydrogen, carbon, etc., is the first step in creating an explosive compound. Most chemical explosives are nitro compounds; oxygen is held in a chemical combination with nitrogen until heat is applied which upsets the stability of the combination. Oxygen is freed to form new gaseous combinations with the other constituents, thereby creating even greater heat and expansion of the products of combustion. If this process is moderately slow it is called 'burning', if very fast is called an explosion. The faster the action and the greater heat, the more violent the explosion.

The most common explosive compounds used were gunpowder, cordite, guncotton, lyddite, picric powder, and fulminate of mercury. These explosives can be divided into three classes: propellants, disruptives or high-explosives, and detonators.

The most common propellants include gunpowder and cordite. These act much slower than the other two classes, as it is essential that the inertia of the projectile is overcome gradually, preventing damage to either the projectile or gun. As an example, a cordite cartridge ignited in the open burns away rapidly but harmlessly, but if the cartridge is confined to prevent the gas from escaping, the pressure increases and an explosion takes place. It is this explosion that can damage the gun, or in the worst case, cause the barrel to explode.

Disruptives or high-explosives include guncotton, dynamite, lyddite, etc., and are intended to detonate. Because of the speed of their detonation, such materials are unsuitable as propellants. Detonation is a different process to the action of explosion. The latter combustion is confined to the surface and takes place layer by layer, whereas detonation takes place instantaneously throughout the whole mass, thereby greatly increasing the power of the explosion and creating a shockwave. Different disruptives produce waves of different speeds, but on average they travel at approximately 4 miles a second. The damage caused to a human body by such a wave is truly devastating.

Fulminate of mercury is the most common detonator. Its action is even faster than that of disruptives, and as a result it lasts a much shorter time and has no incendiary effect. This class is used to initiate the explosion or detonation of other explosives, via a detonating wave.[12]

Propellants

It is the action of the propellant that forces the shell from the barrel of the gun. During the war, the main propellant was cordite, a product made by combining guncotton and nitro-glycerine in a process that is messy, complicated and dangerous. In an 1895 edition of *The Strand Magazine*, William G. FitzGerald described cordite as 'that new and terrible explosive which eminent experts tell us will increase a hundredfold the carnage on the battlefield…'.

The first step in manufacturing cordite is the making of guncotton (or nitrocellulose). The cotton was originally a by-product of the cotton mills, often dirty and containing impurities. It had to be washed, teased and dried, before being immersed in three parts sulphuric acid and one part nitric acid for several hours. The cotton would then be washed, boiled, and pulped to resemble 'porridge', which would be dried in specially built stoves and pressed into disks. This was guncotton, used as part of cordite, but also as an explosive in weapons such as 'jam-tin' bombs made by the troops at the front.[13]

Nitroglycerine was first created by Professor of Applied Chemistry Ascario Sobrero in 1847, when a small sample of the yellowish oil blew up unexpectedly. It was found that it affected the 'vessels of the brain and heart [which] were suffused with blood and much distended'.[14] It is an effective treatment for heart problems (angina) and is still used today in this regard.

Nitroglycerine is made by treating glycerine, an oily substance, with nitric and sulphuric acid in a process known as nitration. Sulphuric acid and nitric acid are poured into a big lead-lined, water-cooled tank called the nitrator, then using compressed air, glycerine is sprayed onto the acids. The reaction creates heat, which if allowed to rise above 22°C, causes the mixture to explode. After nitration, the acids are drawn off and the mixture is washed at least four times to remove any remaining acidic traces. Then it is moved to the 'washing-house' where is was washed a further five times. In the making of cordite, the nitroglycerine was then ready to be mixed with the guncotton.

Acetone is an organic compound, colourless and highly flammable and serves as a solvent in the blending process. It was originally produced by dry distillation, or by the heating of solid materials to produce a gas of acetates, also known as salts of acetate. Later in the war the production was increased by using a fermentation method pioneered by Dr Chaim Weizmann which speeded up the manufacture of Acetone.

Cordite was first created in the late 1870s by Sir Frederick Abel and Sir James Dewar. It is remarkably similar to Alfred Nobel's 'Ballistite'. Thirty-seven parts of guncotton are mixed and kneaded by hand with fifty-eight parts of nitroglycerine to form a cordite paste, with the addition of five parts of a stabilizer such as mineral-jelly or Vaseline. The jelly also reduces the temperature of the cordite at the point of explosion, thus causing less erosion to the barrel. Conversely if too little is added, the barrel suffers greater erosion and the copper driving bands are stripped off, making the shell tumble when leaving the gun and possibly fall short of its target.

Once made, the cordite was cut to size, dried, and blended. The solvent acetone was used to promote the blending process and to ensure consistency of the product. The cordite was placed in something that resembles a pasta-making-machine and squeezed out into reels, similar to macaroni, then moulded into shapes depending on the weapon it was to be used for.

Cordite produces a greater volume of gas and a higher temperature than gunpowder, therefore a smaller amount is required to match the same muzzle velocity of that produced by the latter. The extremely high temperature of the cordite, due to the large percentage of nitroglycerine, causes the bore of the barrel to rust and erode, and necessitates a high level of maintenance. The cordite would be ignited by gunpowder or guncotton, and on the larger guns would produce a back-flash as the breech was opened. [15]

While the use of cordite had many advantages, being smokeless, safe to handle if not confined, not affected by moisture, and a better propellant than gunpowder, it also had significant disadvantages: the erosion it caused to the bore of a gun, the bright muzzle flash it gave off on detonation, the back-flash, the deteriorating effect the high temperature and sweating of the substance could have on the guns.

When used for standard breech-loading guns, the cordite cartridges were encased in silk or shalloon—the silk being stronger, but the shalloon more permeable to the detonation flash. In any event, it was vital that the explosive compounds were created on a uniform basis, as even the slightest deviation could make the ranging and targeting of the gun impossible to determine.

Shell Content

The contents of the shell form the aggressive element of the projectile. The shell could contain various components, but they would primarily be shrapnel and high-explosive. Shells containing shrapnel were known as 'carrier shells' and would be fitted with a fuze that was designed to detonate the bursting charge after a pre-determined period of time had elapsed; the time period equated to the distance that the shell would have travelled based on the weight, calibre, and size of the propellant. Those containing high-explosive would use a fuze that would be detonated on impact or one designed to explode after a pre-calculated period of time, much in the same manner as a shell containing shrapnel.

The most common explosives used as bursting charges were as follows:

Gunpowder

This is created by mixing saltpetre, charcoal, and sulphur, creating black, brown or sulphurless gunpowder, depending on the amount used of each of the constituent parts. Gunpowder ignites at between 550°C and 600°C and is regarded now as a general purpose low explosive, burning at a rate of 1,200 feet per second.[16] It can be ignited on impact or by friction and accordingly there are a number of precautions for its storage and use that have to be strictly observed.

High-Explosive

High-explosives are mixtures of ingredients that produce a substance that is capable of instantly releasing large amounts of energy; the most common explosive during the war was TNT, Tri-nitro-toluene or Trotyl, which was first prepared by German chemist Julius Wilbrand in 1863. Although less powerful than nitroglycerine, it is also less sensitive, and therefore advantageous during shell manufacture as it can be safely poured in a liquid state into shell cases.[17]

TNT is produced in a three-step process: toluene is nitrated with nitric and sulphuric acid to produce mononitrotoluene (MNT), which is separated and then re-nitrated to produce dinitrotoluene (DNT). Lastly the DNT is nitrated using nitric acid and oleum to produce TNT, before being treated with aqueous sodium sulphite to provide stabilization.[18]

TNT produces gas instantly on detonation, 1,000 times the original volume; therefore one gram of TNT would produce one litre of gas; this rapid expansion blasts its way out of the shell casing, producing a shock wave that destroys everything in its path, radiating outwards at a speed of 6,900 metres a second, or approximately twenty times the speed of sound.

The size of the shell determines the amount of the bursting charge. For example, a 3-pdr QF shell would contain nearly 5 oz. of explosive (overall weight 3 5/16 lbs), a 14-pdr QF shell would hold about 1 lb 1½ oz. (overall weight 13½ lbs), and a 30-pdr breech-loaded shell would contain about 3 lb 14½ oz. (overall weight 30 lbs). When detonation takes place, the shell is torn into a large number of pieces, which fly off in all directions—not just forward as in a powder-filled shell. These fragments, often called 'shrapnel', are very effective against personnel, but as their velocity degrades quickly, they have little effect upon defences.

The bursting charge surrounds a long exploder fitted down the centre of the shell, which in turn is usually filled with a fulminate detonator, as this produces the best explosive effect. From a manufacturing point of view the shell cannot be detonated by flame or by heating in an open vessel.[19]

The high-explosive shells were used to destroy the enemy's breastworks and trench systems, and were necessary for cutting the barbed-wire entanglements. Their use of which became a point of disagreement as the war progressed.

Shrapnel

In the late eighteenth century, Lieutenant Henry Shrapnel of the Royal Artillery adapted the principle of the cased-shot, similar to a shot-gun cartridge, which burst as it left the barrel, to a shell-casing that had a long-range use. Shrapnel was used extensively in the colonial wars that Britain fought throughout the nineteenth century, and was especially effective against native warriors in the open. In the First World War, it was not particularly effective against barbed-wire entanglements, and unless it could explode directly over a manned-trench, it had limited effect against trench systems. However, it was formidable against assaulting troops and in preventing reinforcements from reaching defences that were being attacked.

The canister shell can hold a variety of fillings, but this book limits itself to shrapnel, the term used for the 'shrapnel bullets' of lead. Each bullet was comprised of seven parts lead and one part antimony, with a diameter of half an inch. They were contained in the shell casing and would be released via a fuze and bursting charge over the heads of troops in the open or directly above trenches. The shell casing, which forms approximately 48 per cent of the shell, dictated the number of bullets that could be contained within. For example, an 18-pdr shell would contain 375 of these bullets, although larger bore guns naturally held more, such as the 60-pdr which held 990 bullets. The space between each bullet was filled with a resin. The bursting charge, most commonly consisting of lyddite, a picric acid (a pale yellow crystalline substance formed by the action of nitric acid on phenol), was required to blow off the head of the shell and to drive out the bullets, which were carried forward with the remaining velocity of the projectile. As an example, the bursting charge in a 60-pdr shell would be 4½ oz. The remaining velocity would degrade quickly, but would have to be at least 60 foot pounds[20] of kinetic energy to be effective against personnel, producing an effect similar to that of being hit by a rifle or machine-gun bullet. The advantage of shrapnel was that a vast number of bullets could be delivered together instantaneously.[21]

Fuzes

The fuze is the timing mechanism of the shell, determining where and when the shell will explode, or as the *Treatise on Ammunition* describes:

> The bursting charge of a shell is ignited by means of a fuze designed so as to act at any particular moment during its flight, or upon or after impact.[22]

Fuzes may be divided into three classes: percussion fuzes, time fuzes, and time and percussion fuzes. Percussion fuzes, or direct action fuzes, require a heavy impact to make them act, and are fitted with a copper disk supporting a needle over a detonator, that is required to be crushed into the detonator to explode. Time fuzes are designed to act at the end of a determined period of time by the burning of a length of slow-burning compound. The compound is set in a ring which is moveable, the moving of which makes the length of the compound shorter or longer and thereby lengthens and shortens the burn time before it explodes the shell. Time and percussion fuzes provide a timed fuze that has the added benefit of detonation should the shell hit or graze something before the time fuze is activated.

All fuzes are greatly affected by weather conditions and the manner in which they have been stored, that is to say a damp or wet fuze will take longer to burn, extending the time before detonation, whereas an over-dry fuze will detonate earlier.

The Guns

The guns were classified according to size of the shell that they fired; a 1-pdr fired a shell weighing 1 lb and a 15-inch howitzer fired a shell that had a diameter of 15 inches and weighed half a ton. Based on the specifications of the gun, the more propellant used, the further the shell could travel. Maximum ranges are shown below: [23]

Equipment & Weight	Shell Weight	Maximum Range
18-pdr (Mk 1) 1.25 tons	18 lbs	6,525 yards
4.5-inch howitzer 1.45 tons	35 lbs	7,300 yards
4.7-inch field-gun 3.75 tons	45 lbs	10,000 yards
60-pdr (Mk 1) 4.5 tons	60 lbs	12,300 yards
6-inch howitzer 3.63 tons	100 lbs	11,400 yards
6-inch (Mk 19) field gun 10.2 tons	100 lbs	18,750 yards
9.2-inch (Mk 1) howitzer 13.3 tons	290 lbs	10,060 yards
14-inch rail gun (Mk 3) 248 tons	1,400 lbs	34,600 yards
15-inch howitzer 10.7 tons	1,400 lbs	10,795 yards

As the war progressed, the calibre and range of artillery increased; in 1918 the 'Paris Gun' was introduced, which for the time, had a phenomenal range of 130 km (80.78 miles).[24] The loading of the guns, especially the breech-loaders, was heavy work, as recalled by Gunner N. Tennant, 11th Howitzer Bty, West Riding:

> They were five-inch breech-loading Howitzers—great, clumsy old weapons. And they fired 56-lb high explosive shells. You had to thrust the shell into the breech, ram it home, and then push in the charge that would fire it, which was explosive held in a canvas bag shaped something like a mushroom with two smaller charges in a canvas bag behind it. They were called 'cores' and it was hard physical work. The gun drill was just as it had been in the old days and the weapon was really obsolete. Once you'd loaded the gun it was fired by pulling a lanyard and, of course, the guns themselves took a fair bit of man-handling.[25]

Pre-War Munitions Supplies and Manufacture

The Waterloo Campaign, when the Seventh Coalition defeated the French Army commanded by Napoleon, was the last time that Britain had participated in a continental war. Since then, Britain had mostly fought colonial wars acting almost as a police force through the British Empire. These wars had often been fought with mobile weapons, which although devastating to lesser-armed opponents, bore little resemblance to the type of weapons and warfare that was coming. The British had relied upon her Royal Navy to maintain her isolation, and although the Army had the excellent 18-pdr field gun, they had very few medium or heavy artillery pieces.[26]

The manufacturing base for munitions called for a relatively small, steady supply of readily available ammunition via the Royal Ordnance Factories such as Woolwich, and several private companies that supplied them in accordance with their licenses. This form of supply also relied upon other countries to supply component parts; it was a system that worked well in peacetime, when Britain and her Empire were the dominant global economy.

The unification of the Second German Empire precipitated the rapid industrialisation of the country. Their leaders were bent upon Germany becoming the economic powerhouse of Europe and replacing Britain in supplying the rest of world with its steel and chemical products. Germany's output rose significantly since unification: coal production grew from 34 to 277 million tons, pig-iron production from 1.3 million to 14.7 million tons, and steel production from 0.3 to 14 million tons.[27]

The steelworks and arms factories of Krupps at Essen had employed 16,000 workers in 1873; by 1900 this had increased to 45,000, and 70,000 by 1912, making it the largest industrial complex in Europe.[28] In contrast, British industry, the dominant global economy of the nineteenth century, was out of date. It was comprised of a relatively large number of medium-sized firms relying on antiquated technology and lagging behind Germany, which was becoming predominant in manufacturing precision machine-tools, light engineering products, electrical goods, and—relevant to the future need of high-explosives—chemicals.[29] Britain still had the largest empire, holding authority over one-fifth of the world's landmass and one-quarter of its people, but by 1914, Germany had equalled Britain's coal output, pig-iron was a third-higher, and steel production was now twice that of Britain.[30] Added to this was the capitalist nature of Britain's industry, based on competition opposed to co-operation for the common good.

Britain in particular needed to invest in new machinery, retrain labour and step up explosives production 'for which,' as asserted by Saul David in *100 Days to Victory*, 'the denial of German chemicals proved a crucial bottleneck'.[31] The Government's method of controlling the manufacture of materials used in warfare was incredibly complicated, with civil servants over-regulating every aspect.

Peacetime Control of Munitions

Prior to the war, the supply of munitions was controlled by the Master-General of the Ordnance (MGO), a post that had been created in the fifteenth century and ran until 1855, when it was temporarily discontinued until 1904, when it was reinstated. The MGO from 1913 to 1916 was Sir Stanley von Donop, who sat on the Army Council as its fourth military member, advising the War Council on military matters.

The MGO was responsible, via the Director of Artillery, for all types of field and fixed guns, relating specifically to pattern, design, manufacture, inspection, and employment. In addition, the MGO had various technical bodies under his control, such as the Ordnance Board, the Small Arms Committee, and production establishments of the Royal Ordnance Factories (ROFs) at Woolwich, Waltham Abbey, and Enfield Lock. The Quarter Master General (QMG), via the Director of Equipment and Ordnance Stores (DEOS), was responsible for receiving, storing, issuing, and repairing artillery equipment and ammunition. The Director of Army Contracts (DAC), under the responsibility of the Finance Minister, was responsible for the purchase of all the army's requirements, although his power was restrained by the insistence that the military branch had to agree to any purchases before they could be made.

Orders were placed with the ROFs and some private civilian companies to relieve the manufacture pressure on the ROFs and give other outlets experience in production of equipment and munitions in case of war. When non-Government outlets were used, the ROFs would act as quality controllers, and monitor the prices charged. Before the orders could be placed with the private civilian companies, they first needed to get on the List of Contractors, satisfying eligibility rules in areas such as fair wages, sub-contracting, agents and middlemen, financial control, quality control, and plant inspections.[32]

Once accepted, the firms were allowed to inspect 'sealed patterns' and were given the specifications of the product, all of which were highly standardized. Tenders could then be provided to the MGO via sealed envelopes dropped into a locked metal tender box on a given date. They would be opened in public at the appointed hour and the details of each tender would be listed, signed, and witnessed. To ensure fairness and protect against corruption, '...the established principle of public purchase [was] competition and the acceptance of the lowest offer.'[33] Under normal conditions, with a relatively small requirement, this procedure worked well, ensuring that reasonable prices were charged for the standardized products.

The Liberal Government and the Declaration of War

The Pre-War Government

The Liberal Party had been formally created in the late 1850s by the amalgamation of groups of Radicals, Whigs, and Tory Peelites, who advocated civil liberties and free-trade, and reduced Government regulations in private transactions. Under Gladstone, the party formed four successful governments, although there were disappointing defeats in between, as well as almost a decade in opposition ending in the 1890s. The party nearly split towards the end of the century as an imperialist faction, including Herbert Henry Asquith, Sir Edward Grey, and Viscount Richard Burdon Haldane, set itself against a pro-Boer faction. It was the skills of the Liberal leader Sir Henry Campbell-Bannerman that kept the divided party whole, bringing it back to its traditional platforms.

The Liberals found themselves in power when Arthur James Balfour, the head of the Conservative Government, suddenly resigned in December 1905, and the General Election of 1906 gave the party their landslide victory of 399 ministerial seats—a majority over the Conservatives of 143 seats.[1] Campbell-Bannerman became the first politician to bear the title of Prime Minister, just five days after it was officially recognised (previously the head of the government was known as the First Lord of the Treasury). Asquith became the Chancellor of the Exchequer, Grey, the head of the Foreign Office, Haldane, the War Office chief, and David Lloyd George the President of the Board of Trade.[2]

Two years before the landslide victory, Winston Leonard Spencer-Churchill had 'crossed the floor' to join the ranks of the Liberal Party. He had suffered at the hands of his Conservative colleagues, especially Joseph Chamberlain and Balfour, regarding his views over the economy, imperial policy, and the future of the Conservative Party. In early 1904, Balfour was in the House of Commons being pummelled by the Liberal opposition for not calling a general election over an issue of free-trade. Lloyd George led the attack, and when Churchill—still a Conservative MP at that point—rose from the benches intent on criticising Balfour, 'a nasty look came into [Balfour's] face,' wrote a parliamentary commentator, 'which transfigured it in the same way that the claws do a cat's paw'.[3] The First Lord of the Treasury, having decided that he had put up with enough from Churchill, strode with uncharacteristic haste from the chamber, quickly followed by the other ministers and most of the back-benchers, leaving Churchill still standing. Instead of blaming Chamberlain for dividing the party over an unrealistic imperial scheme, Balfour and others found it easier to turn on Churchill, making him the scapegoat.

In March 1904 Churchill resigned from the Conservatives and joined the ranks of the Liberal Party. He was initially offered the position of Financial Secretary of the Treasury, but instead he requested the lesser post of Under-Secretary to the Colonial Office, a position that in his eyes he understood far better than the financial one.[4]

The Pre-War Army

In 1906, Haldane, the new Secretary of State for War, looked to the Army, swollen by the Boer War, as a source of reducing the burden of his department on the economy. In the same year the Cabinet decided that the annual cost of the Army should be reduced to £28 million at the most. For other Liberals, this cost-cutting exercise '…was only the beginning and that they meant to get the figure down to 25 million at the most'.[5] Lieutenant-Colonel Charles à Court Repington, a correspondent of *The Times* newspaper, fought back in an article on 5 July 1906:

> The cost of the Army had risen from 15 million in 1861 to 29½ million in 1906. But the profits assessed to Income-Tax was 371 million in 1865 and nearly 903 million in 1904. We, therefore, had to compare a rise of 15 million in the cost of the Army in forty-three years with the rise, in ascertained and taxed income alone, of 474 million in eighteen years. I then pointed out that the annual charge on the National Debt in the year 1815 stood at 32 ½ million for a population of 17 million at that time, and that it was now 30 ¾ million for a population of over 42 million with infinitely greater resources…. I concluded that our immense resources justified any expansion of our armaments that our situation required.[6]

The article was written at a time when newspapers held enormous power—there was no television, radio or internet, and the public relied solely on newspapers for up-to-date information on the majority of issues—and *The Times* was at the peak of its influence. Abraham Lincoln named the newspaper as 'one of the greatest powers in the world—in fact, I don't know anything which has much more power—except perhaps the Mississippi'.[7] Repington's article had hit its target, and without a suitable response, the suggested reductions in the Army expenditure were quietly dropped from the Commons calendar.

From the military perspective, the reversal of the budget reduction was a success; however, further increases in expenditure were not permitted, with many proposals being rejected due to their impact on the budget. One such proposal was made to upgrade, at a cost of £3,618,000, the munitions manufacturing equipment to produce the 'Quick-Firing' or 'QF' ammunition. The use of this type of ammunition would reduce the overall cost of artillery ammunition and speed up the rate of fire, but the upgrading cost was seen as prohibitive. The short-term alternative of converting the 15-pdr guns at a cost of £1,200 per battery was implemented instead, but this only delayed the full expenditure which by 1910 had been made, allowing 'QF' ammunition to be used in field guns as well as some howitzers.[8]

Army numbers were also reviewed, with Haldane looking to have the army supported by a separate force, to be known as the 'Territorial Force', that could be called upon in the event of war, but whose members during peace time would continue to be civilians. The forming of the Territorials would reduce peacetime expenditure, while ensuring that the Army could be enlarged with the minimum of delay. Sir John French would later extol the virtues of the scheme: 'Without the assistance which the Territorials afforded between October 1914 and June 1915, it would have been impossible to hold the line in France and Belgium.'[9] However, Field Marshal Lord Horatio Herbert Kitchener took a different view, referring to the Territorials as 'a town clerk's army' created by Haldane to encourage amateurism.[10]

It was the creation in January 1907 of the Expeditionary Force that would become Haldane's best-remembered achievement while at the War Office. This would allow a permanent military force, along with supporting troops, to be used for continental interventions, and would comprise of 6,494 officers and 160,200 men, a maximum of 136,159 of which could be held in the field at any one time. This force would be supported by 456 guns, 168 machine guns, 62,216 horses, and 7,938 vehicles.[11]

Prime Minister Herbert Henry Asquith

On 3 April 1908, a seriously ill Campbell-Bannerman lay in his bed at 10 Downing Street, gathering his strength while dictating a letter to the King:

> Sir Henry Campbell-Bannerman with his humble duty to Your Majesty submits his resignation of the appointments of Prime Minister and First Lord of the Treasury.[12]

Five days later Herbert Henry Asquith succeeded him as Prime Minster, providing the opportunity for Lloyd George to take over the Exchequer, and the Board of Trade to go to Churchill, who at the age of thirty-three had gained his first cabinet position.

Lloyd George introduced the 'People's Budget' in 1909 on the platform of social reform, marking a final move away from Government spending reductions and instead redistributing the tax burden to finance social provisions. One of the more alarming clauses for the landed gentry included a requirement for land-valuations to take place and a 20 per cent tax on land transfers. The Conservatives believed that this should be replaced with tariffs on imports. The budget was rejected by the majority of land-owning members of the House of Lords, creating the first constitutional crisis of the twentieth century and forcing the Government to call a general election.

The election, held in January 1910, resulted in the Conservatives winning more votes than the Liberals but not more seats, thereby producing a 'hung-parliament'; the Liberal Government only remained in power via the support of the Labour Party and the Irish Nationals. Without a clear majority, a further general election was held in December 1910, with the Liberals seeing their small margin reduced to just one seat, and them retaining power only with the support of other parties.[13]

The period between the 1910 election and 1914 was to become known as the 'Great Unrest' as strike upon strike rolled across the major industries; the mines, docks, and railways were all affected by industrial action. At the end of 1913, three powerful unions—the Miners' Federation of Great Britain, the National Union of Railwaymen, and the National Transport Workers Federation—formed a 'Triple Alliance', agreeing to support each other as the threat of a general strike raised ever higher during 1914.[14]

The support of the Irish Nationals in 1910 had come at a cost: namely, the abolition of the House of Lords' veto over the Irish Home Rule Act. This forced Asquith to introduce a third Home Rule bill in 1912, and the consequent opposition, led by the Ulster Unionists, would bring the country to the brink of civil war.[15] In addition, the Government was discredited by an attempt to influence the First Lord of the Admiralty, Edward Marjoribanks, 2nd Baron Tweedmouth, during Anglo-German arms talks by none other than the Kaiser himself. The Kaiser sent a private letter to Tweedmouth, his personal friend, clearly stating that it was not Germany's intention to challenge Britain's fleet, but that they were concerned with the British programme of naval expansion currently in progress. This letter was clearly meant to influence Tweedmouth and it was made all the worse by not being divulged to the British public or Parliament. Repington, having discovered the contents, wrote an open letter to *The Times*, which resulted in the matter being raised in the House of Commons, where Asquith was forced to state that it was a private affair.[16] Tweedmouth was replaced in 1908.

The arms talks with Germany continued until February 1912, when they collapsed due to the unabated British naval build-up.[17] Germany was unable to keep up with the British naval construction programme, and switched their resources to enlarging their army.

The Balkan Wars

Two strategic alliances paved the road to the Balkan Wars and onward to the First World War: the Triple Entente between France, Britain, and Russia, which declared a no separate peace pact between the nations; and the Triple Alliance between Austria-Hungary, Germany, and Italy, which promised mutual support between parties in case of a Russian attack. The Entente was later strengthened by the inclusion of Portugal, Brazil, Spain, Japan, Canada, and the US, while the Central Powers would rally around the Triple Alliance, although Italy would ultimately join the Allied cause in 1915.

The retreat of the Ottoman Empire presented opportunities for the Balkan states to expand their individual empires.[18] The first of the Balkan Wars erupted with Russia mobilizing 50,000–60,000 reservists along the Austro-Hungarian border with Poland. The Russian Foreign Minister observed that were it to come to a conflict, Russia could 'probably rely on the real support of France and England.'[19] The German ambassador in London wrote to the Kaiser warning that Britain '…could under no circumstances tolerate being crushed'.[20] In the margin the Emperor scribbled, 'She will have to'.

The Treaty of London in 1913 brought the First Balkan War to an end, with former Ottoman territory ceded to the Balkan League and Albania being declared an independent state. However, unresolved disputes remained within the Balkan League, and even before the Treaty was concluded, Greece and Serbia formed a military alliance against their former partner, Bulgaria, resulting in the Second Balkan War. During this second war, Serbia consolidated her gains from the first war, but was forced to withdraw under threat of military action by Austro-Hungarian forces.[21]

On 28 June 1914, the Serbian Holy Day of Mourning, a thin, pale, sunken-eyed nineteen-year-old, Gavrilo Princip, stepped towards the rear of the stalled limousine transporting the Archduke Franz Ferdinand and his wife Countess Sophie Chotek to the town's hospital. The car was in the process of turning round in Franz Joseph Street when Princip fired two shots into the back of the vehicle. Within 15 minutes the Archduke and his wife were dead.[22] The touch-paper that would lead to the 'War to End All Wars' had been lit. Ferdinand had been a pragmatist, an arch-conservative who understood that 'Austria-Hungary [was] a brightly coloured glass bauble liable to shatter into fragments at a single blow'.[23] His death allowed more bellicose individuals in the Austro-Hungarian Government to propel the Empire to a war that Ferdinand knew they could never have won.[24]

It was quickly established that Serbia had supplied training for the assassins, as well as a box of revolvers and bullets marked 'Royal Serbian Arsenal'. Austria-Hungary blamed the entire Serb nation for the acts of a few individuals, and issued a list of demands that were impossible to meet unless Serbia surrendered its sovereignty.[25] The Kaiser and his Chancellor, Theorbald von Bethmann Hollweg, believed Austria would overpower Serbia quickly, and provided a document in support of any aggressive action. This would become known as the 'Blank-Cheque', a document that would promote a small conflict into a huge European war.

The British Cabinet had been concentrating on the Irish Home Rule Act that was slowly making its way through Parliament, leaving other matters to those ministers who were responsible for them. Therefore the Balkan matter was left to the Foreign Department until a copy of the Austro-Hungarian ultimatum to Serbia was delivered to the Foreign Secretary, which he read to the Cabinet, as Churchill recalled:

> The quiet grave tones of Sir Edward Grey's voice were heard reading a document which had just been brought to him from the Foreign Office. It was the Austrian note to Serbia.... This note was clearly an ultimatum; but it was an ultimatum such as had never been penned in modern times. As the reading proceeded, it seemed absolutely impossible that any state in the world could accept it, or that any acceptance, however abject, would satisfy the aggressor. The parishes of Fermanagh and Tyrone faded back into the mists and squalls of Ireland, and a strange light began ... to fall and grow upon the map of Europe.[26]

Under an agreement signed in 1904, France relied on England to protect the Channel and north French ports in the event of war. Grey had extended this agreement in 1912, without the specific approval of the Cabinet, resulting in the agreement not being binding upon the

Government.[27] With a possible war on the horizon, Grey had no option but to request that the Cabinet ratify the extension to the treaty, confirming that in the event that France was invaded, England would support her. After much discussion the treaty was extended, but the act of doing so almost split the Cabinet, with some ministers resigning. Sir John Simon, the Attorney General, made it plain that should too many ministers resign they would face a coalition government, 'which would assuredly be the grave of Liberalism'.[28]

In a telephone conversation that proved to be somewhat unreliable, Grey offered Germany a guarantee that Britain would not enter the war if Germany did not mobilize against France. Unfortunately Grey had not spoken to the French; under the treaty signed in 1892, France was duty-bound to mobilize against Germany if they declared war against Russia. Germany was under the impression that Britain had brokered the deal and that France was in agreement. The misunderstanding earned Britain the title of 'Perfidious Albion'; despite this, Grey continued his ministrations to reduce the friction between the parties, hoping to prevent war.

Serbia accepted most of the terms set out by Austria-Hungary and proposed alternatives for those that they could not accept. The latter were rejected out-of-hand and therefore Austria declared war on Serbia. The dominoes started to fall as Serbia's 'big brother', Russia, counter-threatened Austria, and in turn Germany threatened Russia, and by extension, their ally France declared war on Germany.

France sought clarification of Britain's commitment, but Britain was unable to promise any more than locking the German fleet out of the Channel, thereby protecting the northern ports from Germany. Grey now faced a bitter choice: to enter into a continental war or to abstain and face a continent ruled by a military power, intent on expansion and war. Lloyd George was fearful of a rampant Germany sitting across the Channel in Brussels and Paris, while Sir Walter Cunliffe, the Head of the Bank of England, was sure that a war would wreck Britain's mercantile-based economy.

If Britain did not act as Germany defeated France then Russia, she would be faced with a new European order consisting of vassal states under German authority, the mass migration of Europeans to German industrial centres, the rise of German influence and trade at the expense of Great Britain's, and a serious threat to Britain's command of the seas. A decision not to enter the war would only serve to postpone Britain's involvement, allowing a victorious Germany to take control of the whole of Europe and pick Britain off at its leisure. Asquith wrote in his diary, 'Are we to go in or stand aside? Of course everybody longs to stand aside.'[29] The decision would soon be out of his hands as the clock to war was ticking; the Kaiser instructed Helmuth Johann von Moltke (the younger), Chief of the German General Staff, to activate the Schlieffen Plan.

The Schlieffen Plan

Since their defeat during the Franco-Prussian War, the French had been building powerful fortresses, such as Lonwy, Verdun, Épinal, and Belfort, along their border with Germany to prevent any attack in the future. The Schlieffen Plan, or deployment plan number 17, was named after its author, the Chief of the Imperial German General Staff from 1891 to 1906, Count Alfred von Schlieffen. It called for a swift invasion of France using most of the German Army, advancing through neutral Belgium via the southern appendage of equally neutral Holland, thereby bypassing the forts, while the French Army would be lured into attacking the thin screen of German forces defending the Alsace-Lorraine region. The German Army would sweep in a great arc across northern Europe to envelop Paris, as they had done towards the end of the Franco-Prussia War. France would be forced to sue for peace—the terms of which would be stringent and punitive, with heavy financial reparations—before the majority of the German troops would leave, moving westwards as quickly as possible to meet the mobilized forces of Russia. The Germans were banking on 'best case scenarios' in each of the elements of the plan, and set a timetable of just six weeks for the invasion of Belgium and defeat of France.

Schlieffen retired after a riding accident and was succeeded by von Moltke, who amended the plan by increasing troop numbers in Alsace-Lorraine and abandoning the plan to invade Holland. In doing this he reduced the possibility of attacks to his right flank from the Dutch, but he neglected to appreciate that by funnelling troops only through Belgium, the narrow roads could easily become choked.

The German Army, well-trained, well-armed, and well-motivated, consisted of conscripted men over the age of twenty years, with those over seventeen years eligible for service with the *Landstrum*, or Home Guard. Each regiment was numbered and often carried the name of the district in which it was formed. The numbering was reproduced on the cloth covers of the leather helmets worn by the soldiers, and their belt-buckles bore the words '*Gott Mit Uns*' (God With Us).[30]

The Invasion of Belgium

To prevent French expansion, Belgium was formed from French and Dutch territories after Waterloo by the 'Concert of Europe', a group of countries that joined together to retain the balance of power in international relations. France was later to join this group, and as a result the Treaty of London officially recognised the independent Kingdom of Belgium and, at Britain's insistence, its neutrality. In 1839 the Treaty was co-signed by Great Britain, Austria, France, the German Confederation (led by Prussia), Russia, and the Netherlands. It would become known as the 'Scrap of Paper'.

On 3 August 1915, Grey received a communiqué from the Belgian Legation in London:

> Germany sent yesterday evening at seven o'clock a note proposing to Belgium friendly neutrality, covering free passage on Belgian territory, and promising maintenance of independence of the kingdom and possession at the conclusion of peace, and threatening, in case of refusal, to treat Belgium as an enemy. A time-limit of twelve hours was fixed for the reply. The Belgians have answered that an attack on their neutrality would be a flagrant

violation of the rights of nations, and that to accept the German proposal would be to sacrifice the honour of a nation. Conscious of its duty, Belgium is finally resolved to repel aggression by all possible means.[31]

In issuing this demand, Germany was disregarding its international obligations, forcing Belgium to appeal to the other signatories under the Treaty. Germany still could not believe that Britain, after not supporting France in their declaration of war, would then go to war over this 'scrap of paper'.

The British Ultimatum

In his 1914 novel *The World Set Free*, H. G. Wells wrote, 'Every intelligent person in the world knew that disaster was impending and knew no way to avoid it.' Grey gave the speech of his life to the House of Commons on 3 August, presenting the Government's case for war. Shortly afterwards, the mobilization of Regulars, Special Reserve, and Territorials was ordered. Later that day, a Council of War was held at 10 Downing Street, chaired by Asquith and including members of the Cabinet and soldiers Lord Roberts, Lord Kitchener, Sir Charles Douglas, Sir Douglas Haig, Sir James Grierson, Brigadier-General Henry Wilson, and Sir John French.[32] That morning, Repington was also active: '…with the approval of the editor of *The Times*, Mr Geoffrey Robinson, I made the first proposal in the Press that Lord Kitchener, who was at home on leave from Egypt, should be appointed War Minister'.[33] The Council decided that in the event of Germany not responding, a British Expeditionary Force consisting of one cavalry and four infantry divisions should be sent to France as quickly as possible. Due to the uncertainty regarding the Irish Home Rule issue, it was decided that two infantry divisions would be kept back for the purpose of home defence.[34]

On 4 August, Germany declared war on Belgium and crossed the frontier at Verviers, near Aix-la-Chapelle. The German Foreign Secretary sent a telegram to the ambassador in London:

> Please dispel any distrust that must exist on the part of the British Government with regard to our intentions by repeating, most positively, the formal assurance that, even in case of armed conflict with Belgium, Germany will not, under any pretence whatever, annex Belgian territory. Please impress upon Sir Edward Grey that the German Army could not be exposed to a French attack across Belgium, which was planned according to absolutely unimpeachable information.[35]

Asquith told the House that this was not 'in any sense a satisfactory communication':

> [I] repeated the request we made last week to the German Government that they should give us the same assurance with regard to Belgian neutrality as was given to us and to Belgium by France last week. We have asked that a reply to that request and a satisfactory

answer to the telegram of this morning, which I have read to the House, should be given before midnight.[36]

War is Declared

When Big Ben struck at 11.00 p.m., Germany had not answered Britain's ultimatum and had not withdrawn its forces from Belgium. Britain therefore had no option but to declare war on Germany and Austria. Churchill instructed the Navy at 11.02 p.m. to 'commence hostilities against Germany'.[37] King George V wrote in his diary:

> I held a Council at 10.45 to declare war with Germany. It is a terrible catastrophe but it is not our fault. An enormous crowd collected outside the palace; we went on to the balcony both before and after dinner. When they heard that war had been declared, the excitement increased.... Please God it may soon be over.[38]

But as George Orwell said, 'The only quick way to end a war is to lose it!'[39]

Britain was at war. The parties that had started the 'twelve days' sleepwalk' to war— Austria and Serbia—were the last to declare war on each other. It was hardly noticed. Grey, standing with John Alfred Spender in his office, watched as the night-watchman lit the gas- lamps in the street.

> The lamps are going out all over Europe; we shall not see them lit again in our lifetime.[40]

A Government at War

War with the Central Powers now placed the Liberal Government in a position that could jeopardise the very existence of a party 'whose guiding principles were international conciliation, personal liberty, and social reform'.[41] Internal battles seemed to rise from the beginning as individuals and institutions vied for control over the strategic direction of the war.[42] Asquith's Government constantly had to contend with journalistic criticism, often inciting revolt of the parliamentary members.[43] But it was the general public, whipped into mindless frenzy at the prospect of a war about which they knew nothing, who began leading the way with enormous numbers attending the enlistment offices.

It was then decided that Lord Kitchener, aloof, formidable, and immensely popular, should be appointed as the new Secretary of State for War. He would be the only soldier ever to hold the position. Margot Asquith, wife of Herbert Asquith, wrote in her diary: 'He is a man of good judgement and bad manners; a man brutal by nature and by pose; a man of no imagination, though not without ideas'.[44] The appointment was based on military reasons, but criticism from the Conservatives was restrained by the fact that Kitchener was a Tory at heart.[45]

At the outbreak of war, Kitchener's duties expanded exponentially. He was now responsible for overseeing the strategic and political aspects of the war throughout the world, equipping the Army with everything from uniforms to heavy guns, recruiting the vast number of men that would be needed, signing off on war related expenditure, and innumerable unforeseen details that demanded his attention.

Despite the British military pledging their allegiance to the King or Queen on the throne at the time, the Government of the day had always tried to control their activities. Communication had been the biggest obstacle to this, as battles took place at such a distance that politicians had to rely on generals to manage the conflict. It was the advent of the telegraph that gave an apprehensive Government during the Crimean War the ability to dictate operations hour by hour; this interference caused massive problems, with decisions being made based on political instead of military criteria. In order to prevent a repeat of this, the War Council was created to provide war direction policy which the military would strategize. The appointment of Kitchener, a soldier, would blur the lines between these two roles and cause problems as the war progressed.

The members of the War Council, an extension of the long-established Committee of Imperial Defence,[46] were traditionally appointed by the Prime Minister of the day. The purpose of the War Council was to discuss and determine the long-term policy of the war. It also provided the administrative departments to support the Army Council and the Board of the Admiralty. These included the Office of the Secretary of War, the Central Department, the Imperial General Staff, the Department of Master General of the Ordnance, the Military Secretary Department, the Department of Finance & Parliamentary, and the Department of the Quartermaster General. The Army Council consisted of a mixture of politicians and the military, made up of those holding the following appointments: Secretary of State for War, Parliamentary Under-Secretary, Financial Secretary, Chief of the Imperial General Staff, Adjutant General, Quartermaster General, Master General of the Ordnance, and Secretary of the War Office.

Britain had last fought a continental war in 1815, and it was therefore considered by many that the war would be short, sharp, and bloody, fought in the same manner as the German Unification wars, and lasting at most a few months—'over by Christmas' was the popular chant.[47] However, Kitchener persuaded the Cabinet that the war would not be quickly or easily won, and he became the chief proponent of a mass recruitment drive.[48] Kitchener's unblinking face began to stare out of the famous poster from 7 August 1914, declaring, 'Your Country Needs You', with his imperious finger beckoning the nation to war. To the public, Kitchener personified stern British determination and the desirable virtues of honour and duty that had highlighted his distinguished career. In the first eight weeks of the war, some 761,000 men joined up, far exceeding the 100,000 that was originally sought.[49] In the next two years, the recruitment campaign would attract over three million, all joining the adventure of defending Britain against 'the German menace'.[50] The majority were Christians, who saw the war as a battle of right versus wrong—a battle of honour, integrity, and a chance to assert their patriotism.[51] There was no greater honour for a young man than to fight for his King and Country, and those refusing the call to arms brought shame and humiliation on themselves, their friends, and their families. Soldiers from India, Canada, the West Indies, and other outposts of the Empire answered the call.

The Reservists, having already completed a term of duty, rushed to their regiments, as recorded in the Rifle Brigade Journal:

> The Army Reserve was called out on August 2, but a very considerable number of Reservists had already joined up when the order was issued. The Depot scheme for mobilization allowed for an influx of eight hundred men on the first day, but, as a matter of fact, so great was the rush of men to re-join that by the evening of August 5 over three thousand had reported. To accommodate all these men in the Rifle Depot itself was impossible and large numbers spent the night in churches, schools and college buildings, and many even slept in the streets. The next day the rush of re-joining continued and, in order to make room to deal with the equipping and clothing, batches of five hundred at a time had to be marched to the Depot football ground.[52]

An Army at War

When war was declared the British Army consisted of 247,482 regular officers and men, 316,094 territorials, and 228,120 conventional reservists that included 3,000 ex-regular officers on reserve.[53] These were divided into armies, divisions, corps, brigades, and regiments. An army consisted of two or more corps and other supporting units and services, and a corps consisted of two or more divisions plus supporting forces under the command of a lieutenant-general. The identifying numbers for a corps were written in Roman numerals. Each division was almost a miniature army under command of a major-general, containing three brigades of combat troops and sufficient supporting units for it act independently. The brigade was comprised of four battalions commanded by a brigadier-general and assisted by headquarters staff, and would often include a territorial battalion.

Each regiment, steeped in tradition, was comprised of battalions of soldiers and the depot, the regimental headquarters where recruits would assemble and be trained. Each battalion was commanded by a lieutenant-colonel, and consisted of twenty-nine officers and 977 other ranks. The battalion was further divided into four companies, with four platoons, each commanded by a 2nd lieutenant, to each company. Each platoon consisted of four sections, with each commanded by a non-commissioned officer. In addition, two .303 machine guns were issued to each battalion, being commanded by a junior officer in two sections of six men.

The Rifle Brigade was, and still is, an infantry regiment comprising of several battalions and not a brigade. At the outbreak of the war, the four regular battalions, in accordance with the rules set out in the Cardwell System, were equally distributed between the United Kingdom and Foreign Services:

1/Battalion: part of the 4th Division (Eastern Command) was in barracks at Colchester awaiting a move overseas in September;

2/Battalion: was at the end of overseas service of seventeen years, which included the Sudan and South African campaigns. It was currently in India, waiting until 29 October to sail back to England;

3/Battalion: as part of 17 Infantry Brigade, 6th Division was stationed at Cork;

4/Battalion: having completed ten years of foreign service, the battalion was at Dagshai near the Northern Frontier of India, awaiting instructions to return.[54]

The British Army artillery consisted of:

Royal Horse Artillery: relied on mobility, using light guns, including 13-pdr, 18-pdr, 4.5-inch howitzers, and medium guns.

Garrison and Siege Artillery: heavy guns including the 6-inch and larger calibre, firing over distances of 6,000 to 10,000 yards.[55]

The artillery brigade consisted of three or four batteries commanded by a lieutenant-colonel, with each battery having four or six guns. The number was often reduced when guns with a calibre larger than 12 inches were used.

The British Expeditionary Force (BEF)

The BEF was the global term for all the British Army units in France, Flanders, and Italy serving in the First World War. In overall command at the start of the war was sixty-two-year-old Field Marshal Sir John Denton Pinkstone French. From the perspective of those in the Army, he was not a particularly popular choice; however, he was articulate, charming, and comfortable around politicians. Initially the four infantry divisions, with a cavalry division under command of General Allenby totalling some 81,000 soldiers, would be centrally commanded by General Headquarters. A further corps, entitled III Corp, under the command of Major-General William Pulteney, was formed of two more divisions and sent to France at the end of August.[56] Therefore by the end of September, six divisions had arrived in France, adding to the total number of combatants of the Triple Entente, which numbered 120 divisions—a mass of three million soldiers in the battlegrounds of Belgium and France.[57]

The size of the British Expeditionary Force had been set at one cavalry and six infantry divisions during the Anglo-French army staff talks of 1906. However, the size of the force and its original placement on the left flank of the French Army committed the BEF to being a virtual subordinate of the French. This would not be acceptable to the British public; in an effort to counter the situation, Sir John French's instructions made it clear that his '... command is an entirely independent one, and that you will in no case come under the orders of any Allied General'.[58]

On August 12, the King bade farewell to the Expeditionary Force at Aldershot:

You are leaving home to fight for the safety and honour of my Empire. Belgium, whose country we are pledged to defend, has been attacked, and France is about to be invaded by the same powerful foe. I have implicit confidence in you, my soldiers. Duty is your watchword, and I know your duty will be nobly done.

I shall follow your every movement with deepest interest and mark with eager satisfaction your daily progress. Indeed, your welfare will never be absent from my thoughts.

I pray God to bless you and guard you, and bring you back victorious.

George, R.I.[59]

In August 1914 the British soldier might have passed for a gamekeeper in his soft cap, puttees, and pack. He walked into battle armed with a rifle and bayonet and grenades (or 'bombs') that were difficult to use. These would be supplemented by trench-made 'jam-tin bombs'. For support he could call only on the shrapnel-firing field guns of the Royal Artillery. That summer, as they marched to the railway stations, the men received a send-off fit for heroes. 2nd Lieutenant Brian Horrocks, barely eighteen, marched his men of the Middlesex Regiment down to the railhead at Chatham amid cheering crowds. He wrote that he 'felt like a king amongst men'.[60] His only anxiety was a commonplace one at the time—that the war would be over before he got to it. Lieutenant Charles Sorley of the Suffolk Regiment recalled that 'after two hours in an oily ship and then in a grimy train, the "war area" was a haven of relief'.[61]

The Opening Stages of the War

1914—The First British Clash

The German forces, divided into five armies, had charged into Belgium and France three days before the BEF landed on 7 August. The First Army, commanded by General von Kluck, advanced through Liège before sweeping past Brussels and Mons and down into Northern France. The German advance met stiff resistance at the French ring of forts defending Liége and the bridges over the River Meuse, slowing their progress and stopping them from reaching Brussels until 20 August. By 22 August the British Expeditionary Force had disembarked in France and taken up positions near the fortress town of Maubeuge, approximately 12 miles from Mons, to form the extreme left of the Allied line, with the French Fifth Army on their right. The BEF's position had been agreed in pre-war plans; they faced the German First Army's advance towards Paris, as determined by the Schlieffen Plan. This, the largest of the five German armies committed to the plan, was already wheeling past Brussels towards Ath and Mons.

The British infantry took up a thin line of positions along the Mons–Conde canal, while the 4/Royal Irish Dragoons pushed forward two patrols. Corporal E. Thomas of the 4 Troop, 'C' Squadron, opened fire near the château of Ghislain. His was the first British shot of the war fired in anger.

German artillery pounded the British lines with shells and the infantry came under heavy attack, but they had stopped the German advance. That evening, Sir John French was advised by the French Commander-in-Chief, Marshal Joseph Jacques Césaire Joffre, that the French were withdrawing as Tournai had fallen and long columns of German troops had broken through, opening a wide gap between the BEF and the Fifth Army. The BEF had no option but to undertake a general withdrawal in the direction of Cambrai in an effort to re-establish contact with the French.

The retreat from Mons continued, and as the German advance neared Paris, the French Government fled. General Snow wrote about the retreat after the war:

The retreat of 1914 was not, as is now imagined, a great military achievement, but was a badly bungled affair only prevented from being a disaster of the first magnitude by the grit displayed by the officers and men. Things took place during the retreat which never ought to have taken place in an army supposed to be trained, things which cannot survive the impartial searchlight turned on them by the historian.[1]

The Allied forces stopped the German advance at the River Marne, where British, French, and Belgian troops combined to push the enemy back towards the River Aisne between 5 and 12 September. The German commander, General Erich von Falkenhayn, had issued the order to retreat to Soissons to form a new defensive line at Aisne, having suffered 250,000 casualties.[2] Not prepared to fall further back and lose the territory he had so far gained, Falkenhayn ordered trenches to be dug to provide protection from the Allied artillery and a frontal assault. By 28 September, the Aisne front had stabilised and the BEF began to withdraw to Abbeville in Flanders.

The Schlieffen Plan had failed because of the inadequacy of the transport of the period to move the vast numbers of soldiers and their equipment with the necessary speed and efficiency. Added to this, Russia mobilised far faster than the Germans estimated, and by 17 August, two Russian armies had invaded Prussia, broken the front, and advanced more than a hundred miles into German territory.[3] An article in the *Observer* newspaper of 31 July 1915 analysed the failure of the Schlieffen Plan:

> The German plan of dealing with France first had greatly underestimated the speed of Russian mobilisation, and the invasion of East Prussia by the Russians and the arrival at Berlin of crowds of refugees came as a great shock to the Germans … the defects of the original German plan, which left the eastern frontier weakly guarded for the sake of a great blow in France. At the beginning of September the plans of campaign with which the Germans had started the war were completely wrecked, and von Molke, Chief of the General Staff, was so discredited that he had later to resign, and his place taken by von Falkenhayn.

The term 'Race to the Sea' describes the attempts by the equally matched Franco-British and German armies to out-flank the each other through Picardy, Artois, and Flanders, finally ending on around 19 October, when the last open area from Dixmude to the North Sea was occupied by Belgian troops. The opposing forces each entered into the costly and ultimately indecisive battles of Yser (16 October to 2 November) and the First Battle of Ypres (19 October to 22 November), while local operations were carried on in preparation for the bigger battles and to improve the tactical positions. On 22 October, British infantry and cavalry divisions, together with French troops, faced two German armies amounting to some twenty-four divisions at Ypres. The Germans advanced singing '*Deutschland über Alles*' into the defences of professional British soldiers trained to fire fifteen rounds a minute; they cut the advancing troops down as if they were corn. Any territory gained was quickly lost. The last attack was made on 11 November along the Menin Road by eight regiments of German guards, who suffered the same fate as those involved in the first attacks.[4] Following these battles, Falkenhayn concluded that a decisive victory could not be achieved on the Western Front, and he abandoned the strategy of annihilation and replaced it with a strategy of attrition, which would allow the front to be held by a smaller number of troops, allowing the transfer of others to the Eastern Front.

New defences were built behind the front line from the North Sea to the Swiss border in the south, stretching approximately 475 miles, although if all the trenches—assault, frontal, communication, etc.—were laid end to end they would have reached approximately 25,000 miles, with the only gap in the line between Ypres and La Bassée.[5] Mobile war would now revert to ritual siege methods of old, with artillery attempting to smash a breach in the enemy earthworks, prior to the infantry launching a desperate assault. The form of battle would be labelled 'attrition', as each side endeavoured to wear down the other by persistent shelling.

Trench Systems

The German *Graben*, or trenches, were dug to ensure the Germans could protect and retain the land that they had gained in the early part of the war. In much the same manner of the Allied trenches facing them, they were constructed to be about 3½ feet wide at the top and around 7 feet deep, with the sides cut as steep as possible. The Germans had the benefit of constructing their trenches on higher ground than those of the British, who in the Flanders area had to contend with a very high water-table. Along the British lines, a trench dug more than one or two feet deep would instantly fill with water, ensuring that the British soldiers' feet were rarely dry. This terrain forced the British to use sandbags filled with mud to build breastworks above a shallow trench; however, these could block the view of no man's land from the rear and expose the soldiers to enemy fire as they climbed over the top. The Germans, on the other hand, were able to dig deep trenches, sometimes with more than one level, using wicker-hurdles to prevent the mud from falling into the trench.

British trenches were built with a parapet to the front facing the enemy, building the earth or sandbags up over the initial lip of the trench and sloping the earth towards the ground. This parapet deflected bullets and the blast of shells, but it had to be 5 feet thick to stop a bullet. To the rear, a parados—a build-up of earth—was created to protect the trench from shells exploding to the rear of the position and to prevent silhouettes of soldiers standing on the fire steps. To enable the soldiers to fire above the parapet, a fire step was formed from compacted mud, allowing him to see across no man's land. Loopholes were created to allow observation and the sighting of machine guns, and for sniping at the opposing trenches. They were disguised and camouflaged to avoid detection by the enemy.

A direct hit on a trench would result in scorching-hot metal, shards of wood, earth, and body parts flying through the confined space. In order to mitigate this danger, traverse trenches were dug. These gave the trench system a castellated appearance from above, protecting the occupants from enfilade fire sweeping its length and minimising the blast damage from the explosion of a shell. If a section of a trench was captured by an enemy, their progress through the trench would be restricted and frequent corners would allow defenders and launch a counter-attack.

Behind the front line were second and third lines connected by communication trenches, dug at right-angles to the main trenches, allowing for movement of troops, supplies, and the wounded. However, they often became congested during battle. Sap trenches (a short cul-de-sac) were also dug at right-angles to the front line into no man's land. They were used for observation and as a method of advancing troops out of sight of the enemy. They also provided emplacements for machine-gunners to sight their weapons across the front of advancing troops, thus providing racking enfilade fire into the enemy flanks. Those digging the saps became known as sappers.

Barbed Wire

To provide further protection, barbed wire, invented by American cattle farmers, was strung between posts across the front of the trenches. These were not simple strands used for agriculture, but vast fields of entanglements designed to be impenetrable. The barbs were often the thickness of a man's thumb and placed at less than a two-finger width to prevent men gaining a solid grip. These fields of barbed wire were the first part of the defence system encountered by an advancing enemy, channelling them through gaps upon which machine guns had been sighted.

The wire was fixed in position by wooden stakes driven into the ground, the fixing of which was a dangerous occupation, but from 1915 onwards a metal screw-picket invented in Sweden allowed the fixing to become almost silent. The belts of barbed wire varied in height and depth, but ideally were about 3 feet high. Behind the first line, a second band was usually laid. It was also often laid in shell holes and water-logged ditches. These bands of intermeshed wire were so dense that they can clearly be seen on the aerial photographs of the trenches taken from several thousand feet altitude.[6]

No Man's Land

The space between the trenches was known as no man's land, an area that belonged to neither combatant and which was constantly fought over—a place of death. The constant shelling resulted in it becoming a quagmire, and shell holes and craters quickly filled with water. The width of no man's land ranged from a matter of feet—enough for bombs to be thrown into the opposite trench—to half a mile or more. At night, patrols explored the land, cutting the wire in preparation for an attack, or repairing damaged wire in anticipation of one. They listened to conversations and sometimes captured an enemy guard. The fighting taking place in no man's land was nothing like the heroic battles that were reported to the British public—it was not a war of dash and movement, but one of slaughter fought over a swampy patch of land.

Army Reorganisation

After the enemy's postponement of their offensive, the Allies did not have the resources to launch an attack. Therefore all the combatants settled down to constructing their fortified trenches and other obstacles, resulting in a monotonous and miserable impasse, destined to continue during the whole winter of 1914/15.

An extensive reorganisation of the BEF was initiated on Boxing Day 1914, with General Douglas Haig being placed in command of the First Army, which now consisted of I Corps, IV Corps, and the Indian Corps. General Sir Horace Smith-Dorrien was placed in command of Second Army, consisting of II Corps, III Corps, and V Corps. Both had been promoted to full generals. Sir John French had originally opposed Smith-Dorrien's appointment to command II Corps in favour of General Herbert Charles Onslow Plumber, but Smith-Dorrien was a protégé of Kitchener's, and the Secretary of State for War overruled the BEF commander. There was bad blood between French and Smith-Dorrien, emanating from disagreements during the retreat, which would continue for the next five months.

The intrigues continued as French felt that Sir Archibald Murray should be replaced by Sir Henry Wilson as Chief of the General Staff (CGS). However, Haig felt that Wilson had 'been intriguing to get poor Murray withdrawn,'[7] and suggested instead that the appointment should go to Sir William Robertson. Both Kitchener and Asquith agreed, feeling that Wilson was the wrong man for the job and that Robertson, who had been promoted through the ranks and was currently Quarter Master General, was ideal. Just as Haig wished, Robertson got the job. Shortly after the appointment, at a dinner with French and Wilson, Asquith remarked, with surprisingly little grace '… it is a curious thing, Field Marshal, that this war has produced no great generals.' To which Wilson quickly replied, 'No, Prime Minister, nor has it produced a statesman.'[8]

Firepower Kills!

It was the 13-pdr and 18-pdr guns, often firing over open sights, that had decided the early battles such as at Le Cateau. The shell expenditure during these battles completely outweighed expectations, thereby causing the first shell shortages. The reliance on small-calibre guns as well as this lack of munitions had resulted in the British often being outmatched during the battles of 1914. After the initial months of the war, the French came to the conclusion that the bombardments had to be of longer duration and have more destructive power; they began dedicating much of their industrial production to heavier guns. Marshal Ferdinand Foch, at the time assistant Commander-in-Chief of the French forces, began to adopt the mantra, 'The artillery conquers, and the infantry occupies.' Henri Philippe Pétain, commanding the XXXIII Corps, was known to quote his favourite maxim, '*le feu tue*'— firepower kills![9]

Now that the war had become one of attrition, high-explosive shells would be needed to destroy the barbed wire entanglements and the enemy trench and breastworks. Shrapnel would be used to burst above the trenches and prevent reinforcements moving from the rear. To achieve this, a 50 per cent ratio of high-explosive over shrapnel was needed, but this was rejected by Kitchener, who had used shrapnel extensively while serving in South Africa.[10] As a result, early battles of 1915 would be fought with a ratio of 90 per cent shrapnel over high-explosive, a ratio that could not deliver the devastation to the defences that was needed to allow a breakthrough.[11]

The Initial Management of Munitions

Following the outbreak of war, Britain's access to the chemicals needed for the manufacture of explosives was cut off as the main supplier, Germany, was now the enemy. This placed the Allies at a disadvantage as they had to establish the necessary facilities to manufacture chemicals before they could build the shells. The British industries in this area were few and their equipment was out of date. Chemical works, dye works, gas works, and very careful laboratory experiments would be needed to bring the production up to the critical mass needed to satisfy the expanding munitions requirements. However, in the meantime there was a serious explosives shortage, and without explosives a shell was, in the words of Lloyd George, 'just a harmless steel vase'.[12]

Steel and iron could no longer be imported from Europe, resulting in production being slowed down. Kitchener began to reorganize the state munitions industry and in the process warned the private sector to regard armaments supply in terms of years rather than months, and urged them to invest in their companies by way of modernization, retooling, and the labour force. However, the existing methods of ordering continued, with orders being restricted mainly to a list of approved companies, forcing those companies to compete with one another for raw materials, workers, and machinery.[13]

In the years prior to the declaration of war, Germany, the most modern industrial force in Europe, had prepared itself for conflict. It was Field Marshal Helmuth von Moltke (Chief of the Prussian General Staff) who appreciated how rapid industrialisation would affect the battlefields of the future; his reforms encompassed the railways, telegraph network, and rifle and artillery manufacture, making the German armed forces the byword for military innovation and efficiency.[14] The German Army became the most powerful institution in Germany, and their needs forced industries to upgrade to match their requirements. As an example, they became the world's predominant heavy chemical industry. In Lloyd George's view,

> The Germans and Austrians between them had even at the commencement of the war, much larger supplies of war material and more extensive factories for the turning of supplies than the Allied countries possessed and they have undoubtedly since made much better use of their manufacturing resources for increasing that output. Germany is the best organised country in the world. [15]

Germany had also seen a drain on their resources caused by the early battles. By the beginning of 1915, more and more raw materials needed for the production of munitions were sought, together with materials to make cordite and explosives. Austria and Hungary also had problems with the lack of raw material and completed products, but theirs was exasperated further by a lack of rail transport. Meanwhile, France's industrial might had been severely curtailed following the annexation of Alsace-Lorraine in 1870; now with Germany occupying a huge amount of their heartland, their production of munitions was further impeded.

As the war progressed, Sir John French appealed for increasing numbers of shells. As early as October 1914, the insufficient supply had to be rationed; during the First Battle of Ypres the allocation for 18-pdr shells was reduced to ten rounds per gun per day. By the end of that month, the 4.5-inch howitzers were rationed to two rounds and the 6-inch howitzers to six rounds per day per gun.[16] Stocks were assessed daily, incorporating remaining shells and the new deliveries; allocations were then made depending on priority and planned actions in the area.

First the Royal Ordnance Factories (ROFs) then the private companies became overwhelmed, and it was not solely the pressure of the munitions demand that was the cause. Uniforms were required for the new recruits, which needed buttons made of the same raw materials as munitions; rifles were in short supply, and again more and more were needed as replacements for those lost in battle and for the new recruits; an urgent need for heavy artillery pieces competed for resources; skilled workers were in short supply as many had volunteered for military service (those that didn't were often approached by young women who gave them white feathers to proclaim their cowardice); and unions sought better conditions for their members instead of looking at the common-good, based on the impression that the war would 'be over by Christmas'.

Under pre-war conditions, the existing structure would have coped, but the sudden escalation of requirements pushed demand far beyond pre-war conditions; the Master-General of the Ordnance (MGO), ROFs, and other departments realised this, but the ordering process was still not adapted and production was limited by the existing machinery and supplies. The whole system was jealously guarded by the MGO, Sir Stanley von Donop, and the purse-strings were tightly held by Kitchener. Therefore, the expansion process became bogged-down, and the urgent appeals for equipment and munitions became more desperate. 'General von Donop did his best,' wrote Repington, 'but all I can say is that all deliveries promised in France were late.'[17] The most frequent excuse, especially from the sub-contractor, was shortage of machine-tools. For example, at the end of 1914, when the shipbuilding company Cammell Laird ordered over 200 machines needed to complete orders, they only received twenty-six.[18]

Unfortunately, any further measures to mobilise more engineering resources were thwarted by von Donop, who only had confidence in the pre-war approved companies and was not happy for orders to be placed elsewhere, but after much persuasion, he relented, allowing sub-contracting initially for minor components.[19] Sub-contracting would be difficult to monitor and control, and to ease this process additional civilian members were added to the Army Council, and the MGO branch received a further general officer to visit and report on production capacity and quality. This revision of the process seemed to provide some short-term relief, but the Government maintained that no drastic change was needed. However, it did support the Board of Trade in its discussions with the trade unions to relax their restrictive practices.[20]

The main contractors, such as Cammel Laird and Vickers, were allowed to sub-contract under the new rules, but they remained responsible for the specialist work carried out. At first this did not go well, and it was not until the summer of 1915 that the previous quality was attained; in the meantime, many deliveries arrived late or defective and often both. The acceptance of sub-contracting had a further inherent problem in that the method created a false scarcity and an inflation in the price of the raw materials needed to fulfil the order. A company that tendered for the order had to be sure that it could supply that order if they won the tender; to mitigate the liability all those tendering for an order placed requisitions for the raw materials needed to complete the order. For example, 200 firms would tender for an order requiring 2,000 tons of a given raw material, and each of these firms would place an option with the supplier of the raw materials, but only twenty firms would succeed in having their tender approved. But the supplier of the raw material had received requisitions for ten times the amount that was needed, creating administrative chaos and forcing a rise in the price based on fictitious and unwarranted requirements.

The quality of the completed products were still the responsibility of the approved contractors, but still had to be passed by the ROFs, causing further delays. The officers of the ROFs were also inundated with requests for information and product samples. Many of the standard patterns and specifications were simplified for the sub-contractors, making the process more difficult and time-consuming for the inspectors, especially as most of this had to be undertaken post-delivery, resulting in masses of products lying around in apparent confusion. Kitchener thought that this shortage could be alleviated by opening discussions with Canada, India, and the United States, but these discussions were beset with specification problems, as well as misunderstandings over technical terms and manufacturing methods.[21]

The war had not only 'wrong-footed' the munitions industry, even the white-collar employees of the War Office were in a fog of disorganisation. They often worked fourteen-hour days in overcrowded offices and repeatedly clashed with businessmen who felt that the 'expert-buyers' of the Army Contracts Department were giving unfair advantage to the approved contractors and were biased against sub-contractors.[22]

Skilled Workers

As already mentioned, another problem experienced by approved sub-contractors and ROFs was staff shortage. One reason was purely attributable to war—a result of skilled men volunteering to fight the Germans. In addition to this, the expansion of an industry that desperately required skilled men resulted in workers being enticed to leave their current employer to work for a competitor. As an example, by October 1914 the drain on the engineering industry due to enlistment was 12 per cent, and by July 1915 this had risen to 20 per cent.[23]

The Order of the White Feather, originally founded in April 1914 by Admiral Charles Fitzgerald, prompted women to approach men wearing civilian clothes and present them with a white feather, an act that was aimed at shaming them to join up. Unfortunately this did not take into account the skilled men needed for the war industry, or even those enlisted men who happened not to be wearing a uniform. The chronicle *The Suffragette Movement* reported:

Mrs Pankhurst toured the country, making recruiting speeches. Her supporters handed the white feather to every young man they encountered wearing civilian dress, and bobbed up at Hyde Park meetings with placards; 'Intern Them All'.[24]

Army recruitment posters were printed appealing to women to ensure that their men joined up:

Is your 'Best Boy' wearing Khaki? If not don't <u>YOU THINK</u> he should be?

If he does not think that you and your country are worth fighting for—do you think he is WORTHY of you?

Don't pity the girl who is alone—her young man is probably a soldier—fighting for her and her country—and for <u>YOU</u>.[25]

This drain on the skilled workforce was brought to the attention of the Government, who responded by instructing recruiting officers not to enlist men who were employed in companies engaged in war work or who had certain skills that were required in those industries. But the giving of white feathers continued and it was not until 1916 that those undertaking essential war work were given a silver badge to denote their essential role in the war.

The drain due to poaching continued, with skilled men being offered higher wages and incentives to take employment elsewhere. The industry had not only to find skilled men, but also retain them, or as Major Harris termed it, 'To get them and hold them'.[26] Employers made various proposals to the Government: skilled men should be given two- to three-year contracts to prevent them from being poached; Belgian workers unable to work in their own country due to its occupation should be given employment in British industries; women should be employed on a large scale; and the French system, whereby skilled workers were conscripted by the Government into their jobs, should be adopted.[27]

The problems surrounding staff shortages were illustrated in the minutes of the East Anglian Munitions Committee:

At a meeting of the engineering Manufacturers in East Anglia, summoned for the purpose of making arrangements for carrying out of a contract with the War Office for the manufacture of Shells, universal complaint was made of the practical impossibility of getting men back from military service, under any circumstances whatsoever. The Managers have recently made a thorough tour of the whole of the Engineering Works in this area, and have found in practically all shops machinery standing idle which could be usefully employed on the manufacture of munitions of war were men available to work same. Concrete cases were given by employers throughout, of the refusal of their applications for the return of men. The Committee therefore thinks that the time has arrived when some definite instructions should be given that when applications for the return of the men have been made, these men should immediately be restored with the object of assisting in the manufacture of Munitions in East Anglia…. Unless a large proportion of the men who have left the Works of the firms represented by this Committee are allowed to return, the ability of this Committee to fulfil its Contract with the War Office will be seriously threatened. On the other hand, if the men are allowed to return to the Engineering Shops, the capacity for the manufacture of shells in East Anglia would be very materially increased. [28]

Conscription of any form was against the Liberal Party ethos and Prime Minister Asquith felt that adopting the French or German system could wreck the Government of the day.[29] Still under the impression that the war would be over soon, the unions objected strongly to the immigration of Belgian skilled workers and sought to protect their members' rights. The remaining proposal was to increase the number of women working on the factory floor. Although females had been employed in the industry for some time, their build and strength was often a disadvantage (although their small hands were an asset in some roles). In any event, increasing the workforce was paramount, but it would entail a vast training programme, and it was therefore not an immediate answer to the problem.

Unfortunately, the result of all the muddle and inefficiency in the administration and operation of the munitions industry was not academic. The late arrival of ammunition supplies or the receipt of defective ordnance greatly impacted the soldiers at the front. Repington wrote:

> I shall never forget the look on our soldiers' faces when they came out of the trenches after a long hammering by the German artillery to which ours, at this time, could make little reply, it was a look of utter and complete weariness and it haunted me. They seemed almost dead to the world.[30]

Although Kitchener had understood early on that the war would not be over before Christmas, even he could not have guessed that mobile warfare would stagnate into a war of attrition—a static conflict based on the continuous firing of shells both day and night, using up enormous quantities of ammunition in the hope of battering down the enemy's extensive breastworks. Kitchener had had an illustrious career fighting and commanding in the Mahdist Wars in Egypt, Sudan, and especially at Khartoum, as well as in the Anglo-Boer War, all of which were based largely on mobility of forces, with artillery being used in open warfare. In Repington's opinion, 'Kitchener did not comprehend the importance of artillery in war, [and] took no effective measures to increase our supplies of it.' To make matters worse, he also felt that Kitchener had 'concealed the truth of the situation from his colleagues in the Cabinet'.[31]

By the end of 1914, it was clear that the whole munitions programme was in serious trouble and that the country was not working towards a common end. Something needed to be done. Lloyd George, the Chancellor of the Exchequer, appreciated how this inefficiency was letting down the men who were serving their country at the front. He took up the issue, and he was a man well suited to the task:

[Despite being] an egotistical, untrustworthy, unprincipled opportunist … [Lloyd George was] brilliant, dynamic, and charismatic, such that, when he set about a task, he was able to sweep forwards, inspiring others to go with him, breaking down whatever barriers of conservatism and lethargy might stand in the way.[32]

The Cabinet Shells Committee

As Asquith began to appreciate the munitions problem, he was placed in an invidious position between Lloyd George, who was pushing for some resolution, and the popular Kitchener, who was jealously guarding his role as Secretary of State for War and the power that it gave him. The interim solution was the creation of the Cabinet Shells Committee, to be presided over by Kitchener, and with Lloyd George and von Donop as members.[33]

The Committee met in December 1914, for the sixth time since its inception on 1 October 1914, to debate the need to send munitions to Russia to prevent a military collapse. The committee also agreed on the following interim measures to assist the munitions industry: Belgian workers would be brought in to assist the manpower shortage; labour would be diverted from less urgent industries such as the railways; and pressure would be put on firms not on munitions work to release their men.[34]

These were the last acts of the Committee as Kitchener removed his support in January 1915; it was becoming glaringly obvious that a modern war could not be run by separate departments with a supreme authority who did not have sufficient knowledge to coordinate the whole. Lloyd George felt that the only way forward was to place the whole of the country on a war-footing, applying pressure to this end on Asquith in his letter of 22 February:

I sincerely believe that we can double our effective energies if we organised our factories properly. All the engineering works of the country to be turned on to the production of war material. While this process is going on the population ought to be prepared to suffer all sorts of deprivations and even hardships.[35]

In a speech in Bangor six days later, he made his point in no uncertain terms:

This is an engineers' war, and it will be won or lost owing to the shortcomings of engineers. Unless we are able to equip out armies, our predominance in men will avail us nothing.[36]

Repington highlighted the problem in his diary:

We were also short of heavy guns of all calibres, in which the enemy enormously outnumbered us, and of shells for those which we possessed; we were short of trench mortars, of maxims, of rifle and hand grenades, and, in fact, of almost all the necessary instruments and materials for trench warfare.[37]

The discussions between the Board of Trade and the trade unions began to produce results. During March an agreement was reached that included recommendations to avoid strikes and the temporary relaxation of demarcation and dilution rules.[38] These agreements allowed the trade unions to show the public that they were behind the war effort and could be seen to be 'delivering the goods' and 'doing their bit'. However, Lloyd George thought that this was not sufficient and sought the assistance of Lord Northcliffe, owner of *The Times* and the *Daily Mail*, to force Asquith and Kitchener's hand.[39] In early March, Arthur Balfour, the industrialist and previous leader of the Conservatives, wrote to Lloyd George saying that he could see no possibility of improvement in the supply of shells and rifles, 'unless you will take in hand the organization of the engineering resources of the country'.[40]

The continued political pressure was increased following the Battle of Neuve Chapelle, placing Kitchener in such a position that he could no longer conceal the problem. During a speech to the House of Lords on 15 March 1915, he admitted that the production of munitions was facing serious challenges:

> … progress in equipping the new armies and forces in field is hampered by failure to obtain sufficient labour and by delays in production of plant, largely due to enormous demands…. Labour has a right to say that their patriotic work should not be used to inflate the profits of directors and shareholders and we are arranging a system under which the important firms come under Government control. Men working long hours in the shops by day and night, week in and out, are doing their duty for King and Country the same as those on active service in the field.[41]

In an effort to protect his position, Kitchener created the Armaments Output Committee chaired by the Liverpool ship owner George Macaulay Booth. However, this organisation was outflanked on 12 April when Asquith created a 'Treasury Committee' under the name of Munitions of War Committee, an entity that was an embryonic 'Ministry of Munitions', chaired by Lloyd George and excluding Kitchener.

The Battle of Neuve Chapelle

In March 1915 the German Army was still in possession of a large chunk of Northern France and Belgium; they only needed to keep it to claim victory. Their position also allowed them to continue to threaten Paris, attacking the city at a time convenient to them, or even to use the threat as the trump card to secure advantageous peace terms.[1] Therefore Marshal Joffre had no choice but to attempt to drive them out:

> The best and largest portion of the German army was on our soil with its line of battle jutting out a mere five days march from the heart of France. This situation may be clear to every Frenchman that our task consisted of defeating this enemy and driving him out of our country.[2]

Comparative firepower strength in France and Flanders on 29 December 1914 was as follows:[3]

Country	Guns	Effective Rifles
British	924	156,000
French	5,100	1,044,000
Total Allies	6,024	1,209,000
German	4,852	700,000
Difference in favour of Allies	1,172	500,000

However, even this suggested superiority did not place the Allies in a position to penetrate the German defences until the spring of 1915, when reinforcements and stocks of equipment and munitions became available. Holding the Allies in place had also suited the German command, as this strategy allowed it to release 100,000 much-needed troops to strengthen the sixty-four divisions serving on the Eastern Front, where a major offensive was to take place between Gorlice and Tarnow.[4] It was suggested that if the relocation of German troops continued, the Allies would have superiority in numbers by April 1915, ranging between 1,900,000 to 2,450,000.[5]

Despite the stagnation, an inability to break the enemy defences, and the almost continual loss of life, the British public were given the impression by the censored British press that

1915 would be another *annus mirabilis* (year of wonders or miracles) and that the Kaiser would soon be defeated.[6] But those in Government, unfettered by the censor and acquainted with all the facts, knew this was not the position and doubted that a breakthrough would take place any time soon. Illustrating this, Haldane wrote to his mother on 7 January 1915: 'Oh the war! If it would only cease!'[7]

Kitchener wrote to Sir John French on 9 January, 'As you are well aware, the result is still far from being sufficient to maintain the large number of guns which you have under your command adequately supplied with ammunition for offensive purposes.'[8] But in any event, Kitchener was of the opinion that even with more guns and adequate munitions, the line could not be carried by assault: 'The French have an almost unlimited supply of ammunition and fourteen divisions in reserve, so if they cannot get through, we may take it as proved that the lines cannot be forced.'[9] French was of the opposite opinion, believing that with sufficient guns and high-explosive shells, the line could be forced.[10] However, even with the much-needed increase in heavy guns, Sir John French made it very plain that, 'unless an adequate supply of ammunition can be ensured, it is useless to add to the number of guns in the field'.[11]

The impasse on the Western Front prompted the Government to start considering other theatres where a breakthrough could be made. It was suggested that a strong reserve remain on the Western Front, while the bulk of the armies, plus the new volunteer armies as they became available, be used to strike at the enemy in some other place. Kitchener wrote to French, who noted the communication in his diary: 'Another incomprehensible letter arrived from K. to-day. He apparently contemplates the possibility of standing entirely on the defensive in France and using troops for offensive purposes in other parts of the world.'[12] French responded in detail, giving the reasons why a British offensive against the Central Powers could not succeed through any other way of approach than that of France and Belgium, or, in other words, that the war would be decided on the Western Front.[13] Repington wrote in his diary: 'By dividing our armies between France and the Dardanelles it seemed probable that we would be too weak for victory in either theatre.'[14]

The Spring Offensive

Given the relocation of German troops to the Eastern Front, now was the time for the Allies to undertake an offensive. Joffre therefore planned for a spring offensive with the French Tenth Army striking between La Bassée and Arras; in support of this the British would attack a salient around the village of Neuve Chapelle, with the intention of cutting away the salient and investing the village. The plan also presented the even more tantalising opportunity of investing Aubers Ridge.

Aubers Ridge protected the plain of Douai, essential to the German war machine in providing extended supply and communication lines among the long, straggling lines of canals, roads, and railway lines. Joffre saw this as an 'Achilles' heel' of the German occupation of Northern France.[15] In describing the plan in correspondence to Lieutenant-General Sir Henry Seymour Rawlinson, commander of IV Corps, on 2 March, General Haig stated:

Our objective is not merely the capture of Neuve Chapelle. Our existing line [is] just as satisfactory for us as if we were in Neuve Chapelle. I aim getting to the line of the La Bassée road to Lille and thus cut off the enemy's front. It seems to me desirable to make our plan in the chance of surprising the enemy and with the definitive objective of advancing rapidly (and without any check) in the hope of starting a general advance.[16]

If the French and British were successful, the plain would be open to the cavalry, and the benefit of the logistical network would be taken from Germany. This would lead to the French city of Lille being returned to the Allied sphere of influence and provide the much sort-after breakthrough, forcing the enemy to retreat. Despite receiving only a half-hearted approval from the War Council, Sir John French instructed Haig to prepare detailed plans.[17]

Before any action could take place, the men had to be made mobile. The winter of 1914/15 had been hard and unpleasant, and the troops, especially those from warmer parts of the Empire, had suffered badly from the rain, cold, and mud. The battalions to be used in the initial assaults were withdrawn for what was termed 'rest', consisting of drill, route marches with full packs, extensive training, and physical fitness regimes.

Neuve Chapelle—The Battlefield

The Neuve Chapelle salient in French Flanders had been formed out of the battles of October 1914, when the German Army's unsuccessful attempt to occupy the Belgian and French coast had resulted in the British Army being transferred to Aisne. Five days later on 25 October, Smith-Dorrien was at Givenchy, beginning a wheeling movement round La Bassée towards Lille, but his forces were prevented from advancing beyond the Aubers Ridge by a strong German effort, reinforced by troops and guns released from Antwerp. It was a bitter struggle; the German Sixth Army took Lille, while the Fourth Army attacked the exposed British flank at Ypres. In the south, the enemy directed their attack towards the occupation of Neuve Chapelle. Neuve Chapelle was a small village of neat villas with gaudy shutters, a few estaminets (small coffee bars), a red-brick brewery and, on the outskirts, an old white château set among walls, gardens, and orchards.[18] The village laid about midway between the towns of Armentières and Bethune, approximately 23 miles south of Ypres and less than 10 miles west of Lille, located on the other side of Aubers Ridge.

The battle of 25 October was one of attack and counter-attack that went on all day, resulting in the village becoming a ghastly scene of destruction and death. In the streets and ruined houses there was constant and desperate hand-to-hand fighting with rifle and bayonet. The German troops were successful in occupying the village, but the Indian troops fought on and retained occupation of a cross-roads known as Port Arthur. The occupation of the village created the salient into British lines on 27 October, before the fighting moved back towards Ypres. It was during this battle that the Germans first tried using chemical weapons, when they filled artillery shells with sneezing powder and fired them into the British lines.[19] The experiment was ineffective but it gave an indication of what was to follow.

The village is situated on the junction of two main roads: one from La Bassée to Estaires, located at the south-west end of the village, and the principal road, leading via Croix Blanche and Fleurbaix to Armentières. Within the boundaries of the village, smaller roads linked to these formed an irregular diamond-shaped island. The village was between the crooked main road, Rue Tilleloy, and the partially artificial watercourse, which was anything between knee to waist deep and grandly named the River Layes, also referred to as Layes Brook and Riviére des Laies. It ran between Armentières and the network of watercourses flowing out of the Riviére La Loisne and criss-crossing the district north-east of Bethune.[20] Rue Tilleloy led north from the junction at Pont Logy, with the Estaires–La Bassée road, past orchards and a large farm on the outskirts of the village, known as the Moated Grange (La Ferme Vanbesien), to Fauquissart.[21]

To the south-east of the village is the woodland of the Bois du Biez, with hamlets La Russe and Les Brulots situated respectively north and south of the wood. Immediately behind the wood the plain becomes broken and begins to rise gently through a 10 per cent gradient (this calculation is based on Neuve Chapelle's altitude of 20 metres against the 35 metres of Aubers Ridge).[22] The ridge is 6 miles in length running in a north-easterly direction from the Bois du Biez and the villages of Piètre and Aubers, and begins from a point 2 miles south-west of Lille. When the ridge reaches the village of Fournes, two spurs run out, one due west to a height known as Haut Pommereau, and the other following the line of the main road to Illes, overlooking the plain towards Lille, Roubaix, and Tourcoing.[23]

The area between the village and the Bois du Biez was, and still is, made up of fields with an incline towards the woods. The terrain consists of deep wet soil heavy with clay and with a water-table barely a foot below the surface. Hedges and watercourses abound the plain, along with, in 1915, the old Smith-Dorrien trench, which had been the scene of bitter hand-to-hand struggles the previous October.

In the spring of 1915 the British lines ran more or less parallel with the Rue Tilleloy as far as the grounds of the Moated Grange—the farm buildings themselves were in no man's land.[24] In the opposite direction, the line ran towards the Estaires–La Bassée road and along that road before circling around the British strong point known as Port Arthur, before running almost due south to Festubert and Givenchy. The German defences drew an approximate line from Port Arthur in the south past Signpost Lane, Sunken Lane, and the Moated Grange, and some cottages that went by the imaginative name of 'Nameless Cottages', before continuing past Fauquissart and onwards to Bois Grenier and Armentières.[25] These consisted of three lines of trenches with no man's land 80–300 yards between them, with communication trenches, machine-gun saps, and intricate barbed wire entanglements. The whole area was covered by the defences located in the hamlet to the front of Bois du Biez, the densely wooded area behind, as well as strongholds at Piètre Mill and the bridge over the River Layes.

Opposite: Sketch map of Neuve Chapelle with major locations noted. (*Based on sketch map published in the* Daily Mail, *19 April 1915*)

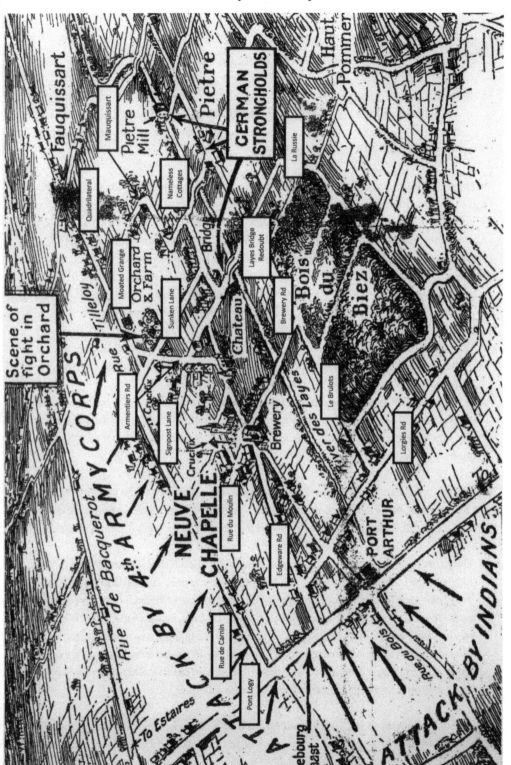

The British Plan

The Times History of the War describes the importance of the village of Neuve Chapelle:

> Neuve Chapelle formed the gateway which gave access to the ridge. The capture of Lille
> would indeed have been of the highest importance. It would have placed the allies in a fair
> position to move against the Germans between that point and the sea. For this the capture
> of Neuve Chapelle was a necessary preliminary.[26]

In general terms, the plan called for the British line to be straightened, eradicating the salient
and incorporating the village within British territory, before advancing through the wood
to attack and invest Aubers Ridge. The cavalry would be loosed and the towns of Lille and
Armentières would be attacked during a two-week campaign. Commander of the IV Corps
Lieutenant-General Sir Henry Rawlinson had dragged his feet through the planning stage,
wanting to restrict the action to the capture of the village only, and attempted to delegate
responsibility to his divisional commanders, who wanted to attack incrementally, nibbling
away over a series of days.[27] A peeved Haig urged him to think in broader terms:

> The advance to be made is not a minor operation. It must be understood that we are
> embarking on a serious offensive movement with the object of breaking the German line
> and consequently our advance is to be pushed vigorously....
>   The idea is not to capture a trench here, or a trench there, but to carry the operation right
> through; in a sense surprise the Germans, carry them right off their legs, push forward to
> the Aubers Ridge with as little delay as possible, and exploit the success thus gained by
> pushing forward mounted troops forthwith.[28]

In a letter to Kitchener sent on 6 March, Rawlinson appraised him of the situation regarding
the forthcoming battle, which could be seen as a political action to protect himself should the
breakthrough fail. In any event, the letter was sent over his commander's (General Haig's) head:

> Things look hopeful I think for an attack on Neuve Chapelle which is tentatively fixed for the
> 10th but if the wet continues it will be absolutely necessary to postpone the date. We shall have
> a very considerable predominance of Arty and infantry, assets which we have never before
> possessed and we certainly ought to be able to force a big hole in the enemy's line. Whether
> we shall be able to follow it up and get the Cavy through behind him is another matter but I
> think there is a reasonable prospect of our being able to do so. Anyway conditions are more
> favourable than they ever have been before and if we cannot obtain a distinct success now, we
> never shall be able to in this theatre of trenches, wire and mud.[29]

The British front was spread over 13 miles from Neuve Chapelle, running north-east to Bois
Grenier, and held by two of the three corps of the First Army: IV Corps and the Indian
Corps, each comprised of two divisions. [30]

IV Corps commanded by Lt-Gen. Rawlinson: the 7th Division under Maj.-Gen. Thompson Capper and the 8th Division under Maj.-Gen. Francis Davies.

Indian Corps commanded by Lt-Gen. Sir James Wilcocks: The Meerut Corps under Lt-Gen. Charles Anderson and the Lahore Division under Maj.-Gen. Henry D'Urban Keary.

7th Division

20th Brigade   **Brig.-Gen. F. Heyworth**
1/Grenadier Guards
2/Scots Guards
2/Border Regiment
2/Gordon Highlanders
6/Gordon Highlanders (TF)

21st Brigade   **Brig.-Gen. H. Watts**
2/Bedfordshire Regiment
2/Yorkshire Regiment (Green Howards)
2/Royal Scots Fusiliers
2/Wiltshire Regiment

22nd Brigade   **Brig.-Gen. S. Lawford**
2/Royal West Surrey Regiment (The Queen's)
2/Royal Warwickshire Regiment
1/Royal Welch Fusiliers
1/South Staffordshires Regiment
8/The Royal Scots (Lothian Regiment) (TF)

8th Division

23rd Brigade   **Brig.-Gen. R. Pinney**
2/Devonshire Regiment
2/West Yorkshire Regiment
2/Cameronians (Scottish Rifles)
2/Middlesex Regiment

24th Brigade   **Brig.-Gen. F. Carter**
1/Worcester Regiment
2/East Lancashire Regiment
1/Notts & Derby Regiment (Sherwood Foresters)
2/Northamptonshire Regiment

5/The Black Watch (Royal Highlanders)(TF)
4/Cameron Highlanders (TF)

25th Brigade   **Brig.-Gen. A. Lowry-Cole**
2/Lincolnshire Regiment
2/Royal Berkshire Regiment
1/Royal Irish Rifles
2/Rifle Brigade
13/London Regiment (TF)

Meerut Division—Lt-Gen. C. Anderson

Dehra Dun Brigade   **Brig.-Gen. C. Jacob**
1/Seaforth Highlanders
2/2 Gurkhas
1/9 Gurkhas
4/Seaforth Highlanders (TF)

Garhwal Brigade   **Brig.-Gen. C. Blackadder**
2/Leicestershire Regiment
1/39 Garhwal Rifles
2/39 Garhwal Rifles
2/3 Gurkhas
3/London Regiment (TF)

Bareilly Brigade   **Brig.-Gen. W. Southey**
2/The Black Watch (Royal Highlanders)
6 Jats
41 Dogras
58 Vaughan's Rifles
4/The Black Watch (Royal Highlanders) (TF)
2/8 Gurkhas (Div. Troops)

Lahore Division

Ferozepore Brigade   **Brig.-Gen. R. Egerton**
1/Connaught Rangers
9 Bhopal Rangers
57 Wilde's Rifles
129 Baluchis
4/London Regiment (TF)

Jullundur Brigade　　**Brig.-Gen. E. Strickland**
1/Manchester Regiment
47 Sikhs
59 Scinde Rifles
4/Suffolk Regiment (TF)

Sirhind Brigade　　**Brig.-Gen. W. Walker VC**
1/Highland Light Infantry
15 Sikhs
1/1 Gurkhas
1/4 Gurkhas
4/Liverpool Regiment (The King's)(Extra Reserve)

TF = Territorial Force

In addition to the infantry, General Headquarters (GHQ) supplied the heavy artillery, the medical and engineering support units, and other units being transferred temporarily from other corps.[31] It was the intensive artillery barrage that would provide the element of surprise—a barrage that, in terms of fire power per foot of enemy trench, was to be the most powerful seen to date, a claim of dubious pride that would remain until 1917. Haig hoped that this barrage would cause the defenders to panic, break, and run.[32]

Discussions continued over the various elements of the plan: the commander of the First Army Artillery wanted compartmentalised bombardment over four days, whereas Haig wished to 'compress the fire into a sudden outburst for three hours—and follow it with a sudden rush of our infantry'.[33] Rawlinson's preference was for a barrage of just thirty minutes.

Royal Flying Corps (RFC) observation planes were to be used to spot the fall of shells and identify the movement of reinforcements; this close support work would be carried out by the First Wing under the command of Lieutenant-Colonel H. M. Trenchard, who would report directly to the First Army Headquarters.[34]

Opposite the British and Imperial troops in their defensive positions were the following enemy forces:[35]

VII Corps

Corp Troops	11 Jäger Battalion	
13th Division	25th Brigade:	13 Regiment
		158 Regiment
	26th Brigade:	15 Regiment
		55 Regiment

14th Division	27th Brigade:	16 Regiment
		53 Regiment
	79th Brigade:	56 Regiment
		57 Regiment

6th Bavarian Reserve		
(BR) Division	12th BR Brigade:	16 BR Regiment
		17 BR Regiment
	14th BR Brigade	20th BR Regiment
		21st BR Regiment

Despite the length of the front, Haig had decided to make a concentrated attack in depth along a relatively narrow portion, with 'holding' attacks taking place at La Bassée, aimed at deceiving the Germans, while simultaneous actions to the north and south would pin down the enemy.[36] In addition, I Corps would extend their front on the southern flank, while the Canadians would replace IV Corps in the north.[37]

Haig's plan was made up of three stages:

First Stage: A wire-cutting bombardment of ten minutes followed by an initial thirty-five-minute barrage targeting the enemy trenches. Haig had concluded that this would be sufficient to eliminate the centres of opposition faced by the first stage assault troops. Simultaneous attacks would be launched along the Moulin de Piètre–Piètre road, and on the right flank, the Meerut Division would attack the German trenches from Port Arthur. The force would then advance further to meet the assault troops in the village.

Second Stage: This would be followed by a barrage to prevent German reinforcements from moving towards Neuve Chapelle itself, and finally there would be a twenty-five-minute barrage on the village before the 25th Brigade would assault the trenches to the front of Rue Tilleloy. Once these were consolidated they would act as 'jumping-off' points for the second wave of assault troops who would attack and invest the village. Any further artillery barrages had to be specifically approved by Haig's First Army Headquarters on a case-by-case basis.

Third Stage: By now the salient would have been eradicated, removing the danger of the enfilade fire from the German positions situated around its edges. Artillery would be moved forward to lay support fire for the advance. The Indian Corps would advance across the wetlands to the hamlet and through the Bois du Biez behind, while the IV Corps progressed from the west and north-west towards the Aubers Ridge. Intelligence had ascertained that the ridge was held by two seriously weakened divisions of the German VII Corps who were not concentrated on the ridge but spread over the whole 13-mile front. It was estimated that the three corps involved in the attack would muster 87,000 men and be opposed by approximately 20,000 German soldiers, supported by a small reserve which could not easily access the front line.[38] This advantage could not last long, for once the battle started, enemy reserves would be brought in from other areas to prevent a breakthrough. It was therefore imperative that British reserves be brought forward as soon as possible; if they were not, the momentum of attack would falter, and the advantage would move to the enemy.

Fourth Stage: Once the ridge was taken, the cavalry would charge onto the plain, leading the advance, cutting through the lines of communication and creating the mobility needed to break the stalemate.

After a meeting with the key commanders, Haig wrote in his diary of 5 March:

We are embarking on a serious offensive movement with the object of breaking the German line. There is no idea of merely taking a trench here, or a trench there. My object is to surprise the Germans, and push forward to the Aubers Ridge with as little delay as possible, and exploit the success thus gained by pushing forward mounted troops as quickly as possible so as to threaten La Bassée from the northeast in which direction there are no fortifications.

The Keynote of all work is offensive action. Bombing parties must act offensively trying to get forward on to the flanks. Infantry will advance first to Enemy's front trenches, then beyond the village, next to the Bois de Biez and Aubers Ridge.

Commanders must therefore carefully consider the employment of their reserves so as to maintain the forward movement.[39]

Battle Preparations

The trenches behind the Rue Tilleloy were modified to include forward saps and forming-up trenches to shelter and hide the mass of troops that needed to be in position prior to attack. Ladders were put in place to assist in the process of getting the troops out of the trench and into no man's land, while portable bridges were built to enable the troops to get over the communication trenches and watercourses which littered the marshy area.

The Royal Artillery quietly began moving the 342 artillery pieces of the IV and Indian corps, augmented by the light 13-pdr guns from the cavalry, into a horse-shoe shape behind the British Lines to the west of the village.[40] The heavier artillery pieces were installed to the rear of the horse-shoe configuration and lighter artillery pieces. Sir John French had ordered two of the mammoth 15-inch howitzers to be brought to the sector, but unfortunately only one was to arrive, and with very little ammunition, much of which proved faulty. The lack of heavy guns was further exasperated by the delay of the eight 6-inch howitzers of the 59 and 61 Siege Batteries of the VII Siege Brigade, which by mid-February were still in Britain.[41]

On 9 May 1915, General Haig wrote a special order to all the troops of the First Army:

We are about to engage the enemy under very favourable conditions. Until now in the present campaign, the British Army has, by its pluck and determination, gained victories against an enemy greatly superior both in men and guns. Reinforcements have made us stronger than the enemy on our front. Our guns are now both more numerous than the enemy's are and also larger than any hitherto used by any army in the field. In front of us we have only one German Corps, spread out on a front as large as that occupied by the whole of our Army (the First). We are now about to attack with about 48 Battalions a locality in that front which is held by some three German Battalions. It seems probable also that for the first day of the operations the Germans will not have more than four Battalions available as reinforcements for the counter attack. Quickness of movement is therefore of first importance to enable us to forestall the enemy and thereby gain success without severe loss. At no time in this war has there been a more favourable moment for us, and I feel confident of success. The extent of that success must depend on the rapidity and determination with which we advance.[42]

From the previous evening, troops marched silently along the roads from Laventie, Richebourg, and St Vaast, lost in their own thoughts, through villages that had been shattered from almost incessant bombardment over the last few months, left roofless and open to the elements, with their inhabitants driven away. Once in place, hot coffee was passed round, for some a warm supper, and for many, thoughts turned to breakfast.[43] With short-form wills completed and the last letters home collected, packs were exchanged for haversacks, overcoats were discarded, and ammunition, bombs, rations, sandbags—to be filled when captured trenches were consolidated—were distributed from the stores that had accumulated over the last weeks. Fixing bayonets on the end of their Lee-Enfield Mk3 rifles, the troops waited.[44]

The night had been cold, and the heavy surge uniforms were wet with the damp air; the men's boots and puttees[45] were covered in the thick, yellow, gloopy mud of the area. Caps were jammed on heads—there were no steel helmets for the British troops.

In the pre-dawn, the sudden deep booms of British guns could be heard as they started the 'registering' process—checking that their ranges were correct, rather like a cricketer will hit a few balls in the nets before going into bat. Meanwhile, across no man's land, the Germans kept watch, the dawn being an obvious time in which to launch attacks. A *Hauptmann*[46] became suspicious of unusual movement and discovered that the trenches to his front were filled with troops.[47] He sent an urgent request to the battery commander for artillery to target the trenches, only to receive the reply that the Corps Commander had to authorise such requests and that he was asleep.[48]

Haig wrote in his diary: 'By 06:30 hours clouds seemed to be lifting so I ordered the plan to be carried out as arranged namely, bombardment to begin at 07:30 and attack by infantry at 08:05 hours.'[49]

The Battle—10 March

Dawn broke softly through the veil of clouds, which slowly moved away, and the silence was broken at 0730 hours when the 15-inch howitzer, christened 'Granny', situated at

Sally-sur-la-Lys, fired a 1,400-Ib shell signalling the start of the barrage.[50] It was the first of 61,219 shells that the Royal Artillery were to fire that day, of which 41,000 came from the 18-pdrs.[51,52] Shells in their hundreds, of every size and calibre, flew over the British trenches, some from the lighter guns passing only 3–4 feet above the soldiers in the trenches, making the air hot like an inferno in the cold, damp dawn. A flail of deadly eruptions crashed down on the enemy positions; the British hoped they would sweep everything living from their path. Great gouts and fountains of flame, scarlet and green and gold, and a noise that numbed the senses and stupefied the brain—that was the barrage. Charles Tennant of the Seaforth Highlanders recalled, 'the din was terrific, the whole air and the solid earth itself became one quivering jelly.[53] 2nd Lieutenant Pennefather of the Rifle Brigade said, 'the [most] unholy bombardment the Lord ever saw [went] over the position, seeing the shorts kill many in the Berkshires line and several [of our] rifleman.[54] 'Shorts', or short-falling shells, would be a continual problem for British forces in 1915. These shells were either badly manufactured or damaged in some way during transport or storage. On 10 March, despite the losses incurred by shorts, a devastating barrage pulverised the enemy trenches opposite the Rifles and Seaforths, and the barbed wire was cut as if it were twine.[55]

A Royal Flying Corps observation plane flew over the battlefield, reporting on the fall of the shells and identifying enemy targets. The plucky pilots dodged the white balls of exploding shrapnel while trying to keep their altitude high enough to evade the artillery shells, or 'Iron Ration' as it was known, pouring into the German lines.

First Stage

Forward observation officers watched the barrage from two towers in the area, as well as other improvised sites to ensure that it was effective. The barrage continued until 0805 hours, when, after a slight delay, the guns were trained on the next targets and the sounds of officers' whistles—which could be held in the mouth, leaving the hands free—resounded throughout the British lines, signalling for the assault troops to scramble out of the trenches into no man's land, and dash towards the German trenches.

Along the Estaires–La Bassée road, the Garhwal Brigade of the Meerut Division left their trenches and advanced towards their objectives in the German front lines. The 1/39 Garhwal became disorientated almost immediately, attacking and securing a 200-yard section of German trench that had not been their objective, despite barbed wire and most of the parapets remaining undamaged. Their Garhwali colleagues on the right had taken their objective at a rush, working hard with bayonet and rifle, almost heedless of the bullets whizzing around the field. The citation of Rifleman Gobar Sing Negi, who was posthumously awarded the Victoria Cross, reads: '[he] entered their main trench, and was the first man to go round each traverse, driving back the enemy until they were eventually forced to surrender.[56] They finally took part of the Smith-Dorrien trench at 0900 hours, but finding it flooded, dug a replacement closer to the River Layes. The division occupied a front from Brewery Road on the left to Lorgies Road on the right. The 2/3 Gurkhas and 2/39 Garhwal Rifles occupied the position on the left and the 1/39 Garhwal and 2/Leicesters occupied that on the right, but the 1/39 and the 2/Leicesters were separated by a gap of some

300 yards of trench. This had been the original objective of the 1/39, but it remained full of German soldiers who almost continuously attempted to dislodge them.

The Garhwal Brigade had reached their objectives in record time; despite being ready to advance against the village from the south and Bois du Biez, they had to wait, as the barrage had not ended.

The assault troops of the 2/Lincolnshire and 2/Royal Berkshire regiments were waiting in their positions along the Rue Tilleloy, with a front of 400 yards from which the British barbed wire had been removed (the uprights were left in place to confuse the enemy). The 1/Royal Irish Rifles were in assembly trenches to their rear, close to Signpost Lane, with the 2/Rifle Brigade to their right, astride a small road that led past the heap of rubble that was once the church, at the very heart of the village.

As the barrage ended the Lincolns and Berkshires advanced towards their objectives situated in front of the village, through thoroughly destroyed wire and pulverised breastworks. They discovered only lightly held trenches, but as noted by 2nd Lieutenant Pennefather, they had suffered severely from short-falling shells. Lieutenant-Colonel Feetham's report stated: 'one shell buried twelve or fifteen men, who were only extricated after the advance, some dead and others badly wounded.... Casualties from "shorts" continued till the first objective was reached'.[57] They continued their advance for another 200 yards, carrying four lines of enemy trenches, which although were severely damaged by the barrage, still laid down significant machine-gun fire.

The 2/Cameronians (Scottish Rifles) and the 2/Middlesex were located along a 400-yard front to the north of Signpost Lane, opposite German trenches manned by the 11 Jägers. The barrage in this sector had not been successful, with the barbed wire and enemy trenches left largely untouched. It had been the responsibility of the 59 Siege Battery, which had been delayed in Britain and therefore had arrived with insufficient time to prepare for the battle.[58] The gunners had not been able to register the guns properly, making the fall of their shells between 5,200 and 7,000 yards indistinguishable from other projectiles.[59] Added to this, all the new 6-inch howitzers of the 59 and 81 Batteries suffered from poor quality shells, manufactured with inconsistent propellant composition. In addition, the barrels of the 4.7-inch guns were worn out. Rawlinson had referred to the problem in his letter to Kitchener of 6 March: 'We want … better 4:7 shells. We have had several driving bands strip (4.7), which drop the shell 3,000 yards short of the target and the other day we killed some of our own men in this way. Then again we burst a 4:7 gun three days ago owing to the shell exploding in the gun.'[60]

The assaulting troops ran straight into the murderous machine-gun fire laid down by the enemy from their undamaged trenches. Sergeant Daws of the Middlesex Regiment later wrote:

> The front line advanced and as they leave their trenches we shout, 'Go on the Middlesex. Go on the Die-Hards!' They are met by terrible machine-gun fire. Few reached the German wire, but these tore in vain at the thick entanglements until their hands were torn and bleeding and their uniforms in rags. The second line fared no better and were decimated.[61]

The second wave comprising of the 2/Devonshire and 2/West Yorkshire regiments ran into the same murderous fire, having to step over the bodies of their brigade comrades. Lieutenant Malcolm Kennedy of the 2/Scottish Rifles wrote:

> ... the two supporting companies [C & D] had come up and were breaking their way through the hedge, closely followed by men of the Devons and West Yorks. It must have been a nerve-racking ordeal for them advancing under heavy fire over that bit of ground, thickly strewn as it was with our dead and wounded, and with little bunches of our dead hanging limply in the tangled mass of barbed wire.[62]

The advance faltered and then stopped, leaving the right-hand flank dangerously exposed, and even worse, leaving the strong points at Mauquissart and Nameless Cottages undamaged. From these positions, the Germans began laying down enfilade fire across most of the battleground.

Second Stage

The barrage created a curtain of shrapnel directly behind the enemy lines, preventing reinforcements from coming forward. At the same time, other batteries bombarded the village and identified strong points, while the heavier guns began counter-battery fire and targeted other strong points. Prisoners later reported that all German attempts to reinforce the front line were checked.

The riflemen of the 2/Rifle Brigade and the Royal Irish Rifles had waited in their assembly trenches, moving up to the front line once the Lincolns and Berkshires had left them to assault the enemy trenches. The 2/Rifle Brigade had had a last meal in the early morning at Croix Barbee, and received a last ration of rum as they watched the barrage start to fall on the village before going over the top.[63] Once the report was received that the front line objectives had been secured, the 1/Royal Rifles were the first out of their trenches following the blasts from Captain Graham's French postman's horn. They charged to the village outskirts where they had to wait for the barrage to stop. The 2/Rifle Brigade were the first into the village, and almost immediately Captain R. O. Bridgeman heard the familiar calls of '*Namaste*' (Hello) and '*Tapai Kasto Hunu, Huncha*' (how are you?) as they met the 2/39 Garhwal Rifles and the 2/3 Gurkhas, with whom they had served in India.[64]

Neuve Chapelle was a scene of devastation. It looked as if an earthquake had struck the village; the chaos was so complete that the street lines were all but obliterated. The church in the centre was a bare shell of a structure, standing delicately above a huge mound of debris. The little graveyard had also been hit and the bodies of the long dead lay scattered among the grey-green dead of the German infantry and British soldiers.[65] John F. Lucy of the Royal Irish Rifles recalled: '... the bodies of the men of our battalion [killed in October 1914] had been blown out of the ground after five months, and their copses, bearing the same buttons and badges, lay mingled with those of the newly killed men.'[66] Amazingly, a tall crucifix remained standing above the churchyard, its surface pockmarked with bullet holes but largely intact.

The reception from the enemy was mixed. Some were emerging from cellars and dug-outs wounded or dazed with the hands up, while others endeavoured to escape by dodging around the shattered houses. Some resisted, firing down on the riflemen. Many of the enemy were killed in the 'mopping-up' operation that was taking place among the din and devastation. On the whole, the resistance was fairly half-hearted and was quickly overcome, but nonetheless, each deadly isolated pocket of resistance had to be dealt with. With the village invested, the right flank of the 25th Brigade was secure.

The Rifle Brigade and Royal Irish continued their advance towards the next objective, but ran into serious danger from their own barrage and had to pull back. Pennefather wrote: 'We simply boosted through the village capturing about 200 Deutschers. Byatt, Verney, Bulkley-Johnson were shot in this part.'[67] By 0850 hours the 2/Rifle Brigade were between the village and the River Layes. Their scouts and bombers had punched out as far as a section of the Smith-Dorrien trench, which was soon occupied by 'B' Company, but at the loss of its commander, Captain R. C. Burton, who had been killed on the way across. Lieutenant E. H. Leigh took command of the company, while Major Harrison took command of the trench as 'C' and 'D' companies set up support positions to provide covering fire. Seeing a white flag being raised a couple of yards to the right, some riflemen were sent to capture some thirty-three of the enemy.

Meanwhile, 2/Royal Irish Rifles moved to occupy the area slightly north of the château, across Signpost Lane and with the Sunken Lane to the front. The area was known as 'Road Triangle' because of the juncture of the three roads. The men of the 2/Royal Irish soon realised that the Middlesex and Scottish Rifles were still receiving intense fire from the German line that had been left undamaged by the initial barrage. They asked permission to attack the flank of the enemy; this was refused and they began to receive heavy machine-gun fire from the strong point on the bridge over the River Layes. Their flank was by now dangerously exposed.

By 1100 hours the village and the roads leading northward and south-westward from the eastern end of that village were in British hands, and consolidation of the ground gained was in progress. Lieutenant Stacke and his men of the 1/Worcesters reconnoitred the area. Working their way from the village, they dashed for the remnants of a lane, and Stacke reported they could not detect any movement in and around the Bois du Biez.[68] This coincided with the view of the 2/Rifle Brigade, who reported very little opposition to their front; from what they could see, the enemy were either dead, captured, or fleeing towards the wood, mostly without their equipment. In Lieutenant-Colonel Reginald Byng Stephens' view, commander of the 2/Rifle Brigade, this was a golden opportunity to exploit the situation; the enemy could be driven from what was left of their defences, as was outlined in the original battle plan:

> As soon as the village of Neuve Chapelle has been captured and made good, the 7th and 8th Divisions, supported by the Indian Corps on their right, will be ordered by the Corps Commander to press forward to capture the high ground.[69]

Accordingly, Stephens reported to Brigadier-General Lowry-Cole, commander of the 25th Brigade, at Brigade Headquarters that their objective had been consolidated and that the situation was ideal to undertake a further advance against a broken enemy. He requested permission to precede. He was advised that the left of the line, the 23rd Brigade front, was held up, and that until that line had come forward the Rifle Brigade must stand their ground.

Communication is the life-blood of battlefield command and control, and without situation reports and adequate communication of orders, those commanding the battle have no real way of knowing what is going on. In 1915, radios were delicate machines and not suited to the battlefield, while telephone lines had to be buried deep under the ground or could easily be cut by shell fire. Semaphore was just too dangerous. That left the messenger or runner, a man who literally ran between the command post and the front line carrying orders, requests, or reports. This form of communication was often unreliable, as once the messenger had left the officer, the officer had no idea whether his message had got through. Snipers were specially trained to recognise and shoot messengers, therefore there was always a large possibility that a runner could be wounded or killed on the way. Once the message was delivered and the commanding officer had issued his orders, a messenger had to get back to the front line. Until the reply was received, the front line officer could not know whether his original message had been received, and conversely, the commanding officer could not be sure whether his orders had reached the officer on the front line. The whole system was unreliable, and when applied to the Napoleonic dictum that no plan survives first contact with the enemy, it became even worse. It was therefore often down to the officer at the front line to make decisions that could impact the whole battle.

General Haig wrote in his diary: 'The communications trying to illuminate this fog of war now failed.'[70] Brigade Headquarters, waiting for the left flank to be secured, did not pass the report on the Rifle Brigade's success to Divisional Headquarters, who therefore did not order the advance to continue, did not commit the reserves, and did not release the cavalry. It is quite possible that had Stephens been allowed to continue the attack, with the support of the reserves, the gap would have been widened, forcing the Germans into a general withdrawal. Later reports confirmed that there were no German reserves available to meet such a manoeuvre.[71]

The 2/Rifle Brigade, in conjunction with the 1/Royal Irish Rifles, now continued digging in. It was unbelievable: 'the Rifle Brigade were navvying!'[72] The Smith-Dorrien trench was deemed uninhabitable as it was too waterlogged and further breastworks were built with sandbags and debris from the village. Lieutenant Pennefather wrote more caustically: 'We could have gone to Berlin at least if there had been anyone behind, but as you know our brilliant staff had two men and a boy behind and also 20,000 Cavalry which they refused to let go because they said it was too foggy, all total balls as there was no fog.'[73]

It was not until midday that, after a new barrage, another attack against the trenches of the Moated Grange was made by the surviving Middlesex, augmented by the 2/West Yorks, who advanced over the dead bodies of their regimental colleagues and those of the Scottish Rifles that had fallen during the earlier attacks. The 1/Worcester, 2/East Lancashire, and 1/Notts & Derby (Sherwood Foresters) regiments, supported by the 2/Northamptonshires of the 24th Brigade, pushed the attack further, consolidating the area around the Moated Grange, the farm buildings, and orchard. But like the Rifle Brigade, they were then told to wait.

The whole front had now reached their objectives and were ready to advance, but instead they were held in place while receiving fire from the Bois du Biez and the strong points of Piètre and Layes Bridge. Casualties were mounting. At 1400 hours, after a further barrage over the Bois du Biez, the 3/Gurkhas of the Dehra Dun Brigade advanced, kukris in hand, to the scraggy fringe of trees on the outskirts of the Bois du Biez. Expecting the objective to be unoccupied, they found it was anything but. Within the shattered houses of the hamlet were machine-gunners who laid down a withering fire, while the unsuppressed strongholds to the north poured enfilade fire across the front of the wood. The delay in moving forward had allowed a partial reorganisation of the enemy who had reinforced the trenches with two companies of the 11 Jägers. Interrogation of a captured German soldier provided notice that two regiments of reinforcements were on their way. Meanwhile, with their positions unsupported and receiving heavy fire, the Gurkhas fell back to positions along the River Layes.

The delay in moving forward had also given the enemy to the front of the Rifle Brigade the opportunity to consolidate:

> The Battalion continued to dig all day but lost a good many men from the fire of two field guns and from a Maxim which moved up and down the road in front of the Bois du Biez. One of our mountain guns which was being rushed up into the village was knocked out with all its team by a shell. [74]

A further advance by the Garhwalis, on the right of the Gurhkas, commenced at 1530 hours. They were immediately hit by heavy fire from apparently undamaged enemy trenches to the front. The Indians bravely continued their advance over the 200 yards to their objective, through uncut entanglements, incurring the loss of twenty officers and 350 men killed or wounded. Losing their way, they swung to the right, occupying an enemy trench, which was immediately shelled. The Leicesters advanced at a rush to form a junction with the marooned Garhwalis, using bombing parties to attack the crowded German trenches, forcing them to vacate their defences.

These attacks succeeded in straightening the front, which now ran from Marquissart—approximately 500 yards south-west of the Moated Grange—to the eastern corner of the Road Triangle. From there the line ran to the Smith-Dorrien trench and the River Layes, and finally along the old British front line south-east of Port Arthur.

A general advance was prepared, but it was stopped by darkness. The Royal Irish Rifles history states: 'The chance of a "break-through" that will-o'-the wisp of the first years of the war, had actually arrived, but did not remain long when it was not taken.'[75] The British attack had lost momentum, allowing the Germans to start bringing up their reserves and feverishly build a new line of defence along what was originally their second line, strengthening their strong points at Mauquissart, Nameless Cottages, and at the bridge over the River Layes.

German Reinforcements

One battalion of 13 Infantry Regiment moved to the front between the Moated Grange and Fauquissart to prevent any further exploitation by elements of the 24th Brigade. Just as darkness descended the almost empty defences fronting the Bois du Biez were reinforced with the two reserve battalions (56 and 57) which had been rushed from Violanes and Salomé. Part of the XIX (Saxon) Corp, amounting to one battalion of each of the following regiments, moved forward to assist in a planned counter-attack for the next day: [76]

24th Division:	47th Brigade:	139 Regiment
		179 Regiment
	48th Brigade:	106 Regiment
		107 Regiment
40th Division:	88th Brigade:	104 Regiment
		133 Regiment

The first day of battle ended with the salient having been eradicated, bringing Neuve Chapelle within the British lines, but the larger objectives had not been accomplished; Bois du Biez was still occupied, and the strong points were still a danger to the British positions, with Aubers Ridge tantalisingly close, but still out of reach. Corps command therefore worked through the night to plan a six-battalion attack to be launched at daybreak on 11 March, aiming at Aubers Ridge and Ligny le Grande—situated to the rear of the wood—despite both locations being 2 miles beyond their current positions and requiring them to cross, by now, reinforced enemy positions with the element of surprise having been lost.

The Battle—11 March

Dawn arrived on the morning of the 11 March after a hard, cold, and uncomfortable night for those in the front line trenches. The morning mist obscured the enemy lines and prevented the forward observation officers (FOOs) from seeing the fall of the shells from a short barrage at 0645 hours, which accordingly did little damage to emplacements or barbed wire. New enemy positions had been created overnight, but exact details and locations could not be determined due to the mist; consequently, and in order to conserve ammunition, the new positions were not shelled. This was in spite of Rawlinson's letter to Kitchener before the battle: 'From what I can gather we shall be sufficiently well off for amn to carry on a week's hard fighting and after that the chances are we shall be better off in this respect than the enemy but we want more H.E. shell for the 18-pdr and better 4.7 shell.' [77] In reality, ammunition was rationed to just five shells for the siege guns and fifteen shells for the 18-pdrs for each barrage.

The Dehra Dun and Garhwal Brigades had moved into position during the night for an attack on the Bois du Biez. Unbeknown to the British, the Germans had crept from the wood into a newly dug trench system some 200 yards to its front. On the left flank the Dehra Dun Brigade awaited the arrival of several battalions from the 25th Brigade, who were to replace the Rifle Brigade. The Rifle Brigade War Diary states that they were to 'withdraw when relieved by W. Yorkshire Regiment and to form up with the rest of the 25 Brigade ready to become a reserve to the advance of 24 Brigade. The W. Yorks never took over our trenches and the battalion remained where it was.[78] The 2/West Yorks had instead relieved the Royal Irish Rifles, while the company provided to replace the Rifle Brigade had failed to reach them because of congestion in the trenches. The riflemen therefore were unable to vacate their position, leaving a tired and fed up Rifle Brigade holding a long stretch of trench which had been repeatedly and heavily shelled.

Before the riflemen could be relieved, Brigade HQ became aware of a counter-attack. Lieutenant-Colonel Stephens had orders stating: '… if the enemy counter-attacked he was to attack him in turn and follow him up'.[79] Stephens replied that there was no sign of an attack and proposed alternatively to attack some field guns to his front; he asked for the support of the rest of the brigade as the German counter-attack had not materialised. He received a reply saying, 'the attack cannot be sanctioned at present'.[80]

The original order had called for the brigades all to advance together. Upon seeing 2/Rifle Brigade, Brigadier C. Jacob, commanding the Dehra Dun, mistakenly thought the Rifles were part of the 8th Division that were to attack with him. Jacobs waited for the Rifle Brigade to move, but when they had not done so after an hour, he visited Stephens who appraised him of the situation and his orders. In disgust, Jacob cancelled the whole enterprise. Brigadier-General Lowry-Cole, arriving shortly after Jacob had left, planned to instruct Stephens to undertake an attack that mirrored what he had proposed earlier. However, upon hearing that the Dehra Dun attack had been abandoned, and after undertaking a personal reconnaissance, he concluded that, as any attack would be unsupported, the operation should be cancelled.[81]

Rawlinson instead ordered a fresh attack by the 24th Brigade against the enemy strong points: 'It is most important that the buildings at the Moulin du Piétre and at the Mauquissart–Piétre cross roads should be captured without further delay. Lose no time in getting guns on to them and assaulting the buildings with infantry.'[82] A breakdown in communications resulted in only two companies of the 1/Worcester Regiment receiving the orders. The two unsupported companies spearheaded an attack that was almost immediately brought to a halt by considerable fire. Further attempts were made by the 2/Northamptonshire Regiment and the 1/Notts & Derby (Sherwood Foresters) Regiment, along with two other companies of the Worcesters, but all met the same deadly fate. The attacks failed.

The day ended with British lines much the same as they had been at the beginning of the day. Problems with artillery and poor communications meant that, despite a huge loss of life, no further gains had been made. The Germans kept up a punishing barrage along the whole front, disguising their troop movements. The general transfer of troops to the Eastern Front meant that few reserves were available, but General von Claer of the German VII Corps was able to recall the 6th Bavarian Reserve Division, which had been resting. They were transported back by train. On the British side, the dead and wounded were collected throughout the night, damage to their lines was repaired, positions were strengthened, and communication trenches were dug. Pennefather recalled that the Rifle Brigade 'wired and dug like the devil during the night'.[83]

The enemy retained their principal strong points at the bridge over the river and at Moulin de Piètre, and overnight prepared for an attack to recapture Neuve Chapelle, together with the whole line from the Moated Grange through to Port Arthur. They had now been reinforced and fielded some 16,000 troops, including six new battalions and dozens of heavy guns, all now poised to attack at 0430 hours.[84] Orders issued to the German 14th Infantry Division for the impending assault read as follows:

> Major-General von Ditfurth will carry out the attack on Neuve Chapelle. In case the troops at his disposal are not sufficient for the recapture of our former positions west of the village, the 14th Bavarian Reserve Infantry Brigade is placed at General von Ditfurth's disposal. This Brigade must be in position in the Bois du Biez at 6 am on the 11th [*sic*].[85]

The Battle—12 March

The 2/Rifle Brigade received orders at 0100 hours to prepare to attack, as originally suggested by Stephens on the first day. At 0700 hours, after a pre-dawn preliminary bombardment, the Germans opened fire on the British lines and the village with a ferocious, but largely ineffectual, bombardment that was the harbinger of the long-expected counter-attack. Pennefather named the following infantry counter-attack as 'the most bloody experience the Lord ever invested, it polished off about 50 of us'.[86]

At about 0445 hours the German reinforcements, that had stayed hidden within the Bois du Biez overnight, began to advance against the half-mile front of the 25th Brigade, crossing over the River Layes and the watercourses via portable bridges. Due to poor light, the Germans almost got to the British lines before being seen—some came as close as 50 yards. A surging mass of grey coats—some five battalions, with a further three in reserve—came on through the dawn light.[87] Their large numbers made them unmissable. The slaughter was sickening, as Sergeant Self described:

> At about 5am it happened. A shout, 'They're on us'. And they were. The gunner pressed the button. A stream of bullets, 600 rounds per minute met them, an enemy grenade thrower blew up with his own bombs … the rush was checked.… They did not pass. It was just slaughter. It was again a dose of their own medicine with interest.[88]

The Indian Front received special attention, as the enemy had specific instructions to seize the cross-roads at Port Arthur, which before the battle had been an embarrassing British salient. This task was laid at the door of the battalions of the 16, 56, 104, and 13 German Infantry regiments, amounting to roughly 2,000 troops.[89] Lieutenant-Colonel Merewether of the Indian Corps wrote:

> At 5:45am dense masses of German appeared coming on at their usual jog-trot … but when they arrived within 100 yards of our line, the spikes of their helmets could be discerned. It seemed at first as if no fire could stop them, so impressive was the sight of this great multitude of men. The effect of concentrated machine-gun and rifle fire must, however, be

witnessed to be fully appreciated … piles of wriggling, heaving bodies lay on the ground, and the air resounded with shrieks, groans and curses…. The slaughter was prodigious. In front of the Leicester's, 1st Seaforths and 2/3rd Gurkhas, some 600 dead were counted.[90]

From the prisoners taken, it was established that they had been told that there were only a few British soldiers occupying the trenches.

The Indians and the riflemen began firing into their ranks, the .303 bullets from the rifles and machine guns often not stopping with the intended victim, but going through to hit those in the ranks behind; the deadly rapid fire of the riflemen made the Germans believe that the British had more machine guns than had been thought.[91] The attack was heavily repulsed. Captain Chichester-Constable recalled, 'This was about the finest shooting the Battalion had during the whole war.'[92] And Pennefather said, '… the Deutschers had the audacity to attack us, we polished off about 600, so they did not come any more.'[93] Lieutenant-General Anderson, commanding the Meerut Division, estimated that the enemy losses on the 25th Brigade front amounted to 2,000. The attack had been ill-timed and ill-prepared, and the retreating Germans were pursued back to their lines until fire from the strong point at Piètre Road brought those chasing the Germans to a halt.

The attacks at other parts of the line met with similar results, with the 21 Bavarian attack, led by 'a fat blighter on a horse', being seen off by accurate rifle fire of the 2/Worcesters and 2/Northants.[94] The attack against the defences of the Sherwood Foresters and those alongside Nameless Cottages were successful, creating a salient into the British lines which allowed the Germans to be fired upon from three sides, forcing them to retreat. But the Worcesters were not content with a mere retreating enemy: '[They] chased the Germans up and down that muddy field like terriers after rats. They pursued them with the bayonet round trees.'[95]

British counter-attack

The attack planned for 0700 hours was postponed until 1030 hours with very little notice. The delay provided the Germans with an opportunity to mount a further counter-attack at 0900 hours. This attack was again repulsed with a high level of enemy casualties, and for the rest of the morning wounded German soldiers crawled into British trenches to receive medical assistance.

Again the British attack was postponed until 1230 hours, by which time the enemy were back in their trenches awaiting an attack, it seems perverse that the High Command opposed a plan of attack against little opposition on 10 March, only to insist that an attack on 12 March be resolutely pressed forward at all costs against reinforced and strongly held defences.[96] Nevertheless, this was the case, and following a bombardment at midday, the Indian Corps prepared for an assault at 1300 hours, while on their left the 2/Rifle Brigade were to attack at 1230 hours—the difference was to allow for the 8th Division to attack the strong point at La Russe and those at Piètre Road and the bridgehead over the River Layes. Stephens endeavoured to arrange for co-operation between the riflemen and the Indian Corps, but was not successful. To the troops, the whole enterprise seemed uncoordinated.[97]

The 2/Scots Guards, 1/Grenadiers, 2/Borders, and the 2/Gordons of the 20th Brigade advanced towards the lines, making stout progress right up to the houses around the Moulin de Piètre. Meanwhile the 1/Royal Irish Rifles' attack on the redoubt at the Layes Bridge, which forty-eight hours earlier had been lightly manned, came up against fifteen machine guns positioned behind a forward projecting bastion and deep barbed wire entanglements. The attack faltered: 'Almost every man who exposed himself was instantly shot down....'[98] Lowry-Cole came forward to investigate why the attack had faltered, and when he realised that it was useless to attack the location during daylight, he gave instructions for it to be halted.

After a very thin bombardment over their objective, the 2/Rifle Brigade attacked at 1230 hours with the Royal Irish on their left. They advanced towards the north-west corner of the Bois du Biez and Layes Bridge, some 400 yards away over ploughed ground intersected by dykes and watercourses. Stephens had excellent first-hand knowledge of the terrain and had therefore requested permission to attack parallel to the direction of the dykes and at right-angles to the river, but permission to do this had been denied. The orders stood, leading the unfortunate riflemen directly into the apex of the new enemy trench and enfilade fire from Layes Bridge, across dykes and watercourses on the diagonal.

'A' Company, commanded by Captain Sherston, and 'B' Company, under Lieutenant Leigh, led the assault with the line commanded by Major Harrison. No sooner had they climbed over the sandbags of the breastworks, they were hit by a devastatingly tornado of crossfire, emanating from the new trench some 400–500 yards away. They also received fire from the hamlet in front of the wood and the Layes Bridge Redoubt, and artillery fire from the Bois du Biez. The disparity of the attacks between the Rifle Brigade and the Indian Corps allowed the guns positioned in the hamlet time to concentrate on the Rifle Brigade before the Indian attack started. Major Harrison and Lieutenant Pilcher were killed immediately, and Lieutenant G. F. Earle was wounded; the leading line of riflemen withered away under the incessant fire. A small contingent of riflemen, including Captain Sherston, and Lieutenants Chichester-Constable, Leigh, and the Hon. H. R. Hardinge, succeeded in covering the 200 yards to the empty and flooded section of the Smith-Dorrien trench, which could not be held. Among the scores of riflemen, more officers were killed, including Lieutenant Gilbey and Captain Fitzherbert-Brockholes, who was mortally wounded. With terrible losses, Stephens ordered the attack to be halted only forty-five minutes after it had begun. The wounded, scattered across the field, dared not lift their heads, aware that the fire from German machine guns, being set at a low level, would give them no quarter.

The brigades of the Indian Corps began their attack thirty minutes after the Rifle Brigade on their left, giving the enemy the opportunity in the first instance to concentrate on the riflemen, and when their attack faltered, to switch their full attention to the Indians. The fire from the Layes Bridge Redoubt, along with fire from the wood and the hamlet, in addition to the artillery fire from beyond Bois du Biez, brought the attack to a standstill, and it was abandoned.

The 1700 hours attack

A report received by First Army Headquarters implied that the junction and strong point at Nameless Cottages had been taken by the 24th Brigade; the suggested status of the general advance in the area further intimated that the Moulin de Piètre was also in British hands.

The First Army staff considered that the attack was forging ahead with speed and vigour against a demoralised enemy.[99] Accordingly, Haig issued the following directive to corps commanders at 1506 hours:

> Information indicates that enemy on our front are much demoralised. Indian Corps and IV Corps will push through the barrage of fire regardless of loss, using reserves if required.[100]

Unfortunately it all appears to have been based on a misunderstanding: it appears that in the confusion of the battle, British prisoners being escorted through enemy lines near Mauquissart seemed to distant observers to be assault troops heading a breakthrough. This led to orders being issued and further attacks taking place. Rawlinson instructed Major-General Capper of 7th Division and Major-General Davies of 8th Division to undertake a determined assault without paying heed to the cost of human lives.[101] A heavy bombardment took place at 1640 hours, largely wasted on the rear areas, as the German front lines, which should have been the target, were by now thought to be in British hands. It proved impossible for the 21st Brigade and part of 20th Brigade of 7th Division to make a co-ordinated attack through the maze of trenches and ditches to the front of the Moated Grange. Therefore they were unable to contribute to the afternoon attack.

The 1/Royal Irish and 2/Rifle Brigade launched their attack, again being hit by a torrent of steel as they clambered out of the trenches. Captain R. Berkeley MC of the Rifle Brigade recalled:

> At 4 pm Colonel Stevens was sent for and ordered to make a second attack at 5:15 pm. There was no opportunity to make any plan. By the time he reached his Battalion with the order it was nearly 5 pm, and a small and inadequate artillery demonstration was already in progress. It was now the turn of C and D Companies. In the spirit of another famous Brigade, 'theirs not to reason why', knowing that someone had blundered badly and knowing their task to be humanly impossible, they hurriedly formed up to obey orders.
>
> Captain Bridgeman of C Company led his men headlong for the machine-guns on the left front. He reached the Smith-Dorrien Trench and found himself with only Corporal Woolnough and Riflemen Rogers, Carbutt, and Jones left of those who had started with him. The rest of number 11 and 12 platoons had been shot down. Beyond Smith-Dorrien trench it was impossible to advance, even had there been anyone.[102]

'D' Company on the right of 'C' Company advanced forward to find uncut barbed wire entanglements blocking their way; as if to add insult to injury it turned out to be British wire. Lieutenant-General Sir C. Wallace and Major R. Cassidy wrote:

> The wire had to be cut and instead of picking a number of men for the 'suicidal task', Company Sergeant-Major Daniels asked his friend—Corporal Noble—to accompany him as he had on many dangerous night patrols in the past.[103]

Along with various types of equipment and ammunition, wire cutters were in short supply. Prior to the battle, secret instructions had been issued:

> The wire cutters will be issued to trained wire cutting men in each platoon and must be tied to the man by a lanyard to prevent loss. During operations wire cutters must be collected from casualties.[104]

The two riflemen, Daniels and Noble, shook hands before climbing over the breastworks and running a few yards to the wire. They arrived unhurt, and laid down on their backs to begin to cut the lower strands of the wire. They seemed to be succeeding, and once the lower strands were cut they took kneeling positions to begin cutting the higher wires. Wallace and Cassidy take up the story:

> It was then that Daniels was hit in the left thigh and dropped to the ground; after a few minutes he heard Noble gasp. Daniels asked: 'What's up, Tom?' to which Noble replied, 'I am hit in the chest, old man'. Daniels managed to roll into a shell hole and apply rudimentary first-aid to his wound; he remained there for four hours before trying to return to the battalion's trenches after dark, when he was seen and picked up by his comrades.[105]

Noble, aged twenty-three, died the following day in a hospital near St Omer. Daniels, a professional soldier who had enlisted in the Rifle Brigade in 1903, was hospitalised in England where he recovered from his wounds. Both men were awarded the Victoria Cross. Their citation read:

> For most conspicuous bravery on the 12th March 1915, at Neuve Chapelle. When their Battalion was impeded in the advance to the attack by wire entanglements, and subjected to a very severe machine-gun fire, CSM Daniels and Corporal Noble voluntarily rushed in front and succeeded in cutting the wires. They were both wounded at once, and Corporal Noble has since died of his wounds.[106, 107]

Despite being severely wounded, both men had accomplished their task. Lieutenant Mansell led his men over the top and almost immediately fell, seriously wounded. Pennefather recalled: 'D [Company] were just off headed by Mansell and myself when the colonel stopped us, Mansell got one in the head there, leaving me in command of "D" Company.... I took a bullet through the hat, which took the hair off my head, I shot the blighter in the head'.[108] Seeing the pointless loss of life, Stephens intervened once more, stopping the attack.

By 1800 hours the cloudy afternoon turned to dusk, followed quickly by darkness. An hour later all was pitchy black. Stephens recalled Captain Bridgeman and his party from the Smith-Dorrien trench. The fighting was now practically over; the Germans had apparently realised that the recapture of Neuve Chapelle and their trenches opposite the Bois du Biez was not achievable and decided to concentrate their efforts on holding their positions protecting the Aubers Ridge. The British advance over the ridge, so fervently desired, could not be progressed, and was now seen as hopeless. Haig, satisfied that no further progress could be made, suspended the operation, issuing First Army Operation Order No. 13 at 2240 hours, officially ending the Battle of Neuve Chapelle. The order stated:

> The 4th and Indian Corps will continue to hold the advanced lines reached by them today. This line to be established as a defensive line and secured against attack including wiring. The general advance will not be continued tomorrow without further orders and reliefs may be carried out within Corps accordingly.[109]

Those soldiers in unsecure forward positions were ordered to withdraw during the night. Practically all the ground gained in the three days battle had been won in the first three hours of the first day. Strengthening of the defences continued, as did intermittent barrages. Pennefather recalled: 'That night was a bloody night as there were no stretcher bearers and all the wounded got left. Bridgeman got wounded by a shell in the evening, also Barton was wounded in the head, and Carle in the finger.'[110]

March 13 was a physically exhausting day. Despite being worn out by three days of fighting, the soldiers continued their work in repairing and strengthening their trenches, as well as entrenching the hard-won ground while the enemy kept up a violent bombardment of the new line. By the end of 14 March, most of the troops that had taken part in the battle had been relieved and were back in their billets.

Casualties

In Sir John French's words, 'the losses during these three days' fighting were, I regret to say, very severe'.[111] The figures were as follows:

Killed	190 Officers	2,337 Other Ranks
Wounded	359 Officers	8,174 Other Ranks
Missing	23 Officers	1,728 Other Ranks

French continued:

> The enemy left several thousand dead on the battlefield which were seen and counted; and we have positive information that upwards of 12,000 wounded were removed to the northeast and east by train. Thirty officers and 1,657 other ranks of the enemy were captured.[112]

Pennefather wrote:

> The next day was quieter and gradually we quietened down, we stopped for fourteen days. We have 12 new officers and 400 men. The Berks had only 7 officers left, the R.I.R. had only 4 left, the Northampton's 1 officer and 100 men left. The Scottish Rifles had all their officers killed.[113]

It had been a hard-fought battle and the cost was high. The 2/Rifle Brigade lost 12 officers and 365 other ranks.[114] Sixty-eight per cent of these were lost on 12 March. In the battle, the British had advanced 1,000 yards at a cost of 12,000 men killed, wounded, or missing. Haig said: 'So many good fellows no more; but it can't be done without incurring loss.'[115]

Reflections on the Battle

The gains and the lost opportunities of the battle hinged on two aspects: communications and munitions. The loss of communication enhances the 'fog of war' in which divisional and even brigade headquarters do not know what is happening on the front line, and decisions taken by officers in the heat of battle affect the front as a whole. In the battle, this was demonstrated when the Rifle Brigade had the opportunity to break through the line, but were refused permission to do so, only to later receive instructions to attack when the enemy defences had been restored and reinforced.

Munitions also greatly affected the battle. It was proved that a surprise heavy bombardment could provide the opportunity to force enemy defences. *The Times History of the War* sums up the battle in these terms: 'The first part of the battle of Neuve Chapelle showed that artillery is under modern conditions the dominating factor.'[116]

The ammunition used during the opening bombardment at Neuve Chapelle exceeded that expended in the two and half years in South Africa,[117] but Sir John French had been required to economise shell usage over the preceding months just to build up sufficient stocks to allow for this expenditure. Further bombardments over the three days used many more shells than the most extravagant estimate, and there were insufficient reserves to keep up the supply.[118] Brigadier W. Kemp recalled:

> We signallers worked for seventy-two hours straight off and I was down and out at the finish. When the battle dies away the battery had fired two hundred and forty shells of 6-inch ammunition and we only had five rounds left between all four guns. They kept one round 'up the spout' for three weeks, ready to give the Germans hell![119]

Reporting to Kitchener, French made the position clear: 'Cessation of the forward movement is necessitated today by the fatigue of the troops and, above all, by the want of ammunition.'[120] Haig, however, was more vehement:

> In my opinion, given sufficient High Explosive gun ammunition we could drive the Germans out of France in six weeks. Instead of having 30 rounds per day per gun and Howitzer, we only have 7. It is a disgraceful state of affairs to be in this situation after over 7 months of War. How can we order Officers Commanding Corps to 'press on with vigour' and at the same time say 'mind you must not expend more than 7 rounds a gun in a whole day!'[121]

As Secretary of State for War, Kitchener had budgetary matters to consider and was becoming particularly sensitive to the repeated calls for ammunition. He also intensely disliked the shortages being blamed for failures on the battlefield, and felt that the cost of the shells fired over the agreed limit was a waste of money. 'The British Army should be able to take positions without artillery,' he said.[122]

Sir John French sent urgent telegrams to the War Council, firstly asking, then demanding, and finally begging for more shells:

> The supply of gun ammunition, especially the 18-pdr, and 4.5 inch howitzer, has fallen far short of what I was led to expect and I was therefore compelled to abandon further offensive operations until sufficient reserves are accumulated.[123]

French had hoped that his telegrams would unblock the delivery of shells, but in a brusque response, Kitchener stated that he considered the use of shells in the first sixteen days of March to have been profligate. He ordered that in the future, 'the utmost economy will be made in the expenditure of ammunition'.[124] This castigation was a severe blow to French's plans to attack again as soon as possible. The shell shortage was not going to go away.

The War Council

The War Council was thankful for the victory, and the censored press repeated Haig's statement to the public:

> The British soldier has once more given the Germans a proof of his superiority in a fight as well as of his pluck and determination to conquer.… We broke the German line and straightened ours. At one period in the fight we had turned the Kaiser's sturdiest and toughest fighters into a disorderly rabble.

But nothing was said about the shortage of munitions or the breakdown in communication and the lost opportunities. The members of the War Council were not impressed by the failure to achieve the extended objectives, and considered the prospect of an all-out victory remote. Added to the gloomy news of the impasse on the Western Front, news had arrived that things were going badly with the Russians in the east, and the Navy's attempt to force the Dardanelles straits had failed.[125]

At the War Council's next meeting, after many hours of deliberation, the only decision made was to ask Sir Ian Hamilton, commander of the Mediterranean Expeditionary Force, what size of force he would need to guarantee the forcing and consolidation of the Gallipoli Peninsula. Sir Maurice Hankey noted that this was 'a question that ought to have been put to him before ever a man landed'.[126]

The Shell Shortage Reaches Home

The Conservatives Withdraw Their Co-operation

On 10 March the Conservative leaders had been invited to attend the War Council's discussion of policy in relation to Constantinople and the future territorial settlement in the Straits region: 'They did not contribute very much,' thought Asquith.[1] When Lord Fisher, First Sea Lord of the Admiralty, suggested that the Conservatives should attend another meeting, Churchill commented, 'I don't think we want a war council on this. It is after all only asking a lot of ignorant people to meddle in our business.' Nevertheless, the Conservatives appreciated that the overall situation was dire, making them determined to take control of the war. Up to this point the Conservatives had been patriotically co-operative, providing an almost semi-immunity to the Government, but they now began to voice their unease about the situation.[2] A section of the party, along with the right-wing press, embarked on a campaign of party warfare, often targeting individual ministers such as Haldane, who was accused of showing a shameful fondness of the Germans, and McKenna, whom they accused of lacking zeal in the hunt for enemy aliens.[3] The *Liberal Magazine* in April 1915 complained of the behaviour of the Conservative Party:

It is not easy at times to remember or to believe that the Party Truce is still in existence. We have no complaint to make of the Unionist leaders or organisations, but in no small or unimportant section of the Unionist Press attacks and criticisms on the Government are being made, the clear object of which is, if possible, not to help towards winning the war, but to discredit Liberal Ministers.[4]

Asquith expressed his concerns that 'under existing conditions, criticism, inspired by party motives and interests, has full rein, and is an asset of much value to the enemy.'[5]

The Ammunition Shortage is Disclosed to the Public

Sir John French gave a press interview on 22 March, which appeared throughout the English papers: 'It is a rough war,' he said, 'but the problem it sets is a comparatively simple one—

munitions, always more munitions; this is the essential question, the governing condition of all progress, of every leap forward.'[6] He made it very plain that the reason the offensive on Neuve Chapelle could not advance further to Aubers Ridge was due to the lack of munitions. Since the battle, the problem of shell shortage had begun to be reported in the public press. On 7 April *The Times* wrote about the Armament Output Committee, criticising it for the

> … extraordinary failure of the Government to take in hand in business-like fashion the provision of full and adequate supply of munitions. The War Office has sought to do too much and been jealous of civilian aid. It should chiefly devote itself to the organisation of the armies and should state its supply requirements and leave to others the far more complex task of organising industry.[7]

A further article on 10 April continued the call for a more organised response to the need for munitions:

> It is that in our previous wars the War Office had been accustomed to rely for all such supplies on the M.G.O. as a sort of Universal Provider. In this unprecedented war the Government ought to have insisted on instant organisation of the whole of our national resources, leaving the War Office to state its requirements and raise its armies.[8]

Munitions of War Committee

Lloyd George proposed that a radical reorganisation of the munitions industry had to take place, but Kitchener opposed this. Lloyd George, with Balfour's support, forced Asquith to apply pressure on Kitchener, who accepted the need for the Munitions of War Committee chaired by Lloyd George, with Kitchener represented by the MGO. It would effectively supersede the Armaments Output Committee.[9] But Kitchener was not to be outdone and effectively 'clipped the wings' of the new committee by refusing to delegate any War Committee responsibility for munitions or, on security grounds, provide any information related to troop movements or those on the front line, thus preventing the committee from calculating estimates of munitions required for any given date. Given this lack of information, the committee was unable to instigate measures to solve the shortage.[10]

Charles Masterman, Liberal MP, journalist, and Head of the British War Propaganda Bureau, told the President of the Board of Trade that there was 'a very strong undercurrent of feeling that some people (no one quite knows who) are exploiting the working classes and making big profits out of the war.'[11] Whether this was true or not, suspicion and resentment of profiteering did exist, and acting on the committee's suggestion, the National Shell Factories were created, controlled by an entity that was in effect the embryo of the Munitions Ministry.[12] As a further measure to solve the shell manufacturing problem, Lloyd George introduced the Defence of the Realm Act II into the House of Commons—'a very drastic measure for the control of private industry'.[13] Seemingly unaware of the dire state of the shell manufacture, Parliament was taken by surprise, with traditional Liberals becoming alarmed by such a large planned encroachment on private enterprise. H. W. Massingham, editor of *The Nation*, asked: 'Is this Government going to end, having begun so well, as a panic Govt?'

Shell Shortage Attracts More Public Attention

In early April 1915 French met with Kitchener at the War Office to press earlier demands for a vital increase in ammunition. However, by mistake or design, French's concerns were misrepresented by Kitchener in a letter to Asquith of 14 April:

> I have had a talk with French. He told me I could let you know that with the present supply of ammunition he will have as much as his troops will be able to use on the next forward movement.[14]

On hearing this, French was angered to say the least, and was convinced that his words had been deliberately misinterpreted. But despite conveying his feelings to Kitchener, the basic terms of the communication were not amended, and the letter provided the evidence upon which Asquith based his speech in Newcastle of 20 April:

> I saw a statement the other day that the operations of war, not only of our army but of our Allies, were being crippled, or at any rate hampered, by our failure to provide the necessary ammunitions. There is not a word of truth in that statement. I say there is not a word of truth in that statement, which is more mischievous because, if it was believed, it is calculated to dishearten our troops, to discourage our Allies, and to stimulate the hopes and activities of our enemies.[15]

Unfortunately, the statement was only too true, as every gunner in the field, knowing full-well the meagre allowance of shells per day for each gun, could have told the Prime Minister.[16] When French was asked whether the letter was a true representation of his meeting with Kitchener, he replied, 'I did not authorize Lord Kitchener to say this. Lord Kitchener never called me into consultation about the shells or mentioned that information was wanted by the Government. If at this meeting shells were mentioned at all it was very casually.'[17] This was borne out by French's diary for 31 March which mentioned a number of matters but not shells.[18] In *Nelson's History of the War*, John Buchan wrote:

> Two days after the Prime Minister's speech the struggle began on the Ypres salient. We were almost without heavy artillery, and what we had was very short of shells. The Germans had at least fifty heavy guns in action, and endless ammunition. We beat off the attack in the end but with a terrible sacrifice. The lives of our soldiers were the price we paid for our deficiency in high-explosive.[19]

The Battle of Aubers Ridge

The Champagne and Artois Campaign

The French offensive in Champagne and Artois was part of a joint Franco-British effort in a three-pronged attack: the French were to attack either side of the La Bassée Canal, while the British would undertake another attack on Aubers Ridge. A heavily reinforced French Tenth Army, comprising fourteen infantry divisions, more than 720 pieces of field artillery, and over 220 heavy guns, would attack between Loos and Arras, within which two ridges formed the most important obstacles—Notre Dame de Lorrette and Vimy.[1] Both of these ridges provided excellent artillery positions from which the Germans could pour shells into the French lines of communication, but by taking these ridges, the French would be able to advance their line to Douai–Cambrai, and occupy the industrial areas of Lens and Douai.

The British attack across the Aubers Ridge would cut the road connecting La Bassée to Lille, and with it the German ability to move supplies to its forces in Artois. Neither Sir John French nor Haig had any great enthusiasm for an assault of this scale at this stage, and would have preferred to wait for further supplies of artillery ammunition. However, the French needed the British attack to draw German reserves from their front.

Aubers Ridge

The occupation of Aubers Ridge gave the German defenders a huge advantage, both in their observation of Neuve Chapelle and Festubert, and their ability to bombard those locations and the British lines of communications. The ridge, running along the eastern edge of the valley, is hardly worthy of the title, rising to only 15 metres above Neuve Chapelle, resulting in a gradient of just 10 per cent. It is a mere crease in the flat lands to the west, which are criss-crossed by deep drainage ditches and innumerable dykes. The portion of the ridge most relevant to the battle runs from the rear of the Bois du Biez, south-west of Neuve Chapelle, in a north-easterly direction towards the villages of Aubers, Fromelles, and Le Maisnil.

Since the Battle of Neuve Chapelle, the Germans had strengthened the defences of the ridge and increased troop density, all of which had been completed by the end of April and had been reported on by Military Intelligence and the Royal Flying Corps.[2] The parapet of the trenches had been raised to 2 yards in height, formed from excavated soil and sandbags, with coiled heavy-gauge barbed wire to the front. The depth of these entanglements was doubled, from 7 to 14 feet, and in some locations it reached over 20 feet.[3] Directly in front of the trench were excavations, formed from the earth needed to increase the height of the parapets. These naturally filled with water and then had barbed wire coils dropped into them resulting in man-traps that could not be damaged by shell-fire. Fire points were constructed along every few yards of trench, formed of large wooden boxes for riflemen and V-shaped boxes for machine-gunners, fronted with steel-rail loopholes, allowing a large, sweeping arc of fire. In order to increase this arc and allow enfilade fire to be brought against the flanks of attackers, forward emplacements were built at right-angles to the line with shallow trenches to provide access.[4]

A second line of trenches was constructed some 200 yards to the rear of the forward trench, with linked communication trenches to allow troop movement; these were often roofed with hurdles or canvas screens to protect and conceal the men. Fire steps were also cut into these, so that in the event that the forward trench was lost, defenders could fight from the second. Concrete pill-boxes armed with heavy machine guns had been put on the third and last defensive lines, providing the retreating soldiers with locales in which to muster for a counter-attack.

Rawlinson had voiced concerns about these updated and very comprehensive defences, but Haig felt that with surprise on their side, a breakthrough was there for the taking, just as it had been at Neuve Chapelle.

The British Plan

The attack against Aubers Ridge was in support of the Second Battle of Artois, in which the French would attack along a 4-mile front with the crest of Vimy Ridge, between Farbus and Souchez, with Notre Dame de Lorette as its objective. These positions would be taken before proceeding into the Douai plain. The grand plan was to take place over two days.

First Day: The French to attack and consolidate the eastern spur of Notre Dame du Lorette; Second Day: The French to widen the gap made the day before and the British to attack Aubers Ridge, extending the breach to the La Bassée–Lille road and preventing reinforcements from being sent against the French.[5]

Accordingly, on 4 May, Sir John French issued the following orders from the British Advanced Headquarters at Hazebrouck:

The First Army will take the offensive on 8 May. Its mission is to break through the enemy's line on its front and gain the La Bassée–Lille road between La Bassée and Fournes. Its further advance will be directed on the line Bauvin–Don.[6]

Haig produced a plan calling for a two-pronged attack to be launched against Aubers Ridge from the north and south of Neuve Chapelle. The two wings were to be approximately 6,000 yards apart, and they were to join in a continuous front enveloping an estimated six enemy regiments, before rolling back the fortified farms and villages and the German front line to the Heute Deule Canal.[7] Control and command of the battle would remain at local level, with officers at the front bearing the responsibility of determining how far the advance could be progressed.[8]

The Indian Corps was to take the southern wing and the IV Corps the northern. The estimated ratio between attackers and defenders was in excess of four to one.[9] The individual actions were planned as follows:

(a.) 47th (London) Division on the 600-yard line south of the front between Chocolat Menier Corner and Cuinchy, was to hold the right flank of the line;

(b.) Meerut Division assembled on the 800-yard front between the Orchard Redoubt (1,300 yards north of Chocolat Menier Corner) and Neuve Chapelle, was to form the first of Haig's wings, advancing towards La Cliqueterie Farm;

(c.) 7th Division, forming Haig's second wing, was to advance towards Aubers Village and Leclercq Farm, before attacking the La Cliqueterie Farm and Le Plouich on Aubers Ridge and linking with the Indian Corps, once a breakthrough had taken place;

(d.) 8th Division was to advance eastwards towards Rouge Banc, establishing a front on the Sailly–Fromelles road to protect the left flank before advancing to Fromelles.

The advance was to be carefully followed by the brigade and divisional staff, along with French, Churchill, and Repington, who watched from the tower of Laventie Church, approximately 2½ miles from the British front. The taking of the objectives was to be signalled by the following:

(a.) White linen strips, 7 feet by 2 feet, to be rolled out after the occupation of Deleval Farm for the pilots of the Royal Flying Corps to see;

(b.) Daylight fireworks to be let off after the capture of Leclercq and Bondel farms;

(c.) Distinguishing flags to be raised to denote general advances.

The German defence was to be controlled from the Fromelle church tower; the slight rise of the ridge, plus the extra height of the church tower provided unrestricted observation opportunities for German officers of the low flat plain stretching west.

The French, as usual, planned for artillery bombardments to be long and powerful; however, Sir John French and General Haig had limited supplies of munitions and therefore had to promote a short but intensive bombardment, in this case lasting forty minutes. Therefore, in support of the two wings, the bombardment would concentrate on cutting the barbed wire entanglements and defences to provide gaps for the assault troops to the front of Fromelles and between Neuve Chapelle and Bois du Biez, before switching to the counter-battery fire.

The British staff felt that the battle plan, based on that of Neuve Chapelle, just on a larger scale and longer front, was basically sound. One officer noted:

…this should be Neuve Chapelle all over again, and much more successful because we have learnt its lessons and shall know what to avoid this time.[10]

Order of Battle

British First Army
IV Corps—Lt-Gen. Sir Henry Rawlinson

8th Division—commanded by Maj.-Gen. F. J. Davies

23th Brigade   **Brig.-Gen. R. J. Pinney**
2/Devonshire Regiment
2/West Yorkshire Regiment
2/Cameronians (Scottish Rifles)
2/Middlesex Regiment

24th Brigade   **Brig.-Gen. F. C. Carter**
1/Worcester Regiment
1/Notts & Derby Regiment (Sherwood Foresters)
5/Black Watch (TF)
2/East Lancashire Regiment
2/Northamptonshire Regiment
4/Cameron Highlanders (TF)

25th Brigade   **Brig.-Gen. A. W. G. Lowry-Cole**
2/Lincolnshire Regiment
2/Royal Berkshire Regiment
1/Royal Irish Rifles
2/Rifle Brigade
13/London Regiment (TF)

7th Division—commanded by Maj.-Gen. H. de la P. Gough

20th Brigade   **Brig.-Gen. F. Heyworth**
1/Grenadier Guards
2/Scots Guards
2/Border Regiment
2/Gordon Highlanders
1/6 Gordon Highlanders (TF)

21st Brigade   **Brig-Gen. H. Watts**
2/Bedfordshire Regiment
2/Yorkshire Regiment (Green Howards)
2/Royal Scots Fusiliers
2/Wiltshire Regiment
1/4 Cameron Highlanders (TF)

22nd Brigade   **Brig.-Gen. S. Lawford**
2/Royal West Surrey Regiment (The Queen's)
2/Royal Warwickshire Regiment
1/Royal Welch Fusiliers
1/South Staffordshire Regiment
1/8 The Royal Scots (Lothian Regiment) (TF)

Indian Corps—Lt.-Gen. Sir J. Willcocks

Meerut Division—commanded by Lt-Gen. C. Anderson

Dehra Dun Brigade   **Brig.-Gen. C. Jacob**
1/Seaforth Highlanders
2/2 Gurkhas
1/9 Gurkhas
4/Seaforth Highlanders (TF)

Garhwal Brigade **Brig.-Gen. C. Blackadder**
2/Leicestershire Regiment
1/39 Garhwal Rifles
2/39 Garhwal Rifles
2/3 Gurkhas
3/London Regiment (TF)

Bareilly Brigade   **Brig.-Gen. W. Southey**
2/The Black Watch (Royal Highlanders)
6/Jats
41/Dogras
58/Vaughan's Rifles
4/The Black Watch (Royal Highlanders) (TF)
2/8 Gurkhas (Div. Troops)

1st Division—commanded by Maj.-Gen. R. C. B. Haking

1st (Guards) Brigade   **Brig.-Gen. H. C. Lowther**
1/Coldstream Guards
1/Scots Guards
1/The Black Watch
1/14 London Regiment (Scottish)
1/Cameron Highlanders

2nd Brigade   **Brig.-Gen. G. H. Thesinger**
1/Northamptonshire Regiment
2/Royal Sussex Regiment
2/King's Royal Rifle Corps
1/5 Royal Sussex Regiment
1/9 King's Liverpool Regiment
1/Loyal North Lancs

3rd Brigade   **Brig.-Gen. H. R. Davies**
2/Royal Munster Fusiliers
2/Welsh Regiment
1/4 Royal Welch Fusiliers
1/Gloucester Regiment
1/South Wales Border

The Royal Flying Corps First Wing under Lt-Col. H. M. Trenchard again supported the artillery via reconnaissance aircraft, but this time they were to use wireless transmitters, via the 30-watt No. 1 Aircraft Spark, to relay the information via Morse Code in its first recorded use in battle.[11]

German Sixth Army

The density of enemy troops had been increased by the VII Corps commander, General von Claer, from two to three divisions. The Sixth Army was under the overall command of Crown Prince Rupprecht of Bavaria. Those opposite the Indian and IV Corps were:

- 6 Bavarian Reserve Division (Lt-Gen. von Scanzoni), which took over the 9,000-metre sector between Bois Grenier at the northern extreme and Fauquissant;
- 13th Division (Lt-Gen. von dem Borne), which took up positions between Fauquissant and Chocolat Menier Corner;
- Three regiments of the 14th Division (Lt-Gen. von Ditfurth), which occupied the 8,000-metre front from Chocolat Menier Corner to Cuinchy.[12]

Each regiment was responsible for a front line of 2,500 metres, instead of the 3,500 metres that they had been expected to hold after 12 March.[13] The German artillery consisted of eight heavy howitzer batteries of the VII Corps, six batteries of the 14th Division, and nine batteries of the 13th Division.[14]

British Artillery

The HAR (Heavy Artillery Reserve) and division artillery of the First Army fielded some 516 field and light guns/howitzers, with a further 121 heavy guns. The following were available for the battle on 1 May:

Type of Gun	Number
13-pdr QF	78
13-pdr/AA	6
15-pdr/BLS (obsolete)	84
18-pdr QF	276
4.5-inch QF howitzer	60
4.7-inch QF (obsolete)	28
60-pdr BLS	20
5-inch Howitzer (obsolete)	20
6-inch Howitzer (old & superseded)	36
6-inch BLS (old & superseded)	4
9.2-inch howitzer	10
15-inch howitzer	3

Note: QF = Quick Firing / BLS = Breech Loading

Of the number of artillery pieces, almost 28 per cent were identified as being either obsolete, old, or superseded by the time of the battle. There was also an unbalanced ratio between heavy and field guns, as highlighted by Sir John French:

> At this time the British Army had but 71 guns altogether above 5 inch calibre against 1,416 below it, and no adequate steps whatever had yet been taken to bring the proportion more nearly to the requirements of modern warfare…[15]

At Neuve Chapelle the German trenches had received a huge bombardment from heavy guns; however, in the planning for the Aubers Ridge attack, the front was extended without the comparative increase in heavy guns. There were therefore insufficient guns to support a similar full-scale attack across the whole front, and as a result it was decided that the short intensive bombardment would be directed only at two ends of the line.[16] In addition, a larger proportion of guns were directed not on the German front lines, but on the positions behind it.[17]

Munitions

The munition stocks were well below what was required, and in addition, they had to be shared with batteries fighting in the Second Battle of Ypres and in other theatres like Gallipoli and Russia. Reserves had depleted to an alarming level. In order to mitigate the problem, leading up to the battle Sir John French ordered ammunition to be rationed to eighteen rounds per battery per day.[18] Lieutenant-Colonel D. H. Drake-Brockman, commanding the 39 Garwalis, recalled:

> If one telephoned up to the gunner officer for a little ammunition to be expended on some bomb, gun or minenwerfer that was annoying us, the reply generally received was, 'sorry, but I have used my allowance!'[19]

In order to breach the enemy heavy defences and cut the barbed-wire entanglements, high-explosive was needed. The majority of the shells, however, contained shrapnel. Although this was an excellent weapon against massed troops in the open or in the prevention of enemy reinforcements reaching the front lines, it had limited valued against defences or entanglements. Kitchener had accrued massive experience fighting in the open expanses of South Africa, Egypt, and Sudan, where shrapnel had a devastating effect on massed troops. He therefore favoured shrapnel over high-explosive shells, which also required chemicals that were in short supply. As a result, a higher ratio of shrapnel was manufactured. The BEF's experience at Aisne, where there was hardly any high-explosive available, resulted in demands for at least a 15:85 per cent ratio. As the war progressed, Repington, French, and numerous generals repeatedly demanded for a more equal ratio, but despite this, by the spring of 1915, only 7 per cent of the shells delivered contained high-explosive. Repington had tried on several occasions to bring this inadequacy to the attention of the British public, but due to the censorship of the press, he had not been able to succeed.[20]

Preparations for the Battle

The particularly high water-table in this area caused the British sappers a major problem, as recalled by Captain J. Cohen:

> Our trouble of course was of drainage. This horrible country is made of mud, water and dead Germans. Whenever water is left in a trench it drags the earth down on either side and forms a fearful sticky viscous matter that lets you sink gently down and grips you like a vice when you're there.[21]

Therefore, instead of digging down to form a trench, the defences were built upwards. After a shallow trench was dug, earth and sandbags filled with mud were used to construct the breastworks, providing a standard trench measuring 7 foot from the bottom of the shallow trench to the top of the parapet and parados. Earth would then be sloped towards ground level, extending the breastwork between 5 and 7 feet. Short ladders allowed access to the top when an attack was made. This form of trench construction provided good protection for those sheltering within, but it meant that when the men rose to 'go over the top' they were standing on a parapet several feet above ground level. They would then descend to the flat ground to form up, while the enemy machine-gunners ranged their weapons on the point where the troops would congregate. The height of these breastworks also obscured much of the action from the view of brigade staff and artillery officers, who required FOOs to advance further to report on the fall of the shells.

Working parties repaired the defences and entanglements and dug assault trenches and narrow passageways through the barbed wire to facilitate the attack through no man's land, a flat expanse crossed with water-filled ditches and devoid of cover. This area was surveyed and reconnoitred by company officers and those leading the lines—a dangerous enterprise and one which increased casualties among junior officers. Siegfried Sassoon wrote in his diary:

> No-man's land fascinates me, with its jumble of wire-tangles and snaky seams in the earth winding along the landscape … pools of dead looking water.[22]

Rows of assembly trenches were constructed to shelter the follow-up troops, held back until the initial assault troops had started their advance to prevent overcrowding and confusion. Many of these assembly trenches were covered in an attempt to disguise the concentration of troops entering the area prior to battle. The men had 'rested' in their billets where they had been subjected to route marches and physical fitness regimes, as well as special training for bombers, machine-gunners, and blocking parties.

Each company would put together a party of about fourteen men, commanded by an NCO, which was to act as a bombing party, advancing with the assault troops. Each bombing party was divided into teams depending on their role:

Bayonet men—to cover the group and take the lead against enemy infantry;
Bombers or Grenadiers—to prepare the grenades and discharge them at the enemy (they needed to keep their hands free for throwing and therefore relied on the bayonet men for protection);
Grenade Carriers—to carry the grenades in special leather buckets with tops that could be closed off to prevent the bombs falling out or foreign objects entering and setting them off;
Blocking or Sandbag Men—to consolidate the gains made by barricading the ends of the captured trenches, before pulling down part of the trench wall to create a more permanent wall.[23]

The Mark I stick-grenade consisted of a brass body with a hook, a cap with a needle and safety-pin, a cast-iron ring, a 16-inch cane handle with a beech wood block and silk braid tail, a detonator holder and detonator containing 30 grains of fulminate of mercury, and a bursting charge of 4 oz of lyddite.[24] The lack of manufactured grenades meant that 'homemade' bombs were made in the trenches from empty tins. They were known as 'Jam-Tin' bombs or 'Tickler's Artillery' from the product name.[25] These were filled with guncotton, sealed, and given a fuze which was ready to be lit at the appropriate time and thrown at the enemy. The famous pineapple-shaped Mills bomb Mark 5 was not issued until later in 1915, and was not available at the Battle of Aubers Ridge.[26]

It was planned that the section of the front assigned to the 13/London (Kensington) Territorial Force, attacking the Rouges Bancs to the left of the Royal Irish, would be mined. Accordingly, two deep mine galleries, 70 feet apart—one 283 feet in length, the other 330 feet in length—were dug through the blue clay by 173 Tunnelling Company Royal Engineers, deep underneath the German lines. Each tunnel was charged with 2,000 lb of explosives, ready to be ignited at the appropriate time.[27]

The men made their way to assembly trenches at 2300 hours, moving as silently as possible to avoid giving the enemy any notice of the impending attack. In *I was there—Great War Interviews*, Richard Tobin writes:

> These last hours waiting were the longest hours, but at the same time the shortest hours in life. Their thoughts centred on; whether they would live long enough to get over the top; would they have enough 'puff in their lungs' to make it across no-man's land in the mad rush; and if I was knocked down, would I have enough courage to get up and to face the leads being fired by the enemy.[28]

By 0230 hours all the troops were jammed into their overcrowded forward trenches. It was a clear, cloudless night. Around 0400 hours, as the dawn rose, the men were fortified by rations of rum and tea.[29] The plan, once the bombardment ended, was for the assault troops to leave their trenches and form up in a line. Each battalion would attack with two companies split across the front that it was responsible for, with the other two companies in support. The leading companies would then be divided into parties of no more than thirty men, who would advance in broken or uneven lines in depth, this formation being less vulnerable to machine-gun or artillery fire.

The soldiers were to attack at zero hour, scheduled for 0540 hours on Saturday 8 May, but phase one of the French attack was delayed by heavy rain and a dense mist. It was therefore decided that the two phases of their attack and the British attack would take place on Sunday 9 May, despite the French bombardment having started on 3 May. Unfortunately the premise that the enemy was unaware of the attack had been spoiled; the huge massing of British soldiers had caught the attention of the Germans, as had the destruction of a factory chimney on the Rue du Bois to provide a better field of fire for the heavy guns. The Germans raised a notice board bearing the words 'Attack Postponed Until Tomorrow' to taunt the British troops.[30] The long wait and the certainty that their attack was expected added to the anxious feeling among the soldiers waiting to go over the top.

The Battle—9 May

As the sun rose at dawn, Aubers Ridge was bathed in sunlight and peace. The villages on the skyline of the ridge stood out clearly in the morning air. At 0500 hours the peaceful silence was abruptly broken as more than 600 guns roared into action; sheets of orange and yellow flames flashed among the black and grey smoke over the enemy defences, obliterating the view across no man's land and making the ground tremble with the explosions. The massed 18-pdr and light batteries pounded the barbed wire with thousands of shrapnel balls from low trajectory shells, intent on cutting a corridor through the fields of barbed-wire entanglements. After ten minutes these moved their fire to join other guns in pounding the enemy breastworks. The heavy guns targeted strong points and fortified farms while the 13-pdrs bombarded the areas behind the front line trenches to prevent the movement of troops. As explosions took place, the billowing smoke, dust, and debris obscured the view of the BE2 reconnaissance planes circling overhead, preventing them from accurately directing the fire and pinpointing strategic targets.

A considerable number of the heavy shells, mostly from the obsolete guns, fell short and landed on the British trenches; worn barrels, faulty fuzes, and inconsistent propellants caused shells to fall short or explode above or in the British lines. After forty minutes, a swirling breeze cleared a view over what was supposed to be devastated and demolished breastworks, but the enemy defences looked to have survived very well. Pickelhaubed-helmed troops appeared to be filing back into positions with their bayonets glinting ominously in the morning sun. Rifles were cocked, machine gun positions were manned, and they waited for the attackers to emerge from their trenches.

Southern Attack

The regiments of the 47th (London) Division were to remain in position defending their front from Cuinchy to Chocolat Menier Corner. The 2nd and 3rd Brigades of the 1st Division would provide the assault troops to the front between Chocolat Menier Corner and the Orchard Redoubt, with the two brigades divided by the cart track servicing the Ferme du Bois. As the barrage intensified for the last ten minutes, the advance troops, consisting of the 1/Northants and 2/Royal Sussex of the 2nd Brigade and 2/Royal Munster Fusiliers and 2/Welsh of the 3rd Brigade, were to advance against the 57 Royal Prussian Regiment and 55 Regiment holding the fortified positions at Ferme Cour d'Avoue and Ferme du Bois. Upon their successful consolidation, the two brigades would regroup and hold the line along La Quinque Rue, linking up with the Meerut Division on their left.[31]

The men of the 1/Northants clambered over the top straight into an inferno of accurate rifle and machine-gun fire. The leading platoons running forward found that the barbed wire was untouched, the enemy breastworks were still intact, and machine-gun emplacements were undetected and undamaged: '[they] came to within 30 yards of the German wire having rushed forward with great dash'.[22] Captain Dickson and twenty men of 'B' Company fought through a narrow breach in the wire to gain entry to the enemy trench, but according to German reports, all perished by grenade and hand-to-hand fighting.

The rest of the battalion, along with the second wave, managed to get half way across no man's land, but were now also receiving enfilade fire from machine guns located at an angle to the German line; they were either 'mown down' or 'trapped and … unable to advance or retire'.[33] By 0630 hours the order was given to withdraw; many wounded had no choice but to remain where they were for the rest of the day.

Positioned on the left of the Northants, the assault platoons of the 2/Royal Sussex emerged from their trenches, and like the Northants, they found themselves immediately in the midst of an accurate hail of bullets from defenders who appeared unaffected by the barrage. Many dead and wounded fell backwards into their own trenches, and few made it more than half way across the 300-yard no man's land, although some with almost super-human effort made it to with 40 yards. One lone soldier reached the enemy parapet before being killed.[34]

The second wave consisting of the 1/5 Royal Sussex moved across the land between their reserve trench and advance trenches among increasingly heavy salvos of fire from German artillery and re-directed machine-gun fire. Once in the advance trench they regrouped and climbed over the top, straight into the same inferno of bullets. Together with those remaining from the 2/Royal Sussex, they created almost a sea of advancing troops against which the German machine guns scythed back and forth, cutting men down as they tried to get across.

The 1/Loyal North Lancs, a reserve battalion, pressed ahead in support of the attack. Reaching the advance trenches, they saw clear evidence of the failure of the attack on this front. Wounded men from all three battalions were lying only 100 yards from the uncut enemy wire.[35] Just before 0700 hours they were struggling to climb over the parapet against a hail of bullets. Their diary reports: 'The enemy fire was terrible. Many machine guns on our left flank. Before 100 yards had been covered the whole line was checked. Some managed to get back.'[36] Under cover of a short bombardment they withdrew under orders at 0745 hours.

The 2/Royal Munster Fusiliers of the 3rd Brigade went over the top at 0535 hours and were met by constant rifle and machine-gun fire. Approximately a hundred of 'B' Company made it to the enemy breastworks through wire that had been severely damaged, but which still caused some delay. They lost some fifty men while forcing their way through. The remaining fifty crossed the water and wire-filled ditch to find a trench filled with the dead and dying of the German 11/55 Regiment, mauled by the artillery fire. Rushing forward, they overran the second line trench, trapping most of the remaining men of the enemy regiment. However, success was short-lived as they were immediately attacked by enemy bombers from the front line trench and from the flanks of their occupied trench, overpowering and killing all but eight, who were taken prisoner.[37]

The 2/Welsh to the left of the Munsters had a shorter stretch of no man's land to cross, but they also had the added obstacles of three water-filled ditches. At 0537 the lead platoons came over the parapets to be met by 'such an increase in machine gun and accurate heavy rifle fire as to make advance impossible'.[38]

The 1/Gloucesters could not proceed more than 40 yards from their own parapet due to the heavy fire, losing two officers and sixty men in the first few minutes. They were ordered to withdraw and regrouped behind the Rue du Bois.[39] The 1/South Wales Borderers had moved up in support of the assault units, but due to the chaos of the disintegrating first attacks, they could not move forward against the confusion of the repelled troops falling back from the concentrated enemy fire. They moved further back, joining the 1/Gloucesters behind the Rue du Bois.

To the left of the 1st Division was the Meerut Division front running from the Orchard Redoubt to and including Neuve Chapelle. Facing both the 1st Division and the Meerut Division front were three companies from the 1 and 3 battalions of the 57 Royal Prussian Regiment under command of Hertzog Ferdinand von Braunsweig, and nine companies from the 1 and 3 battalions of the 55 Regiment under command of Graf Bulow von Dennewitz.[40]

The Dehra Dun Brigade had the objective of attacking the 800-yard enemy front, but they experienced casualties due to short-falling shells. However, they reported that the wire to their front had been satisfactorily damaged.

Under cover of the barrage, the 1/Seaforths and the 1/4 Seaforths climbed out of their advance trenches, forming the line ready to advance stealthily across the narrow stretch of no man's land. Continuing short-falling shells forced them instead to crouch in front of their own parapets, waiting for the barrage to end.[41] They stood to advance once the barrage ended, only to be cut down by a hail of bullets issued from an enemy less than 150 yards away. The fire was intensified by machine-gun fire from the corner of the Bois du Biez.

As the barrage intensified for the last ten minutes, the Jats and Gurkhas ascended their ladders and climbed out of the trench, but while in the process of forming up, they were hit from a range of less than 150 yards by concentrated, inescapable rifle and heavy machine-gun fire, cutting into the leading ranks as they endeavoured to cross the first few yards.

Within twenty minutes of the start of the attack and despite the intensive barrage that was intended to clear the way, the Southern Wing of the pincer movement had failed; all advances were arrested and none of the objectives had been reached. The casualties mounted with wounded men in ragged, dismembered groups, sheltering in craters and ditches as the battle raged over them; the slightest movement brought down a hail of bullets. In total the 2nd and 3rd Brigades lost 83 officers and 2,135 men killed, wounded, and missing, while the Dehra Dun Brigade lost 37 officers and 856 men killed, wounded, and missing.[42]

Generals Haig and Sir John French had received reports by 0800 hours of the stalled actions, but these did not convey the true state of affairs—of enormous losses caused by the hail of machine-gun fire emanating from breastworks that had supposedly been destroyed in the barrage. Orders were therefore issued for a further assault in the southern sector to take place at noon; this was postponed until 1440, and then finally took place at 1600 hours. The fruitless attack called for the 1/5 Sussex to support the 1/Black Watch and the Dehra Dun to attack on their left in an action that was called off an hour later due to the great loss of life.[43]

Northern Attack

The brigades of IV Corps were responsible for the front line between Neuve Chapelle and Bois Grenier, facing four regiments of the 6 Bavarian Reserve Division, from south to north: 17 Reserve, 16 Reserve, 21 Reserve, and 20 Reserve.[44] The plan called for the assault troops to break through the front line and consolidate the Sailly–Fromelles road as the first objective, before advancing up the ridge between the villages of Aubers and Fromelles. The 24th Brigade was to secure Deleval Farm and the Rue Deleval on the right flank, while the

25th Brigade was to capture Fromelles Village and secure the left flank running from the village to La Cordonneries Farm.[45]

The 23th Brigade, plus a brigade of the 7th Division under command of Brigadier-General R. J. Pinney, would advance through this gap before moving south-eastwards towards Aubers Village and Leclercq Farm, then pressing onwards towards La Plouich Farm and La Cliqueteries Farm to meet up with the Indian Corps.[46]

The barrage was provided by the No. 2 Group HAR guns and those guns of the 7th and 8th Divisions, plus the VII Siege Brigade, totalling some 190 field guns and howitzers.[47] In sequence with the southern attack, the barrage began at 0500 hours with howitzer fire directed towards the fortified farms of Deleval and Delange and counter-battery operations against the artillery situated on the ridge, while the guns of the HAR were used to destroy the strong points beyond the range of the divisional artillery. The German breastworks and forward positions were also pounded by the guns of the VII Siege Brigade, with the 18-pdrs targeting the wire and seven of the RHA 13-pdrs sweeping the communication trenches to prevent the movement of reinforcements.

Until the gap in defences had been made, the role of the 23rd Brigade was restricted to holding the section of the line outside the attack sectors of the 24th and 25th Brigades. The 2/Middlesex moved up to a position a mile west of the Sailly–Fromelles road on the Rue de Quesnes, where they held the trenches while being blasted by continual and often heavy counter barrages from the German field batteries.[48]

The 24th Brigade objective was to attack a salient in the German line. Accordingly it was decided that the right section of the salient would be attacked by the 2/Northamptonshire while the left would be attacked by the 2/East Lancashire. Two guns of the 14th Battery, XXII Brigade RFA, fitted with rubber-rimmed wheels, were moved into the salient during the night to target the wire and create a gap before switching their fire to the breastworks. One gun tore several gaps in the entanglements, but the other could not be fired when the weak flooring shattered and collapsed.[49]

The East Lancashire men were assembled in a trench on the south side of the road, at an angle to the line of attack. To mitigate this disadvantage, they began creeping out into no man's land from 0530 hours onwards, in readiness for the charge once the barrage lifted. As it was lifted they came 'immediately under very heavy machine gun crossfire, losing heavily even before crossing the Fromelles Road'.[50] The attack withered away under fire from German riflemen standing on their parapet. Regrouping, the leading companies doubled forward but were 'again mown down before they had gone twenty-five yards, the survivors creeping back as best they could to the trench and sap on Fromelles Road.'[51]

From their assembly points in the orchard near the Rue Petillon, the Northants advanced on a two-company front. The right company found the wire cut, but came under heavy enfilade fire and were reduced to one officer and forty men, who managed to break into and hold a trench. The company attacking on the left found the wire uncut and were soon wiped out under heavy rifle and machine-gun fire.[52]

As the East Lancashires were being smashed against their own parapet, the Sherwood Foresters, Worcestershires, and Black Watch were all coming forward from behind. The trenches became congested and movement became well-nigh impossible. It was made all the worse as the enemy's counter-bombardment landed on the grid-lock. Half an hour later, the Sherwoods launched an attack towards an identified breach on the right of the East Lancashires' position, which turned out to be about a yard wide, the rest being a ditch with immersed barbed wire. The attack got to within 40 yards of the enemy before it was arrested.[53]

By 0700 hours, the 24th Brigade attack had failed and their advance was at a standstill, while the troops, congested in trenches, were in hopeless confusion.

The regiments of the 25th Brigade were situated 400 yards to the left of those of the 24th Brigade, across an approximately 120-yard-wide no man's land. Four regiments of the 6 Bavarian Reserve Division defended a front of equal length.[54] The British line was made up of, from the right: 2/Rifle Brigade, linking up with the Sherwood's on their right, 2/Royal Berkshire, 1/Royal Irish Rifle, 13/London (Kensington), and 2/Lincolnshire holding the far left of the line.[55] The assault troops were formed from the Rifle Brigade, Royal Irish, and the Kensingtons, the former two attacking 9 Company, 16 Bavarian (Reserve) Infantry Regiment, with the Kensingtons facing the 10 Company of the same regiment.[56]

The barrage screamed overhead, creating an air pressure that pushed the caps onto the heads of the men of 2/Rifle Brigade as they waited for the orders to begin their assault. The men went through the same rituals that had saved them in the past: touching a piece of wood; rechecking their weapons; thinking of loved ones.[57] Surely it was madness to risk all by running across no man's land against rifle and machine-gun fire to be horribly maimed or killed? Despite their professionalism and experience fighting overseas, each man struggled with his own private fears, but overriding them was the determination not to let the regiment or his mates down. Suddenly a cascade of short-falling 4.7-inch shells, caused by faulty manufacture, began exploding in among the riflemen of 'B' and 'D' companies, causing significant casualties during the last ten minutes, just as the bombardment intensified.[58]

Officers continued their checks of the men's equipment—rifle fully loaded with one in the breech and the bayonet fixed—before checking their own, ensuring revolvers were fully loaded. The indispensable pipe or cigarette, helping to keep a 'stiff upper-lip', was jammed in the mouths of most officers; it was critical that they did not show signs of fear, a contagion that could cause the line to falter. Checking their watches, they waited: 'This is an attack…. We have got to get over the parapet. We have got to get over the parapet—when the guns lift'.[59]

The call to go over the top was almost a release from the waiting and short-shells exploding in their midst. The call rang out, 'Forward the Rifles!' as Captain Kennedy led 'B' Company and Captain Werner 'D' Company up the ladders and over the parapet of the advance assault saps. They formed their line, with the Royal Irish on their left, making swift progress, despite the yellowish caramel-like mud, which stuck to their boots in great clumps, adding a few inches to their height and weighing several pounds. No man's land was suddenly filled with men covered in mud, rushing, stumbling, leaping forward and shouting as they charged onward, concentrating on their objective.

The German trench ahead was wrecked by the barrage, but the occupants had regained their composure and begun sending a storm of fire into the riflemen, who seemed oblivious to the shells falling and the bullets cracking past. They continued running towards the

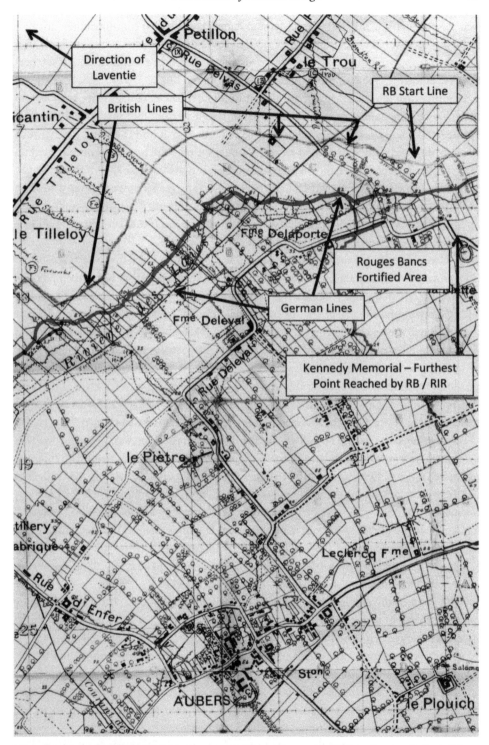

Map of the Aubers Ridge battlefield, showing the Rouge Banc area, the front lines, and the positions of the Rifle Brigade and Royal Irish. (*Based on Trench Map Sheet 35 S.W.1. Laventie*)

trenches through a whirlwind of thunder and flame. The riflemen continued their advance as their mates were brought down around them; the wounded would have to look after themselves, applying their field-dressing over entrance and exit wounds, until stretcher-bearers could get to them or they could crawl back to their lines.

Running through the barbed wire, almost heedless of the entanglements, they ran up the enemy parapet and jumped into the trench. They had been told that after the intense barrage, the enemy would be crushed and cowed, but they found them to be very much alive. As desperate individual hand-to-hand battles ensued, the bombers concentrated on throwing their grenades, relying on their training while mayhem raged about them.

As the German defenders were pushed back, blocking teams moved forward to erect obstacles at opposite ends of the trench, while fire steps were built facing the enemy's second line. The fighting had been hard, with the enemy incurring significant casualties, but 2/Rifle Brigade had secured 80 yards of enemy trench.

'A' Company was led forward by Captain Sherston, while Captain Hargreaves led 'C' Company, with 'HQ' and the battalion machine guns in support. As they began their advance to the newly captured trench, the enemy fire cut into them causing severe casualties, preventing 'HQ' Company and the machine guns from being brought to the captured trench. Despite the absence of the machine guns, the support troops reached the trench. The assault troops regrouped and began their 200-yard advance between the enemy's first and second lines, to the bend of the Rouges Banc to Fromelles Road. The enemy fire seemed to intensify further and casualties began to mount once again; the bombing and blocking parties, known as the 'very best, bravest and steadfast in an emergency'[60] could not replicate their success in taking the first trench. They broke up and were unable to regroup themselves into a coherent force.

Having gained the second objective—the bend in the Rouges Bancs to Fromelles Road—a defensive line was formed, creating a front of approximately 250 yards in all. The riflemen regrouped again before attacking the strong point at Rouges Bancs; viewing the battlefield they realised that, with the exception of the Royal Irish, they were alone. Their position was unenviable; they had progressed far into enemy territory, they had lost their bombing and blocking parties, and they were now receiving fire from both flanks, the rear, and at least two machine guns located in the Rouges Bancs strong point.

More and more riflemen fell, Captain Kennedy among them. By 0800 hours the remaining riflemen began falling back to the captured trench.[61]

At the end of the artillery barrage, 'C' and 'D' companies of the 1/Royal Irish Rifles mounted their parapet along with the men of 2/Rifle Brigade. They formed lines at thirty paces and charged across no man's land into significant fire from the front and flank.

'A' and 'B' companies followed immediately behind, while two platoons led by the regimental sergeant major of 'D' Company attacked the enemy who were laying down enfilade fire from rifle and machine-gun emplacements. The action, at an oblique angle to the main advance, became pinned down with a high number of casualties being incurred, forcing the remainder to withdraw.

The main attack progressed through the enemy's first line and onwards to the second line trench, where there was a pause for reinforcements. The enemy counter-attacked with an onslaught of mortars and grenades, causing very heavy casualties; the Royal Irish, who were commanded by the regimental sergeant major as all the officers had been killed, wounded, or were missing, had to fall back onto the first captured trench. The remainder held the trench until ordered to retire on 10 May.[62]

The 2/Lincolns held the reserve trenches between the Royal Irish and the Kensington battalions, having moved up after the Royal Irish had cleared the parapets. 'W' and 'X' companies followed the Royal Irish across no man's land, littered with hundreds of wounded, dying and dead soldiers. Strafed from the flank by emplaced machine guns, the companies became pinned down and stranded, with casualties increasing from the constant fire. 'Z' and 'Y' companies were instructed to remain in the forward trench.

The 1/13 Kensingtons were about 400 yards to the left of the 1/Royal Irish Rifles and waited while the barrage flew overhead; their War Diary stated that 'it appeared to lack the intensity of the Neuve Chapelle bombardment'.[63] At 0530 hours, a battery of the 4.7-inch howitzers was due to bombard the fortified Delangre Farm, but when the main barrage ended, this had still not taken place.[64] A few seconds later, the mines were detonated: a thunderous explosive force of 2,000 lb in each tunnel expanding by 1,000 times issued a shock wave that flew at twenty-times the speed of sound and forced the earth to heave as mud, debris, and fragmented bodies of the Bavarian Regiment and their shattered equipment were catapulted into the air. The mass seemed to hover before falling back to the ground. These were the largest mine detonations to date and they obliterated 80 yards of front and reserve lines. [65]

Climbing over their parapet, the Kensingtons saw the devastation, but without hesitation they began charging over the ground to take possession of the crater lips, which had formed natural ramparts. Once they had regrouped, 'D' Company pushed forward, overrunning the second- and third-line trenches before launching themselves at the fortified Delangre Farm. The undamaged fortified farm contained dazed enemy soldiers, who soon regained their composure to lay down devastating fire from at least two machine guns and numerous rifles, bringing the Kensingtons' advance to a halt 50 yards short. Those remaining took occupation of a communications trench. The machine guns had been set at a low level, ensuring that their muzzles could not easily been seen, inflicting terrible injuries to the upper legs of the advancing troops.

The enemy on the other side of the crater also quickly regained their composure and started firing into the new ramparts formed by the crater and at the support troops that were crossing no man's land. Enemy blocking parties moved forward to block the Kensingtons' access to trenches that were undamaged by the mines; there they formed a new defensive line in preparation for a counter-attack.

Lowry-Cole Brings Order

The 25th Brigade front had now grounded to a halt, and to make matters worse, the ground between the lines was choked with men and leaderless units, all in great confusion. The British trenches were also blocked with discarded and broken ladders, small bridges, and the dead and wounded. Controlled movement forwards or backwards was impossible. Men in the lodgements were cut-off, and the consolidation of the gains made by the 1/Royal Irish and 2/Rifle Brigade were in the balance. Brigadier-General Lowry-Cole moved up to direct operations personally from the forward positions in the breastworks at about 0625 hours. He ordered two companies of the 2/Lincolnshires to make their way via a sap and a shallow communication trench to the crater rim, and from there work to the right, bombing along the German front to connect with the troops of 1/Royal Irish and 2/Rifle Brigade.[66]

Those of the Rifle Brigade forward of the captured trench, along with the Royal Irish, now heard a shouted order to 'retire at the double'[67] made with great fury and quickly and positively repeated by a 'Captain Dee of the Royal Irish Rifles'.[68,69] Men were seen retreating back from all directions, while German prisoners seen running for cover behind the British lines were immediately mistaken for a counter-attack and fired upon from the British trenches. Brigade staff, including Lowry-Cole, saw the danger of the whole front disintegrating; without a second thought he jumped on top of the parapet walls to order the troops back. Standing erect, calling the men to return immediately, Lowry-Cole was hit and mortally wounded, but his actions nonetheless restored order. Brigade Major Dill, who was with Lowry-Cole, was also badly wounded.

Command of the 25th Brigade passed to Lieutenant-Colonel Stephens, who was ordered back.[70] He crawled to Brigade Headquarters after passing command of the trench to Captain Newport of the 2/Royal Irish, as all the officers of the Rifle Brigade had been either wounded or killed.[71] In the meantime, Stephens corresponded with his staff via runners, one of whom was Rifleman Jones, who despite being wounded three times, managed to carry a message from the captured enemy trench across bullet-swept ground to the British lines.

By 0830 hours the whole of the front had stagnated, with the exception of three lodgements in enemy territory. No advance had been made and a breakthrough was not immediately possible. The lodgements existed because the British had employed a 'Bite-and-Hold' technique, attacking and holding what they could until reinforcements could be brought up to force a breakthrough. Haig described the tactic:

> Bite off a piece of the enemy's line, like Neuve Chapelle, and hold it against counter attack. The bite can be made without much loss, and, if we choose the right place and make every preparation to put it quickly into a state of defence there ought to be no difficulty in holding it against the enemy's counter attacks….[72]

The Northamptonshires had a foothold in a trench in the 24th Brigade front, 2/Rifle Brigade were on the Sailly–Fromelles road, and 13/London (Kensingtons) were close to Delangre Farm.[73] The lodgements were not particularly secure: they were not a continuous line, the flanks were open, and they were receiving attacks from the front and the open ends, both of which steadily caused casualties among the defenders and drained ammunition that could not be replaced. Lastly, the lodgements were deep in enemy territory; the reinforcements that were needed to exploit the advantage had to fight their way to them through falling shells and enfilade fire from rifles and machine guns.

Communication problems surfaced again with divisional staff being unaware of the exact location of the troops in the areas between the British lines, which trenches had been captured, and exactly what was in British hands. Therefore they had no option but to suspend bombardments for fear of causing British casualties. The Germans, however, had defended in depth, allowing the lightly held front line trenches to fall, drawing the attackers into progressively more heavily defended zones. The enemy could fall back to muster points to prepare for a counter-attack, while the defenders were subjected to enfilade fire from the flanks using up precious ammunition and men which could not easily be replaced.

The Rest of the Day

As the Royal Irish were forced back to the captured trench while the Rifle Brigade, under constant attack, endeavoured to consolidate the trench by building substantial blocks at either end. Sergeant Starr, with riflemen Denton, Jones, Watkins, and Windebank, formed an *ad hoc* bombing team which provided some response to the enemy bombing attacks from the flanks. Denton climbed back over the parapet to collect bombs from the dead and wounded to supplement their almost exhausted supply, while Rifleman Watkinson caught three German bombs in the air, throwing them back from where they came. Unfortunately the fourth exploded in his hand.[74]

Haig, removed some distance from the battlefield, could not or would not accept that his army, superior in number and executing a meticulously laid plan, could have failed to such a degree.[75] The French Tenth Army to the south had broken through the German line, and one of the prime British objectives of the battle was to maintain pressure on the German front in his zone to prevent reinforcements being redeployed against the French. Haig therefore instructed Rawlinson to 'try again!'[76] Rawlinson in turn decided that an attack should be made against the 400-yard German trench west of the Sailly–Fromelles road, against which the 2/East Lancashires and 1/Sherwood Foresters had failed earlier. Rawlinson instructed Davies to attack 'with what men you can muster'.[77] Accordingly Davies ordered his reserve battalions of 1/Worcestershires and 1/5 Black Watch to lead an attack at 1330 hours, with 2/Queen's from the 7th Division in support and 2/Middlesex and 1/7 Middlesex of the 23rd Brigade as reserve. At 1250 hours the artillery opened fire on the 400-yard objective, causing casualties among the assembled battalions from scattered short-falling shells. The German artillery, accurately sighted on the front trenches, answered with a barrage of their own, cutting down men where they stood, bringing the attack to a halt even before it had formed, let alone actually started. Three hundred and eighty-one men were lost without even crossing their own parapet.[78] It seemed that the Germans 'owned' the battlefield, making further attacks during daylight hours pointless.

Aware that the men of the Rifle Brigade were in dire need of reinforcements, Stephens ordered two bombing parties, together with seventy riflemen and two machine guns, to join the remaining men in their captured trench. The 15 Field Company Royal Engineers was also instructed to dig a communication trench from the captured trench to Captain Newport's position to allow 'D' Company of the 2/Queen's to provide reinforcements. A further initiative commanded by 2nd Lieutenant W. E. Gray of 2/Rifle Brigade was the only one that succeeded.

2nd Lieutenant Gray

Gray, who commanded the battalion machine-gun section, had gathered about fifty of his fellow riflemen, and crawled out of the forward trench and into an abandoned derelict trench, in which they formed up ready to make the dash across to the forward position. The whistle blew and they rose from the trench straight into intensive fire. Men began to fall immediately and the small force was soon halved, but the survivors continued their advance and twenty managed to reach the forward position.[79] Once there, Gray began repairing a MG8 machine gun which had been captured and damaged in the initial assault. He soon had the machine working, while his fellow riflemen made an attempt at extending the trench along the dyke bordering the Sailly–Fromelles road. The enemy made a concerted effort to prevent this extension and then attacked the ends of the trench, persistently pushing them inwards. Although these were fought off, the action further reduced the critically low supply of bombs, ammunition, and men.

As darkness began to fall, the riflemen, knowing that this was a dangerous time for counter-attacks, became aware of the enemy mustering for an attack. At 1950 hours, 1 Battalion of the 16 Bavarian (Reserve) Infantry Regiment, commanded by Major Arnold, launched their assault. Gray's expertise now paid dividends as the enemy were hit by their own MG8 machine gun in concert with a British machine gun, which together with the rifle fire and the bombs collected earlier, brought the dramatic close-fought attack to a halt.

The French Attack at Vimy Ridge

As a result of their destructive four-day artillery bombardment, the French swept across the hill of Notre Dame de Lorette and thrust down into the Souchez Valley, continuing their attack towards the lower slopes of Vimy Ridge, the bastion of the Douai Plain. Exasperated by the French success and the First Army's lack of a breakthrough, Haig ordered another attack to take place at 1800 hours. Again, the movement of the troops to the congested assembly trenches brought down an enemy bombardment with the shells falling among the troops and preventing any movement towards the front line. The attack was called off, and further alternative plans were discussed at the Indian Corps Headquarters at Lestrem, ending with two courses of action open to Haig: a night attack undertaken by troops unfamiliar with the ground, or an assault in daylight preceded by another mini-bombardment. The latter was accepted, with the generals instructed to work on the specific plans.

Meanwhile, the British-held lodgements were becoming more and more precarious. Under orders to retire, the twenty-six remaining men of the Northants clambered out of the trench that had cost so much and made their way back to British lines. It was hoped that the Rifle Brigade/Royal Irish position could be held overnight so that it could be used as a staging point for the attack planned for the next day.

1. Diagram of a 60-pdr breech-loaded shrapnel shell. (*Reproduced from Treatise on Ammunition 10th Edition War Office, 1915*)

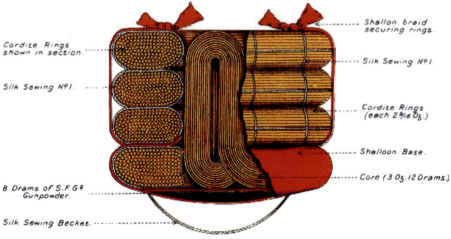

2. Diagram of a cordite cartridge. (*Reproduced from Treatise on Ammunition 10th Edition War Office, 1915*)

SHELL, Q.F. COMMON POINTED 12 & 14 PRS. MARK II.

3. Diagram of a quick firing 12/14-pdr high-explosive shell. (*Reproduced from Treatise on Ammunition 10th Edition War Office, 1915*)

4. Royal Artillery gun and carriage. (*Reproduced from* The Great War Magazine, *1918*)

5. Re-enactor Gary Wise, member of the Rifle Living History Society, in Rifle Brigade uniform of 1914. (*Author's collection*)

6. Royal Artillery fighting the Flanders Mud. (*Reproduced from* The Great War Magazine, *1918*)

7. Six-inch gun battery. (*Reproduced from* The Great War Magazine, *1918*)

8. Example of a German Trench from above at the Passchendaele Museum. Note the rifle loop hole. (*Author's collection*)

9. Example of barbed wire entanglements. (*Reproduced from* The Great War Magazine, *1918*)

10. Modern photograph of the ground that the Rifle Brigade advanced across after taking the village of Neuve Chapelle. (*Author's collection*)

11. View from Layes Bridge, the location of a German stronghold, across the battlefield, showing the River Layes. (*Author's collection*)

12. The loading of a British heavy gun. (*Reproduced from* The Great War Magazine, *1918*)

Above: 13. Gravestones in the cemetery of Neuve Chapelle. The bodies of these five were among those originally buried in the village graveyard, but were blown-up in later battles. (*Author's collection*)

Below: 14. British heavy gun, nicknamed 'Bunty', firing. (*Reproduced from* The Great War Magazine, *1918*)

15. Silk or shalloon-encased cordite cartridges at Royal Gunpowder Mills, Waltham Abbey. (*Author's collection*)

16. From the Kennedy Memorial looking towards Rouge Bancs and onward to Aubers Ridge, which can be seen in the distance by a row of trees. (*Author's collection*)

17. From the Kennedy Memorial towards VC Corner Cemetery, the approximate location of the British lines. This is the ground that the Rifle Brigade and Royal Irish advanced over to their first two objectives. (*Author's collection*)

18. The Kennedy Museum, which marks the furthest point reached by the Rifle Brigade during the Battle of Aubers Ridge. (*Author's collection*)

19. A Vickers machine gun, based on the Maxim gun, at Royal Powder Mills, Waltham Abbey. (*Author's collection*)

20. A German MG 08 machine gun, based on the Maxim gun, at Royal Powder Mills, Waltham Abbey. (*Author's collection*)

21. Fromelle Church, where German staff officers directed the Battle of Aubers Ridge, from the Kennedy Memorial. (*Author's collection*)

22. The Laventie church tower, where Sir John French, Churchill, and Repington viewed the Battle of Aubers Ridge. (*Author's collection*)

23. & 24. Two views of the Passchendaele Cemetery illustrating what 11,161 gravestones actually look like. (*Author's collection*)

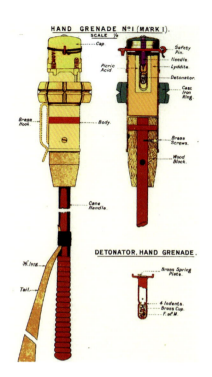

25. Diagram of a Mark 1 British grenade.
(*Reproduced from Treatise on Ammunition 10th Edition War Office, 1915*)

26. Female workers at Crittall Munitions Factory in Braintree, Essex. (*Reproduced from photograph held at the Crittall Archive at the Braintree Distinct Museum, reference BRNTM NEG 3066*)

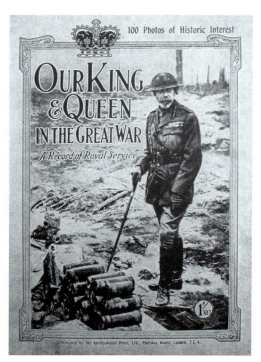

27. Front of special edition of *The Great War Magazine* showing King George V examining shell cartridges on the battlefield. (*Reproduced from* The Great War Magazine, *1918*)

28. Shells awaiting collection having been found by members of the public. (*Author's collection*)

29. The gravestones of unknown soldiers, with one from the Rifle Brigade at the front. (*Author's collection*)

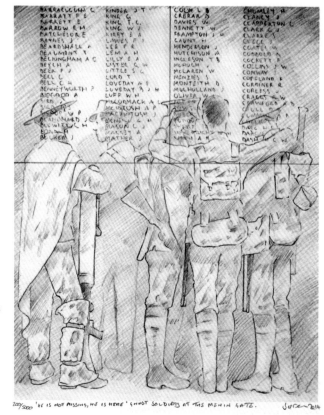

30. 'He is not missing; he is here—Ghost soldiers at the Menin Gate'. Drawing by artist Soren Hawkes, whose great uncle is listed on the Menin Gate. (*Reproduced with kind permission of Soren Hawkes*)

Above left: 31. An 18-pdr shell given to a Crittal worker at the end of the war, now used as a doorstop. (*Author's collection*)

Above right: 32. Memorial in the Passchendaele Museum to the British Empire's Dead. (*Author's collection*)

Final Attack

The forward Rifle Brigade/Royal Irish lodgement was an embarrassment to the enemy, who had no intention of allowing the British to remain there; however, they were also fully aware that they had a formidable adversary to encounter. Therefore, three simultaneous attacks all converging on the position were set out. Companies 1, 2, and 4 of the 16 Bavarian moved off from their reserve positions between Rouges Bancs and 'the house with the white fence' at 2115 hours, arriving at their forming up point around 2215 hours after encountering some navigational problems and suffering casualties from British artillery. Scouts were sent out to survey the area around the British position and forward patrols were put in place to guide the assault troops to the occupied trench. A British artillery barrage forced the attack to be postponed until 0245 hours on 10 May.[80]

Out of the darkness the soldiers of companies 1 and 2 made a determined frontal assault on the trench; the riflemen fired into the night, and with the support of two machine guns, they brought the attack to a standstill. Sergeant Starr and 2nd Lieutenant Gray, operating the two machine guns, took a terrible toll of the enemy troops.[81] Meanwhile, 4 Company, led by Leutnant Gebhardt, attacked and forced the right-end flank of the trench, pushing their way forward in ferocious hand-to-hand fighting using anything they could as weapons. The riflemen manning blocks set up along the trench system fought to prevent the trench being 'rolled-up', but then became aware of a small enemy force led by Leutnant Hock entering the trench from above, some distance from Gebhardt's attack. Hock and his men began advancing with supporting fire from the remainder of 4 Company who picked off the riflemen as their dark silhouettes appeared. The severity of the attack can be measured by the comments of a Roman Catholic priest serving in the German Army:

> ...after two hours fighting, the enemy was beaten back. You can scarcely have an idea of the work this represented. How these Englishmen had in twelve hours dug themselves in! The hundred fellows who were in our trenches had brought with them an enormous amount of ammunition, a machine-gun and one they had captured from us.... Almost every single man of them had to be put out of action with hand grenades. They were heroes all, brave and true to the end, until death ... men of the active English Rifles Brigade.[82,83]

The defenders began to run out of ammunition and casualties mounted to such an extent that the defence became hopeless. Those not incapacitated or captured tried to make a break for the British lines. Starr was captured, but managed to escape and then was wounded in his desperate dash back to the lines. Gray was the last officer to leave the trench.[84] By about 0300 hours it was all over. Fifty men were overpowered and taken prisoner and a further thirty wounded were captured the next day. The remainder of those that had occupied the trench were dead. When Stephens arrived at the British assembly point with the 2/Queen's of the 22nd Brigade, he found that he did not have a battalion to relieve. Lieutenant Gray was the only officer to return from the position along with less than 200 of the mixed force that had occupied the captured trench. Two hundred and twelve were missing, and of these the greater number would be missing forever. It is estimated that less than 100 were taken prisoner, and of these, thirty were wounded.[85]

The Bavarians made good their losses and consolidated their previously lost trench, closing up the line. British gains of the previous morning were lost and the Germans regained possession of the whole of their original line. The British were back where they had started.

Haig Receives Unwelcome News

Despite the setbacks, Haig was still determined to 'press on vigorously', but during a conference held at 0900 hours on 10 May, it was announced that First Army had insufficient shells to undertake two attacks—namely further attacks at Aubers and the forthcoming attack at Festubert.[86] The conference was also advised that the ammunition for the 4.7-inch howitzers was too defective to use.[87] Fuzes on many of the shells (those for the 15-inch howitzers in particular) were deficient and failed to detonate. The worn barrels of the guns resulted in far too many shorts, and although the barrage created a 'curtain of dust and smoke', it did little actual damage.[88]

The Battle of Aubers Ridge was over, and the recriminations, which were to have a devastating effect upon the British public and the Government, were about to begin.

Reflections on the Battle

The battle had resulted in no ground being won and no tactical advantage gained. With the exception of depriving a small number of reinforcements that could have been made available to defend against the French attack, it is doubtful that the Battle of Aubers Ridge had any significant effect on assisting the main French attack 15 miles to the south. In his *History of the Great War, 1915*, Brigadier-General Sir J. Edmonds gets straight to the point: '…Aubers Ridge—certainly as regards May 9—was less a battle than a massacre'. [89] However, the *Manchester Guardian* endeavoured to report the battle with a positive spin in its second edition of 14 May 1915:

> We have had many casualties this week, but if we have not won all we hoped, we have detained on our front a force equivalent to our own, and have greatly facilitated the French offensive on our right. This offensive swept on towards the Arras–Lens road like a flood.

The only guns capable of damaging the defences were the 60 pdrs and 9.2 inch, of which just eighteen were available; many of the artillery pieces were outdated, badly maintained, or simply worn out.[90] The Official History also criticised difficulties in ranging: 'the British Gunners were unable to hit their targets and the counter-batteries and machine guns were not silenced…. According to British aeroplane reports the registration before the battle was useless.' Intelligence about the newly strengthened German positions had been acknowledged, and yet the duration and strength of the bombardment was not capable of breaking the German wire, breastwork defences, and the well-concealed machine-gun emplacements. The German efforts to strengthen their defences had made the Battle of Aubers Ridge 'a very different proposition to that which had confronted the First Army at Neuve Chapelle'.[91] After the battle, Haig put his thoughts to paper:

The defences in our front are so carefully and so strongly made, and mutual support with machine-guns is so complete, that in order to demolish them a long methodical bombardment will be necessary by heavy artillery before infantry are sent forward to attack.[92]

Sir John French's eighth despatch concurred with Haig in that 'a more extensive artillery preparation was necessary to crush the resistance offered by his numerous fortified posts'.[93] The defences and therefore the firepower contained within had been grossly underestimated and the short, intensive bombardment had been inadequate. By contrast, the French had bombarded the enemy in their sector with 1,368 guns—almost 25 per cent of which were heavy guns—for four days, not forty minutes; in duration, the British barrage equated to less than 1 per cent of the French.[94] In *Nelson's History of the War*, John Buchan wrote:

> Our artillery preparation was necessarily inadequate, our men were held up by unbroken wire and parapets, and the result was failure and heavy losses.
>
> On the other hand, the French in their great movement towards Lens about the same date had 1,100 guns firing all day with the rapidity of Maxims. In one restricted area they placed 300,000 shells. As a consequence, the whole countryside was sterilized and flattened, nothing remained but a ploughed field with fragments of wire and humanity, and the infantry could advance almost as safely as on parade. The lesson was writ too plain to be missed. We must pay in shells or in human lives.[95]

In addition to the problems caused by the short barrage was the fact that 90 per cent of the shells fired by British guns contained shrapnel and not the high-explosive needed to destroy wire entanglements and defensive emplacements.[96] The French had used 240 rounds of high explosive shell per field gun per day during their bombardment.[97] On 12 May, Sir John French wrote in his diary:

> [Major-General] Du Cane told me that the success of the French was almost entirely due to their profuse expenditure of HE ammunition. He showed by figures that they used in their attacks of the 9th and 10th four and five times as much as we did or COULD. It is, to my mind, a great question whether we ought not to stand altogether on the defensive until an adequate supply HE is available....[98]

Haig now came to the conclusion that a longer bombardment was required. During the Battle of Festubert, the artillery would provide a thirty-six-hour bombardment before the infantry went in.[99] The toll on the soldiers involved in the Battle of Aubers Ridge and the lessons learnt thereof would influence future plans, especially those for the Somme Campaign.

Casualties

Hundreds of wounded men in agony littered the battlefield; the stretcher-bearers sought them out, rolled them onto a stretcher and brought them to the lines using a 'knee-shuffle'.

They kept their heads as low as possible, half-dragging, half-pushing the stretcher, while bullets flew around them.[100] Writing in *The Guardian* in 1993 about his research for *Birdsong*, a novel set in the First World War, author Sebastian Faulks told a sobering anecdote:

> The old man sitting next to me on the bus took my hand as he explained how it felt to be wheeled on a general service wagon over rutted ground with the two parts of your shattered leg rubbing together.[101]

Private L. Mitchell, 24 Field Ambulance, 8th Division:

> The vehicles were packed jam-full, and sometimes they were coming back full up and the ambulance drivers didn't know where to take the wounded. I never saw an attack with so many men who had bullet wounds as at Aubers Ridge. The Germans just mowed them down and most of the bullet wounds were through the legs. We had a lot of splinting to do.[102]

The low setting of the enemy machine guns had caused an enormous number of wounds to the upper legs of the assault troops, and to these were added the devastating effect of the artillery explosions. Once off the battlefield, the wounded were sent to the Regimental Aid Post, where their injuries would be assessed and morphine would be given before they were moved to a clearing station. It was at this point that wounds were washed with hydrogen peroxide, boric acid, or perchlorate of mercury, and then dressed and splinted, using anything at hand from a chair-leg to an old rifle, old belts, or shoe-laces.[103] The patient would then be moved to either the Casualty Clearing Station, for those unfit to travel, or to the Base Hospital. Unfortunately, by now infection had often already set in and many soldiers died of their wounds weeks after the battle.[104]

As the casualty reports started to filter through, the cost of the day's failure became clear to Haig. This single day of fighting had resulted in an enormous death toll:

Officers: 458
Other Ranks: 11,161[105]

The total casualties therefore amounted to 11,619. In order to appreciate fully what 11,619 deaths represent, I suggest you visit Tyne Cot Cemetery, where some 11,954 are buried from the battles of 1917. The photos taken and included by the author of the cemetery may assist the reader in visualising the number lost.

The overall numbers of lost were broken down as follows:

The 8th Division suffered the following casualties:
Officers   192   Other Ranks   4,490
The Meerut Division suffered the following casualties:
Officers   94   Other Ranks   2,535
2 Rifle Brigade suffered the following casualties:
Officers   21   Other Ranks   629

Almost as a slight against those who fought in the battle was the fact the Germans hardly mentioned it in their reports, instead combining the battle with that of Festubert, under the title: '*Das Gefecht bei Fromelles*'—the fight at Fromelles.[106] Aubers Ridge would remain in German hands for the rest of the war, until it was attacked and captured by the 47 (London) Division in October 1918.[107]

The View from Laventie Church Tower

Repington visited Sir John French, 'not as a correspondent, for no correspondents were permitted, but as a friend',[108] along with Churchill, who had broken his journey from Paris upon hearing of the battle and decided to join his friends.[109] They watched from the battered church tower at Laventie with French and his staff officers as the battle unfolded. They were appalled. Repington particularly could not believe that such insignificant gains had been made for such heavy losses.[110]

In his book, *1914*, Sir John French recalled watching the battle:

On the tower of a ruined church I spent several hours in close observation of the operations. Nothing since the Battle of Aisne had ever impressed me so deeply with the terrible shortage of artillery and ammunition as did the events of that day. As I watched the Aubers Ridge, I clearly saw the great inequality of the artillery duels, and, as attack after attack failed, I could see that the absence of sufficient artillery support was doubling and trebling our losses in men.

I therefore determined on taking the most drastic measures to destroy the apathy of a government which had brought the Empire to the brink of disaster.

A friend was standing by my side on the tower, and to him I poured out my doubts and fears and announced my determination. He warned me that the politicians would never forgive the action I proposed, and that it meant my certain recall from the command in the France. But my decision was made, and I immediately started for my Head-quarters, fully determined on my future course of action.[111]

Upon arrival at his General Headquarters, French received an order to send 20 per cent of his reserve stock of shells to Gallipoli. In his view this was the last straw, and he wrote of it in his diary:

Last night I received an order from the War Office to send 25,000 rounds of artillery ammunition to the Dardanelles (via Marseilles) at once.

I replied that in view of the situation here—hard fighting going on all along my front—I could not accept the responsibility of reducing my stock of ammunition unless it was to be replaced at once.

A reply came this morning to say that the situation in the Dardanelles demanded a supply of ammunition at the earliest possible moment and that whatever was sent would be replaced. It has therefore gone....[112]

An estimate of munitions reserve for 16 May 1915 showed that the British armies had only four rounds per gun in reserve, instead of 150. The situation was disastrous.[113]

French provided two members of his personal staff with copies of his correspondence on the subject of ammunition supply between himself and the War Office, instructing them to proceed to England and deliver the papers to Lloyd George, Balfour, and Mr Andrew Bonar Law, leader of the Conservative Party. As an explanation, he included a memorandum setting out his reasons for demanding a greatly increased supply of ammunition, and showing that, in the particular form of warfare in which the British Army was then engaged, high-explosive shells were more necessary than shrapnel. Repington was also to be supplied with evidence related to the failure of the operations that day.[114] Finally, French instructed Frederick (Freddie) Edward Guest, his Aide-de-Camp and Churchill's cousin, to meet with Asquith to acquaint him with the situation and gain his assistance. In response, Asquith wrote to French on 13 May 1915:

My Dear Sir John,

Freddy Guest is here and has been giving me an account of what has been going on at the front. I deeply sympathize with you that an attack so well-conceived, and so gallantly delivered, just failed of success. No blame to anybody. This is one of the rubs of war.

I note two things – (1) that you find the 4.7 guns practically useless, (2) that you want a substantially higher percentage of high explosives.

I will not forget this. I regret that I am so much preoccupied with a thousand things that I cannot write you a real letter. But I wish you to be assured, as the months go on, my admiration for what you and your men are doing becomes more profound, and my confidence in your own leadership and in your ultimate success has never wavered for a moment. Whenever you would like to come over for a War Council please say so, and I shall be delighted to have you amongst us.

Always very sincerely yours,

H H Asquith.[115]

In the meantime, Repington visited his old battalion, 2/Rifle Brigade, meeting Lieutenant-Colonel Stephens with whom he had served previously. They discussed the battle and Stephens showed Repington a paper stating how they had begun the battle with 29 officers and 1,090 riflemen, and twenty-four hours later were left with:

… only one young company officer who had been in the Cambridge eleven the previous year, and 245 other ranks unwounded. I was enraged by this loss which was attributed by the troops solely to the failure of the guns, due in its turn to want of shells.[116,117]

At this point, Repington decided to expose the truth to the general public, no matter what the cost. He sent a telegram to *The Times* on 12 May without consulting anyone. It included the following fateful words:

…the want of an unlimited supply of high explosive shells was a fatal bar to our success.[118]

The Fallout of
The Times Article

The Press and DORA

The period immediately after the declaration of war was hectic, with the Government looking into every walk of life to determine possible dangers. Despite the removal of civil liberties, Asquith urged Parliament to increase the Government's powers in respect to Home Front regulation, allowing the prosecution of anyone whose actions were deemed to provide assistance to the enemy or jeopardise the success of the operations of His Majesty's forces. The instrument of these powers would be the Defence of the Realm Act, known by the acronym DORA, passed without debate, immediately receiving Royal Assent.

The original Act gave the Government executive powers to commandeer resources such as office space, land, ports, etc., to imprison without trial, and to control the press. It was in itself little more than a paragraph long, but the clauses restricting civil liberties were anathema to the Liberal ethos and threatened to split the party. In respect to the press and publication of matters arising from the war, the most important clause read:

> No person shall by word of mouth or in writing spread reports likely to cause disaffection or alarm among any of His Majesty's forces or among the civilian population.[1]

For several years before the war, press representatives were present at army manoeuvres, but when war broke out the press was restricted and the French policy of refusing journalists permission to attend the front was adopted.[2] Kitchener appointed Ernest Swinton as the British Army's official journalist to the Western Front. Reporting under the pseudonym of 'Eyewitness', his articles were first censored at General Headquarters in France, before being personally vetted by Kitchener; only having passed these inspections were they passed to the press. In addition to the censorship, Swinton was given exacting guidelines within which to operate: he was not allowed to mention place names, names and details of battalions, brigades and divisions, and not allowed to say that he had witnessed the events personally. Lastly, he had to write about 'what he thought was true, not what he knew to be true'.[3] The result was that the British public would read comforting accounts of devastating British gun fire and British gains against a cowering, shell-shocked enemy, with only the positive aspects of any action, successful or not, being reported.

Today's media 'spin-doctors' would have been proud of the manner in which the censored news from the Western Front was manipulated. In *Politicians At War*, Hazlehurst writes:

> When genuine successes followed the rarely reported setbacks, it was equally impossible for even professional observers to form a coherent picture of the trend of events.[4]

When the first-hand accounts of the retreat from Mons appeared in *The Times* they caused the public to react with anger and disbelief.

The restrictions of the Act were also applied to letters written by servicemen to friends and family, often sent from the front. These had to be read and censored by the military authorities, a role that was assigned to the subalterns and lieutenants, requiring them to sign the letter identifying that they were responsible for the censorship, meaning that they could be held liable in the event that a breach of security was discovered.[5] 2nd Lieutenant Robert McConnell recalled:

> I have just censored the letters of my men. By jove! If you could read some of those letters, they would do you good. The tenderness of those great, rough fellows is wonderful. I love them all for it.[6]

Instead of reading the letters, most officers preferred 'glancing over the page and spotting censorable matter without reading line by line,'[7] which can be appreciated as when the war was at its height, some 12.5 million letters in 16,000 mail bags would be sent from Flanders to Britain every week.[8] As for an officer's own letters, theoretically these were to be read by his commanding officer, but by gentlemanly convention they went straight to the anonymous base censor. Both officers and men tried to include clues or codes as to where they were fighting—it became a common game to try and outwit the censorship system.

In November 1914 the Act was repealed and replaced by the Defence of the Realm Consolidation Act 1914.[9] This new Act tightened the regulations, especially in respect to information, upon which it reads:

> (1)   His Majesty in Council has power during the continuance of the present war to issue regulations for securing the public safety and the defences of the realm, and as the powers and duties for that purpose of the Admiralty and Army Council and of the members of His Majesty's forces and other persons acting in his behalf; and may by such regulations authorise the trial by courts-martial, or in the case of minor offences by courts of summary jurisdiction, and punishment of persons committing offences against the regulations and in particular against any of the provisions of such regulations designed:
>
> (a) to prevent persons communicating with the enemy or obtaining information for that purpose or any purpose calculated to jeopardise the success of the operations of any of His Majesty's forces or the forces of his allies or to assist the enemy; or
>
> (b) to secure the safety of His Majesty's forces and ships and the safety of any means of communication and of railways, ports, and harbours; or

(c) to prevent the spread of false reports or reports likely to cause disaffection to His Majesty or to interfere with the success of His Majesty's forces by land or sea or to prejudice His Majesty's relations with foreign powers; or

(d) to secure the navigation of vessels in accordance with directions given by or under the authority of the Admiralty; or

(e) otherwise to prevent assistance being given to the enemy or the successful prosecution of the war being endangered.

[…]

(4) For the purpose of the trial of a person for an offence under the regulations by court-marshal and the punishment thereof, the person may be proceeded against and dealt with as if he were a person subject to military law and had on active service committed an offense under section five of the Army Act:

Provided that where it is proved that the offense is committed with the intention of assisting the enemy a person convicted of such an offence by a court-martial shall be liable to suffer death.[10]

Despite Swinton's appointment and the hardening of DORA, enterprising newspapermen filed reports, known as 'copy' in newspaper speak, from forbidden zones often by illegally entering battle areas. The system of 'eyewitness' accounts was not working and a War Office Press Bureau, or the 'Suppress Bureau' as it became known, was hastily created under the Conservative MP, Colonel Frederick Edwin Smith.[11] The official view of the progress of the war was not acceptable to many, especially Lloyd George, who after a cabinet meeting in February 1915 denounced the press for 'treating the progress of the war as one of almost unbroken success'.[12]

This sanitised version of the war's progress supported the Government's view that the war was being won. After the Battle of Neuve Chapelle, the press gave a one-sided euphoric description of a victorious battle, of gains and prisoners taken, but did not mention the opportunities missed or the casualties incurred.[13] This view quickly became discredited as the casualty lists emerged, provoking fury from some quarters. The *Daily Mail*'s war correspondent attacked the earlier official view:

Sir John French's despatch on the fighting at Neuve Chapelle is the one topic of conversation. On March 10th an official statement was issued that the British Army had taken the important village of Neuve Chapelle and had captured a thousand prisoners and some machine-guns. Two days afterwards a British official despatch described the magnitude of the victory, the effectiveness of our heavy artillery, and the defeat and heavy loss of the Germans when they attempted counter-attacks.

The enemy for the time being was 'beaten and on the run'. The whole incident was painted in 'couleur de rose'. There was an outburst of national rejoicing. Then suddenly the rejoicing paused. Casualty figures were published in daily instalments, and were surprisingly heavy. Rumours spread from mouth to mouth. Every man one met had some fresh story to tell, stories not in keeping with the official description. Many of them were false—but they fell like a pall on the public mind.

Now Sir John French has given us the real story, and not before it was time. His long despatch is a splendid tribute to the courage and devotion of the British Army, and it records a real victory. But it is very different from the tale told in the first accounts.

The advance was a success. The Germans were, for the moment, overwhelmed. We might have swept right through, far on the road to Lille. It was clearly Sir John French's intention that the Cavalry Brigade should pour through the breach in the German lines and get some enemy on the run. But our reserves were not brought up in time. The net result was that our real gain—a very important gain—was made during the first day of the battle. We did splendidly. But anyone who studies Sir John French's despatch with insight can see that his aim was not to capture a village, but to advance to Lille itself. And, but for the unfortunate mist, he would probably have done so.

WHY TRUST THE PEOPLE? Had the real story been told to us at the beginning, all would have been much better.

When the big advance comes, the big advance that would have started at Neuve Chapelle had things gone well as was hoped, losses will be much greater. The nation will not shrink back. But our authorities would be well advised not to try to blind the public, even for a time, by telling of the victories and glossing over reverses.[14]

The reality of the war was beginning to dawn on the British public as it already had to the invaded peoples of France and Russia. Neuve Chapelle seemed to rekindle the public's resolve, with many men now enlisting, while mothers, wives, sisters, and men too old or infirm to fight, increased their efforts to find ways of 'doing their bit'.

The public's anger over censorship continued, but it was only at the beginning of April 1915 that Asquith made any attempt to put the relationship between the press and the Government on a practical working foundation. During the first week of May 1915, six correspondents took up residence at GHQ France, but they were never officially recognised by Kitchener. C. E. Montague, the former lead writer of the *Manchester Guardian*, a newspaper that had supported the Liberal Party in the past and especially Lloyd George, was transferred to Military Intelligence with the rank of 2nd Lieutenant. He was responsible for the compulsory censorship of all messages transmitted by cable, the issuance of official statements, and the dispensing of advice to all journalists who voluntarily sought clearance for proposed articles. The journalists themselves would be responsible for operating within the requirements of DORA and would be subjected to punishments if they strayed outside its guidelines.

Kitchener's anger was often directed at 'official' correspondents, manifested in threats of 'unofficial punishments'. Thomas Basil Clarke of the *Daily Mail* was advised by a local police chief that orders to arrest him had been received, but at the police chief's discretion, he was instead given the chance to leave the area.
A similar order from Kitchener stated, 'should the journalist Philip Gibbs of the *Daily Chronicle* be found near the front line again, he was to be put up against a wall and shot!'[15]

This was the environment that Repington worked in. Even before the war had started he had reported on military campaigns and issues for *The Times*, and was not shy in bringing the Government to task over any matters that affected his beloved military. He was the sort of person that John F. Kennedy was describing when he spoke in October 1963 about the freedom of the press:

> The men who create power make an indispensable contribution to the nation's greatness, but the men who question power make a contribution just as indispensable, especially when that questioning is disinterested, for they determine whether we use power or power uses us.[16]

Charles à Court Repington

Charles à Court was born in 1858 and changed his name to à Court Repington in 1903 to fulfil a requirement in a cousin's will. Educated at Eton and Sandhurst, he joined the Rifle Brigade in 1878 as a newly appointed 2nd Lieutenant before fighting in the Anglo-Afghan War. After returning to England and serving in Ireland, he became a staff officer in 1887.

> ...after a young officer left Sandhurst in those days, his education in the art of war practically lapsed unless he were lucky enough to get on [staff] service, [especially as] the royal road to active service was closed for want of wars.[17]

Repington progressed his career with both military staff and intelligence roles. It was during this period that a Captain Douglas Haig of the 7 Hussars undertook several missions for him in Europe. As a result, and at Repington's suggestion, Haig received his first staff appointment as ADC to the Inspector of Cavalry.[18] Later Repington was appointed Deputy Assistant Adjutant General (DAAG) to the force that was tasked with re-conquering Sudan, first under Sir Grenfell and then with Kitchener during the Atbara and Omdurman campaigns. He was mentioned in despatches and promoted to Brevet Lieutenant-Colonel.

After serving as the first military attaché to Belgium and the Netherlands, Repington returned to the role of DAAG for General Buller's expedition to South Africa, where he raised a force of British immigrants known as the South African Light Horse. He was then involved with the Rifle Brigade in the battles of Spion Kop, Vaal Krantz, and Pieter's Hill. He entered the relieved Ladysmith with the official party, which also included a young Churchill. In his book *Twenty-five years, 1874–1909*, H. Spencer Wilkinson says Repington '...had been widely regarded as the most brilliant young staff officer in the British Army'.[19]

After serving in Egypt on Sir Grenfell's staff, Repington was forced to retire in 1901 over a matter of honour regarding his involvement with a married woman. It was the end of a thoroughly successful career. During his military service he had been made a Commander of Leopold, Officer of the Legion of Honour, and Companion to the Order of St Michael and St George (CMG). He joined the *Morning Post* newspaper writing on military matters, as well as joining a group of Conservative dissidents which included Churchill. He worked with the politician Leo Amery on *The Times History of the War in South Africa*, before publishing reports in *The Times* on the Russo-Japanese War under the banner 'By Our

Military Correspondent'. After war was declared, Repington used his influence and military friendships to gain access to the battlefields and the staff of the French, Belgian, and British establishments, reporting on events and bringing problems to the notice of the Government and the British public. He was also close to Kitchener, saying, 'I was on the best of terms with Lord K. at the opening of the war and told him that I would do my best to support him if he would trust me'.[20] He wrote about complex subjects in an interesting, clear and simple manner, often crossing political boundaries to protect Britain and especially the Army.[21] One politician described him as 'the twenty-third member of the Cabinet'.[22] An article in *The Spectator* referred to him as 'The most brilliant military writer of his day. His pen [was] devoted to the service of England and the army that he loved.'[23]

Repington first visited Sir John French's headquarters on the Western Front on 23 November 1914, on French's invitation.[24] This was a time when journalists held the power of political 'life or death' over politicians and servants of the state, with articles and newspaper campaigns being powerful tools. Henry Wickham of *The Times* wrote in 1908:

> We are *The Times*. We mould today and shape tomorrow, we are where the power lies.… We have got the ear of and influence those who have the ear of the masses.[25]

The Telegram

Following his meeting with Lieutenant-Colonel Stephens, Repington sent a report via telegram to George Geoffrey Dawson, the editor of *The Times*. In accordance with the required protocol, this was passed to General MacDonogh, Sir John French's Chief Intelligence Officer, who removed the specific detail regarding the Rifle Brigade casualties, the lack of heavy guns, howitzers, trench mortars, maxims, and rifle-grenades, before consulting on further censorship with Lieutenant-Colonel Brinsley FitzGerald. After reading the report, FitzGerald said that he 'felt sure that Sir John French would approve' of its contents, despite French not seeing the document.[26]

The telegram's journey continued, being sent to Colonel George Cockerill, Director of Special Intelligence, who in turn sent it to Major-General Sir Charles Edward Callwell, Director of Military Operations, with a request that it be passed. Callwell, loyal to Kitchener, saw no harm in the telegram, and knowing the situation in France, replied, 'All right, carry on'.[27] Thus the telegram was returned to *The Times* for publication.

Sir John French did not see the article before publication, but advised Repington later that he stood by FitzGerald's statement that he would have approved of the wording.[28] The first line of Repington's report read: 'The want of an unlimited supply of high explosive was a fatal bar to our success.' The American editor Isaac F. Macosson, writing in *Adventures in Interviewing*, qualifies these words:

> Never before perhaps in history of the world, certainly of war, have sixteen words in a newspaper produced such epoch-making results.[29]

The Article

The following article was published on the front page of *The Times* on 14 May 1915:

NEED FOR SHELLS

BRITISH ATTACKS CHECKED
LIMITED SUPPLY THE CAUSE
A LESSON FROM FRANCE

"The want of an unlimited supply of high explosive was a fatal bar to our success."

It is to this need that our Military Correspondent, in the message we print below, attributes largely the disappointing results of the British attacks in the districts of Fromelles and Richebourg on Sunday. By way of contrast, he records the fact that the French, in cooperation with whom we made our movement upon German lines, fired 276 rounds of high explosive per gun in one day and levelled the enemy's defences with the ground.

From Our Military Correspondent.

NORTHERN FRANCE, May 12.

It is important, for an understanding of the British share on the operations of this week, to realize that we are suffering from certain disadvantages which make striking successes difficult to achieve.

...To assail these ridges, with their command over lines, their superior facilities for observation, and their numerous lines of trenches, which have hardened week by week, and are provided with every scientific and clever device for arresting an attack, is no light task.

...There are not many points where an attack can be attempted, and at these points the enemy has accumulated defences, has brought into them hundreds of machine-guns, which are skilfully concealed, and has covered the front of every successive line of trenches by barbed wire entanglements. Supported by formidable artillery, and held by good troops, these German lines are not easily to be taken.

LACK OF HIGH EXPLOSIVE

...We found the enemy much more strongly posted than we expected. We had not sufficient high explosive to level his parapets to the ground after the French practice, and when our infantry gallantly stormed the trenches, as they did in both attacks, they found a garrison undismayed, many entanglements still intact, and maxims on all sides ready to pour in streams of bullets. We could not maintain ourselves in the trenches won, and our reserves were not thrown in because the conditions for success in an assault were not present.

The 'conspiracy of silence' over the shortage of shells had been broken.[30] The article was read by a public used to being told of British troops sweeping aside the shell-shocked and dazed enemy. It was seen as proof of a betrayal of the nation's soldiers by the Government, and an indictment on the honesty and competence of both the Prime Minister and the Secretary of State for War. Repington's only regret was that MacDonough, the army censor, chose to remove all reference to the casualties suffered by Repington's old battalion, as well as his remarks 'about the want of heavy guns, howitzers, trench mortars, maxims and rifle-grenades'.[31]

Other newspapers quickly took up the article, with the *Daily Mail* producing the following comments:

> Colonel Repington, *The Times* correspondent at the front, has had the audacity to clear up the mystery of our failure to advance. "We can smash the crust", he says, "If we have the means", and he explains that the means required consist of an unlimited supply of high-explosive shells.... It is lamentable that an action once begun should fail to attain its legitimate result because our gunners are obliged to count every shell instead of being able to blaze away, like the French, until they have achieved their purpose. Thus are our grievous casualty lists lengthened by official lack of foresight.
>
> If there has been slackness it is because the working men have been kept in the dark about the realities of this awful war.
>
> ...It is shown by the manly messages which the Glasgow and West of Scotland Armaments Committee sent in the afternoon to the Commander of the Fleet and the Army in the field:
>
> To Sir John French they give their promise—employers and workmen jointly—to work to "the last ounce" and we have no doubt they will be as good as their word...
>
> It is about time for some newspapers to tell the public the truth when one member of the Cabinet contradicts another on the vital question of whether or not the Army is hampered for lack of high explosive shells....[32]

Kitchener was now forced to explain the situation, giving a periodical review of the war to the House of Lords which was reproduced in the *Manchester Guardian* of 19 May 1915:

> It contained three announcements of the highest importance—first, that the Allies had decided to reply in kind to the German use of asphyxiating gases; next, that despite considerable past delays in the production of shells, our positions in this respect would in the very near future be satisfactory; and, finally, that the time had come for a call for more men—to the number, as the War Minister put it in his business like way, of 300,000.
>
> Offensive operations against the enemy's trenches demand, as we have known for some time, an enormous expenditure of ammunition, both of our usual type as well as of the high explosive pattern that we are now making. Your lordships and the country are aware of the energetic steps that have been taken to produce a sufficient amount of ammunition to supply the army in the field. There has been undoubtedly considerable delay in producing the material we at an early stage in the war foresaw would be required.

This delay is due mainly to the unprecedented and almost unlimited calls that have been made on the resources of the manufacturers of this country. Strenuous efforts have been made by all concerned to reduce as far as possible this delay in production, and I am glad to say that already a very considerable improvement in the output has been the result of the energy and good work of all concerned. High explosive shells for field guns have recently been brought into prominence by comments in the press. At an early stage in the war we took preliminary steps to manufacture these new projectiles, and though the introduction of any new departure in munitions of war naturally causes delay and difficulty to manufacturers, I am confident that in the very near future we shall be in a satisfactory position.

The Times article and the shell scandal were raised in the House of Commons. The Right Honourable Harold John Tennant, the Under-Secretary for War, struck out at those he considered were to blame for what was becoming a very public disclosure, stating that as Repington's telegram had not been censored in England, it was Sir John French who was to blame for the unauthorised release of information.[33] The original telegram, bearing the censor's stamp, as it had reached the offices of *The Times*, was collected to be presented to the House of Commons by Freddy Guest, but before this could take place, Tennant withdrew his statement.[34] However, the accusation against French remained, and the subject was again raised after the war when he was forced in 1919 to write to *The Times* reaffirming his innocence. His role in the affair remains somewhat obscured to this day.

Many members of the two houses felt that they had been 'kept in the dark' regarding the munitions problem. The discussion quickly became anguished, as Frederick Handel Booth, Liberal MP for Pontefract, articulated:

> We are all thinking of a certain position.... If you could look inside the hearts of most hon. Members of this house to-day, you would find that the one word impressed upon them was the word 'shells'.[35]

French received a letter from Mr B. B. Cubitt of the War Office (Repington believed it came from Kitchener himself) advising him that as a consequence of the new fleet dispositions, the Admiralty was no longer able to safeguard the shores of England from invasion by the enemy on a large scale, and in order to protect the home front, the War Office could not fulfil their promises of reinforcements for the army in France.[36] Repington conveyed these facts to Captain Stanley Wilson, a King's Messenger, and asked him to see what he could do in London. In support, Wilson sent a telegram to Bonar Law, and met him together with Mr J. A. Grant MP at the Carlton Club the same evening. Bonar Law and Grant told Wilson that they intended to meet with Asquith at the House of Commons that evening to request a committee to inquire into the exact position of munitions and reinforcements. First, however, they said they would need to meet with Repington so that he could explain the facts first hand as his telegram had been heavily censored. Lord Curzon, Sir Edward Carson, Sir F. E. Smith, and other Conservative leaders all attended a dinner at Bonar Law's house, where he relayed the whole story in great detail: '[I] neither minced my words nor concealed my feelings,' said he. [37]

Having read the article, Lloyd George immediately discussed the situation with Asquith, stating that matters could not continue in this manner. Concerned that Lloyd George was not fully aware of the facts, Repington produced a report for him exposing all the deficiencies in 'munitions and guns of all types, and giving a history of the shortage'.[38]

Admiral Fisher Resigns

While Repington's article was being read and discussed up and down the country, another calamity befell the Liberal Government.

At Churchill's request and over the King's initial objections, Baron John (Jacky) Arbuthnot Fisher had come out of retirement to take the position of First Sea Lord of the Admiralty in 1914 at the age of seventy-three. The King had thought him too old. His career in the admiralty had spanned sixty years, during which he was known for his innovation and support of the dreadnought class of battleships, working with Churchill to recreate the fleet.

The Gallipoli Campaign had originally been Churchill's great plan for changing Britain's fortunes in the war. Turkey, the centre of the Ottoman Empire, had entered the war at the end of October 1914 in support of Germany and the Austro-Hungarian Empire. The occupation of the Dardanelles, the only waterway between the Black Sea in the east and the Mediterranean Sea in the west, would give the Allies direct supply routes to their ally Russia. A victory against Turkey could also entice the neutral states of Greece, Bulgaria, and Romania to join the Allied side. It was further hoped that a powerful Allied fleet sailing towards the heart of the Ottoman Empire might provoke a *coup d'état*. Accordingly, Winston Churchill, as First Lord of the Admiralty, proposed a naval operation to seize the Dardanelles and Constantinople. Had an attack taken place when the idea was first proposed—in late 1914—it probably would have encountered little opposition and may well have changed the course of the war, but it was delayed until early March 1915.

Soon after his initial proposal, Churchill became disenchanted by the Gallipoli Campaign and started to promote a similar target in the North Sea. However, Fisher and Kitchener both promoted the Gallipoli option, and Fisher wrote to a friend that a combined land and sea assault on the strait and the Gallipoli Peninsula could work well, especially with a large commitment of troops.[39] Churchill suggested that the idea should be dropped, saying, 'Germany is the foe & it is bad war to seek cheaper victories & easier antagonists'.[40] But Fisher managed to convince Churchill of the opportunity and on 13 January 1915, Churchill explained to his cabinet colleagues how the new 15-inch guns of the battleship HMS *Queen Elizabeth* could take out the Turkish forts guarding the strait one by one, thereby establishing control. Lloyd George was the first to respond, saying he liked the plan, and Kitchener said that 'it was worth trying'.[41] Asquith also gave his approval. Almost immediately, Fisher began to reconsider the plan, worried that it might fail.[42]

As the fleet was steaming towards the Dardanelles, Admiral Sir Henry Jackson sent a memo to the War Council; the last paragraph read: 'The naval bombardment is not recommended as a sound military operation, unless a strong military force is ready to assist in the operation, or at least to follow it up immediately the forts are silenced'.[43] To satisfy this need, the 29th Division was sent to the Dardanelles instead of the Western Front. It was under the command of Sir Ian Hamilton, who had been ordered to Gallipoli by fast destroyer on 12 March with the following instructions: to cooperate with the Royal Navy; to effect a landing on the Gallipoli Peninsula; and thereafter, to occupy Constantinople.[44]

Fisher's concerns were validated when three of the Navy's older battleships were lost to mines. Meanwhile, the transfer of the division away from the Western Front resulted in Sir John French not being able to relieve the French 9 Corps, causing a delay for their Tenth Army offensive.[45] The naval attack of 18 March on the Dardanelles resulted in almost a third of the Franco-British fleet being put out of action. An infantry landing at Kilid Bahr Heights on the Gallipoli Peninsula was ordered as the only alternative for the successful attack on the objectives.[46] In April 1915, Australian and New Zealand troops joined the large French and British force to fight the Turks.

Fisher lost his nerve after HMS *Goliath* was torpedoed by the Turks on 13 May. Two days later he sent a letter of resignation to both Asquith and Churchill, before setting out to destroy Churchill by feeding incendiary comments to his enemies.[47] On 15 May at Downing Street, Lloyd George met Fisher, who confirmed his resignation. He told Lloyd George:

> Our ships are being sunk while we have a fleet in the Dardanelles which is bigger than the German Navy. Both our Navy and Army are being bled for the sake of the Dardanelles Expedition.

Asquith told Lord Stamfordham, Private Secretary to the King, that Fisher was 'somewhat unhinged otherwise his conduct is almost "traitorous"'.[48] Churchill put it more succinctly to Kitchener: 'Fisher went mad.'[49]

Both Asquith and Churchill tried to convince Fisher to withdraw his resignation, as he had done with the last seven resignations he had made in the previous six and a half months. However, Private Secretary Maston-Smith was accurate in saying, 'this time I think he means it,' and Churchill set about preparing his new Board of Admiralty, convincing Sir Arthur Wilson to replace Fisher, with all the junior members remaining in their positions.[50]

Asquith retreated to his Thames-side house for the weekend. In his biography of Churchill, Jenkins writes, 'Fisher's flounce and the perceived threat to his government was allowed to do no more than postpone his weekend by a few hours.' By late Sunday afternoon, Asquith had deliberated; Fisher had close friends in the Conservative camp, and Asquith now felt that 'the situation was sufficiently serious that the Conservative leader would have to be consulted' if a parliamentary crisis was to be avoided.[51]

Churchill offered his resignation before dining with Asquith and his family.

Asquith Contemplates a Coalition Government

The situation was deteriorating, and Asquith was facing attacks from the Conservative Party which would lead to a general election. He was still unwilling to entertain the option of a coalition. 'It was not so much the politics or policies,' writes Jenkins, 'as the political style and manners of the opposition which he disliked. It was his old Liberal Mandarin spirit.'[52] Asquith explained, 'To seem to welcome into the intimacy of the political household, strange, alien, hitherto hostile figures, was a most intolerable task.'[53]

Booth had raised the question of a coalition government in February 1915, but it had been rejected out of hand. He raised the question again during Prime Minister's Questions on 12 May:

> ...whether, in view of the present War and in view of the steps necessary to be taken in order to grapple with the rearrangement of industry and social life consequence upon a prolonged struggle, he [Asquith] will consider the desirability of admitting into the ranks of Ministers leading Members of the various political parties in this House?[54]

Asquith's answer was brief and pointed:

> The government was indebted for suggestions and help from the leaders of all parties. But coalition was not in contemplation.[55]

Asquith was unaware that the idea of a coalition would meet with 'general assent'.[56]

Lloyd George had a meeting with Bonar Law in which they came to an understanding that the only way forward was for complete co-operation between the parties, preserving a united front in the direction of the war.[57] According to Lord Beaverbrook's account, Lloyd George told Bonar Law, 'Of course, we must have a coalition, for the alternative is impossible.'[58] This was before meeting with Asquith to advise him plainly that the Cabinet should be reconstructed and some senior members of the Conservatives admitted. Never an enthusiast for coalition, Bonar Law was of the opinion that:

> ...with a Unionist Opposition we can stir them up—and stir them up with some effect, but given a Coalition Government we should get callous and careless.[59]

Austen Chamberlain provided the counter-argument:

> If our help is asked by the Govt. we must give it. God knows each one of us would willingly avoid greater responsibility; but the responsibility of refusing is even greater than accepting.... We cannot shirk this job because we don't like it or because we think the risks to ourselves too great.[60]

After a fifteen-minute discussion in which it was decided that the only way to fight the war was with a broad-based government on a united front and complete co-operation between the parties, an agreement was reached. Lloyd George recalled that 'the decision took an incredibly short time'.[61] Bonar Law attended a meeting recorded by Austen Chamberlain:

> Asquith now stated that he had arrived at the same conclusion [that the time had come for a

coalition] and that he had been intending to inform his colleagues at the end of the week. He produced a scheme for the distribution of offices, not complete in itself, but showing that he had been seriously thinking of the matter and had advanced some way in its consideration. He and Lloyd George both stated that it was absolutely necessary to get rid of Kitchener.[62]

Following the discussion, Asquith wrote a memorandum saying that a change in government was necessary to avoid an attack by the Conservative Party. He cited the double crisis as the reason for his party's vulnerability:

> Resignation of Lord Fisher, which I have done my best to avert, and the more than plausible parliamentary case in regard to the alleged deficiency of high-explosive shells.[63]

On 19 May, Asquith spoke for twenty minutes to over a hundred rebel Liberal MPs who looked at the prospect of a coalition with revulsion, explaining why the decision had to be made to reform the Government on non-party lines.[64] His audience was in a 'black and angry gloom', indignant that the Irish and Labour leaders had been approached before their own party. There was some whispering that Churchill was to blame, while others declaimed against Kitchener.[65]

The Coalition Government is Formed

The coalition, unthinkable a week before, came into being with an announcement made to the British public on 26 May 1915. With that announcement came the end of the great reforming Liberal administration of 1906. Repington wrote:

> Thus fell from office the old Glastonian Liberal Party which had never understood foreign politics, and had neither foreseen the war nor prepared for it.[66]

Margot Asquith, wife of the Prime Minister, wrote emotionally to Haldane:

> I confess I have had a sleepless night of misery over H's decision of yesterday. Our wonderful Cabinet gone!! Smashed![67]

With the Coalition formed, Asquith, still head of the Government, was now something of a Tory hostage.[68] However, the responsibility of administering the war, and the resource, resolution, and leadership needed to guide the country, was now shared with the Conservatives. The power of the Government had declined since the outbreak of the war, which cast a long shadow of gloom over its hopes and aspirations; it was blamed for the early setbacks which seemed to reduce the determination that the conflict demanded.[69] Bonar Law told a Conservative meeting '… that the Liberal Government had been losing its hold on the country and, one course they could have followed was to wait for the fruit of government to drop into their hands'.[70] But the route set out by the Coalition was to preserve national unity. The danger to liberal principles was also initially averted as, when Liberal rule came to an end, only men were sacrificed, while for a brief and indeterminate period, principles were spared.[71] But bitterness remained, as Churchill affirmed some years later:

> [Asquith] did not hesitate to break his Cabinet up, demand the resignation of all Ministers, end the political lives of half his colleagues, throw Haldane to the wolves, leave me to bear the burden of the Dardanelles, and sail on victoriously at the head of a Coalition Government.... These were the convulsive struggles of a man of action and of ambition at death-grips with events.[72]

National unity was the reason behind the formation of the Coalition, but this was an illusion; there were still deep divisions between the Liberals and Conservatives. The Coalition seemed to vindicate the Conservatives' pre-war conduct, their hostility towards Germany, their advocacy of a tariff policy against imports—especially those from Germany—and their demand for peacetime conscription and the increased manufacture of armaments. The Conservatives were the more 'patriotic' party, matching the public's mood of nationalism, while the Liberals were identified by their principles of internationalism and free trade, making them appear over-sympathetic to pacifists and aliens, and lacking in the nationalistic fervour necessary for a wartime government.[73]

Negotiations for ministerial positions had begun immediately after the fateful meeting with Bonar Law on 17 May. In her diary, Margot Asquith wrote:

> I could not help watching Andrew Bonar Law, and feeling how tragic it was for Henry [Asquith] to see this third-rate man, who had called him 'liar', 'cheat', 'fraud'—every name under heaven—sitting quietly there, wondering which of his followers he could impose upon Henry ... who was making up his mind which of our men he would have to sacrifice in his new Cabinet.[74]

She did not have to wait long; the cabinet appointments were made between the 25 and the 30 May, were clearly prejudicial to the Conservatives:

Prime Minister	Asquith	Liberal
Exchequer	McKenna	Liberal
Lord Privy Seal	Earl Curzon	Conservative
Home Secretary	Simon	Liberal
Foreign Secretary	Grey	Liberal
Colonies	Bonar Law	Conservative
War	Kitchener	
Financial Secretary to War	Forster	Conservative
First Lord of Admiralty	Balfour	Conservative
Board of Trade	Runciman	Liberal
Munitions	Lloyd George	Liberal

Asquith was determined to keep Bonar Law out of the Exchequer position; his appointment would have left the Conservatives holding the 'purse-strings', an unforgivable situation. However, giving the position to a Liberal without offering it to Bonar Law could have broken the Coalition before it had begun. Both Lloyd George and Asquith had made it plain that Kitchener had to go, and Lloyd George went so far to tell Lord Lansdowne and Austen Chamberlain that Kitchener had 'put lies into his mouth' regarding the supply of munitions.[75] Placing Lloyd George in the role of Secretary of State for War would be a good argument to keep the Conservatives out of the Treasury, sweetened further by offering them the Home Office, Leadership of the House of Lords, and the India and Colonial Offices.[76] But the removal of Kitchener was an impossibility— the man was a national hero to the general public—although it was recognised that his power could be reduced by relieving him of the responsibility for the supply of munitions. Convincing Lloyd George to leave the Exchequer was not easy, and when the new disposition of the Cabinet was formally announced, it came with an important footnote:

> The Prime Minister has decided that a new Department shall be created, to be called the Ministry of Munitions, charged with organizing the supply of munitions of war. Mr Lloyd George has undertaken the formation and temporary direction of this department, and during his tenure of office as Minister of Munitions, will vacate the Office of Chancellor of the Exchequer.[77]

With Asquith's political manoeuvring complete, it appeared, according to Lord Beaverbrook, that the Conservatives had got the 'runt-end' of the deal. From the moment at which Asquith and his principal Liberal colleagues set in motion their scheme to depreciate the status of their new partners, especially Bonar Law, the first coalition was doomed.[78]

The appointment of Lloyd George as the Minister of Munitions, opened a new phase in his career; Churchill referred to him as 'the powerful politician whose action had compelled the formation of the Coalition'.[79] He possessed the qualities that Asquith lacked: the ability to organise the industrial force of Britain behind the war. Only Haldane and Churchill were axed at the specific insistence of the Conservatives, and for Haldane, not even the lowest office was available.[80]

Churchill Resigns from the Admiralty

Churchill had left powerful enemies in the Conservative Party when he crossed the floor to the Liberals in 1904. The Conservatives demanded his exit from the Cabinet as part of their price for entering the Coalition; both he and Fisher were tainted by the failure of the Dardanelles Campaign. Haldane and Churchill resented Asquith's failure to stand by them and neither were to support him again.[81]

Clementine Churchill wrote to Asquith:

> Winston may in your eyes & in those with whom he has to work have faults, but he has the supreme quality which I venture to say very few of your present or future Cabinet possess, the power, the imagination, the deadliness to fight Germany.[82]

In advising Churchill of the formation of the new government, Asquith asked him if he would take office in the new government or prefer a command in France?[83] He was appointed to the minor role of the Chancellor of the Duchy of Lancaster, a position, despite being one of the lowest in the Cabinet, carried with it membership to the War Council, but Churchill regarded the position as insufficient and resigned on 11 November 1915. In his letter to Asquith he stated that he did not 'feel able in times like these to remain in well-paid inactivity'.[84] He left to command the 6 Battalion of the Royal Scots Fusiliers on the Western Front—the man born to be a soldier was going to war.[85]

Northcliffe's Attack on Kitchener

A week after Repington's article and while the ministerial negotiations were underway, Lord Northcliffe, owner of *The Times* and the *Daily Mail*, attacked Kitchener in his role as Secretary State for War, hoping to force him from his job. The shell scandal and military failure at Aubers Ridge had done immense damage to Kitchener's reputation; his political star was waning and he was becoming more difficult to deal with. Asquith and Lloyd George were looking for ways to replace him and Bonar Law was prepared to see him go as well.[86] On 21 May, the *Daily Mail* produced a more sensationalist version of Repington's article, attacking Kitchener personally with the banner headline: 'The Shell Scandal—Lord Kitchener's Tragic Blunder'.[87]

The article was described by Churchill as 'odious and calculated', and Haig called it 'reptilian'.[88] In his diary entry of 26 May, Haig wrote that a conspiracy was behind the article:

> Letter reached me tonight from Major Wigram. He states that there was an organised conspiracy in the Press controlled by Lord Northcliffe against Lord Kitchener; and that Sir J French's personal staff are mixed up in it. Brinsley Fitzgerald and Moore approached the editors of the daily press and asked them to write up Sir J and blackguard Kitchener!
>
> A most disgraceful state of affairs. Wigram thinks I have influence with Sir J and can keep him from quarrelling with Kitchener! I have always put in a word, when I get a chance, advising that we all … should pull together, and think about nothing but the beating the Enemy! I fear such advice from me had no effect. The truth is that Sir J is of a very jealous disposition.[89]

The British public could not believe that their hero 'could have sent the army into battle without shells' but the personal attack was ill-judged;[90] the nation's belief in their war idol was stronger than their belief in the *Daily Mail*, resulting in a ceremonial burning of the edition of the paper containing the headline outside the Stock Exchange.[91] Sales dropped by 200,000 copies, and the share value became seriously affected by a public boycott of the paper.[92] The campaign had precisely the opposite effect to that intended, and it was dropped after a few weeks. Kitchener became more entrenched in his position as Secretary of State for War, with King George V calling him to the Order of the Garter, Britain's oldest order of chivalry.[93] It could be deemed that without the Northcliffe attack, Asquith may have been able to remove Kitchener; however, the fallout from Northcliffe's attack made his position stronger, with the loss of his control over munitions being the only diminution.

Repington's Reputation

Kitchener was furious at Repington for his article in *The Times*, instructing Sir John French that he was no longer to be allowed to visit the BEF Headquarters. Haig told Fitzgerald that 'it was quite wrong to allow such a deceitful fellow to come to the front at all.'[94] His actions had created many enemies in London and he was attacked politically and in print by those accusing him of intriguing to bring down the Liberal Government. In his view it was '... not an intrigue to endeavour to save an army from defeat by a necessary public exposure when all official representations have hopelessly failed.'[95] In his article on Repington, W. Michael Ryan writes:

> ... Repington served as a valuable link between the Conservative opposition and Liberal dissidents in their struggle to unseat Asquith. A widely divergent cabal of political, military and journalistic leaders, all animated by months of discontent over the lack of decisiveness on the part of the Government, were briefly brought into harmony by the shells shortage.[96]

The shell scandal carried Repington to the apex of his fame and influence, and his impact on British politics can hardly be overestimated. Lloyd George was to benefit chiefly; although their personal relationship fluctuated, Repington believed that Lloyd George possessed the energy and enthusiasm to pull Britain through the munitions crisis and the war, saying to him: 'My main hope is you!'[97]

Further Intrigues

The Cabinet was still one-sided, with Liberals taking the more prominent, powerful roles. The Conservatives were not happy with the composition and political cracks began to appear almost immediately. The *Manchester Guardian* of 26 May featured an editorial on the subject:

> I think it right to mention here a very strong rumour that we may before long see another great change in the present Government, and that Mr. Asquith may retire from the Premiership and be succeeded by Mr Lloyd George.[98]

By June, Haldane wrote to his mother: 'The "Times" is now joining with the "British Weekly" in a movement to turn out the poor P.M. & substitute Ll. George.'[99]

The pressure mounted: in October 1915, Asquith suffered a nervous collapse while in Cabinet. His wife recorded in her diary her husband's mood:

> I feel very ill, and have come to the reluctant conclusion I must give up. I sat bolt upright. Henry ill—really miserable, tired, finished![100]

The Ministry of Munitions

Lloyd George Takes Control

The new Ministry of Munitions, created during the forming of Asquith's Coalition Government, temporarily propelled Lloyd George into a position from which he could place the British public on a true war-footing; British industrial power would at last be dedicated to the needs of the war. The *Manchester Guardian* showed its support for Lloyd George's mission:

> Just as every available man, woman and child in Germany is doing something to help on the fight, so the exertions of every capable human being in Britain must be organised to expedite the issue and make it more decisive.[1]

On 20 May, a further article in the newspaper confirmed support for Lloyd George as a politician of action:

> No Ministry now formed can hope to render its full service to the nation which does not give full and free scope to the contriving genius and the powerful initiative of Mr Lloyd George.... For the particular work which now above all needs to be done—the organisation of the whole industrial resources of the nation for the purposes of the war—there is no one in or out of office who can approach him in capacity.[2]

The home front would be impacted as war demands reached every street, town, and city across the country, uprooting tradition, and above all bringing change. Free-market ideology was replaced with State intervention; new state factories were set up to supply munitions, modern assembly-line methods were introduced, and semi-skilled labour was employed *en masse*, including large numbers of women.[3]

Repington had ensured that Lloyd George was fully acquainted with the problem in the supply of munitions and the urgent need for high-explosive shells. In his diary of June 1915, Francis Bertie, 1st Viscount Bertie of Thame, wrote:

Lloyd George, I understand, has been convinced that French is right and Kitchener wrong as regards the supply of shells. However, had it not been for the *Daily Mail* and *Times* revelations about the absence of high explosive shells, the cries of French and his officers would have been unheard and there would not have been a Ministry of Munitions to put matters on a better footing.[4]

However, the act of creating the ministry would not solve the crisis overnight, as Sir John French wrote in his book *1914*:

> The actual supply in May [1915] proved to be less than one half of the War Office estimate, which was the only one ever furnished for our guidance. Such failure made it quite impossible to make any reliable forecast of the condition of the ammunition supply at any particular date. This state of uncertainty rendered the formulation of plans for co-operating with the French most difficult, if not impossible.
>
> I begged that His Majesty's Government might be informed that, if their object was to drive the enemy off French and Belgian territory during 1915, no progress towards this objective could be obtained unless and until the supply of artillery ammunition should enable the Army to engage in sustained operations. The official reply which I received to this letter was an injunction to use the utmost economy....[5]

The companies that accepted orders for the supply of munitions and equipment had contracted for more than they could deliver, and this resulted in shortfalls amounting, by June 1915, to 12 per cent for rifles, 19 per cent for artillery pieces, 55 per cent for machine guns, and 92 per cent for high-explosive shells.[6] The ministry had to solve the delay in supply while increasing production. The *Manchester Guardian* wrote:

> If we are to save life and limb for scores upon scores of thousands of our men, not to speak of saving hundreds upon hundreds of millions sterling, we must work more strenuously than ever to multiply the guns and amass the ammunition.... We must have more guns and howitzers and more again. We must have more shells and still more shells and shells without end.[7]

The Beginnings of the Ministry

Lloyd George first entered his office in the Ministry of Munitions on 27 May:

> There was a table—I forget whether there were one or two chairs, but by the orders of the Board of Works, there was no carpet. I believe I had a greater struggle over getting a carpet that I had over getting £50 million for munitions. I said to my assistant: "Look at that table, look at those chairs." "Yes" he said: "What is the matter with them?" I said: "those are the Ministry of Munitions."[8]

Asquith's political manoeuvring had dug deeply into Kitchener's control as Secretary of State for War, but he seemed unconcerned with the loss; either he failed to appreciate just how much of his empire had slipped away, or he was just glad to accept Lloyd George's support in what had become such a 'hot potato'. He wrote to Lloyd George on the day of his appointment: 'Delighted to hear you are coming to help me.'[9]

Within five days of his appointment, Lloyd George was rousing the nation to face the reality of his radical reorganisation:

> We are fighting against the best organised community in the world. The best organised community whether for war or peace and we have been employing too much the haphazard go-as-please methods, which, believe me, would not have enabled us to maintain our place as a nation—even in peace—much longer. The nation now needs all the machinery that is capable of being used for turning out munitions or equipment, all the skill that is available for that purpose, all the industry, all the labour, and all the strengths, power and resources of everyone to the utmost.[10]

This was the start of the biggest social reform Britain had ever known.[11] Lloyd George began to exercise ever more control over capital, machinery, raw materials, and labour, forcing manufacturers to co-operate with the new ministry if they wanted contracts. The ministry soon eclipsed the control that Kitchener had wielded over the manufacture of munitions, with Lloyd George assuming more industrial power than any previous politician.[12]

The ministry was organised as if it was a private company, and the power that the civil servant mandarins had exercised was reduced and in many cases extinguished completely. Lloyd George wrote:

> ...from first to last a businessman's organisation. Its most distinctive feature was the appointments I made to chief executive posts of successful business men to whom I gave authority and personal support that enabled them to break through much of the aloofness and routine which characterised the normal administration of Government Departments.[13]

Within five months the ministry's staff rose from 137 to 2,350.[14] The country was divided into seven main areas, which were then sub-divided and placed under the responsibility of Boards of Management, whose duty was to place orders with suitable producers at prices and under conditions agreed with the Ministry of Munitions. The whole of the organisation was under the control of the Director of Area Organisation (DAO).[15]

East Anglia Munitions Committee

Industries not involved in war work were pressurised to start producing munitions or equipment, with representatives of the ministry arranging meetings to discuss ways in which their operations could be adapted. One of the first meetings took place at the Great Eastern Hotel in Liverpool Street, London, with representatives of nineteen manufacturers operating in East Anglia.[16] Two proposals were put to the group: they could either be amalgamated into a National Factory or work together as a co-operative producer. The latter was chosen, and the co-operative consisted of the following limited liability companies:

R. Boby & Co.	Torbinia Engineering Co.	E. H. Bentall & Co.
J. Chambers	Crompton & Co.	J. W. Brooke & Co.
Boulton & Paul	Crabtree & Co.	The Crittall Manufacturing Co.
R. Garrett & Son	Elliott & Garrood	National Steam Car Co.
R. Warner & Co.	R. Hunt & Co.	Ransomes, Sims & Jefferies
Lake & Elliot	Reavell & Co.	The Hoffman Manufacturing Co.
Richards & Co.	Davey, Paxman & Co.	The Marconi Wireless Telegraph Co.
Laurence Scott & Co.	Ransomes & Rapier	E. R. & F. Turner
A. Webber	Chas. Burrell & Sons	

The joint-managers of the co-operative, Messrs Crittal and Stokes, undertook a week's tour around the manufacturers in their area, as well as some due diligence. An example of an 18-pdr shell was acquired and cut in half, then examined and reverse-engineered.[17] The co-operative agreed to supply 200,000 18-pdr shells at a price of 22 shillings per shell for the first 20,000 and 20 shillings per shell thereafter, all to be delivered within six months. This original order was accomplished and accordingly further contracts totalling 2,133,000 18-pdr shells were agreed and fulfilled.[18]

Plans were agreed for the construction of a depot, sidings, and a railway line to bring in the raw materials and send out the completed shells. By August, the depot, employing a workforce of between 300 and 400, mostly made up of women, was completed and shell production was in full swing, making East Anglia the first co-operative to deliver shells.[19] Encouraged by the result of the 18-pdr contract, seven of the firms within the co-operative agreed to supply 4.5-inch shells, and ultimately produced in excess of 1,074,400 shells for the ministry.[20] Other contracts followed, including ones for 60-pdr, 6-inch high-explosive, and 13-pdr shells. The co-operative also produced fuzes, practice shot, percussion fuzes, and primers. For example, a contract was agreed in July 1915 for 250,000 No. 100 fuzes with the adaptor at a price of 15 shillings each, with the War Office supplying copper at £90 0s 0d a ton, zinc at £105 0s 0d per ton, and bar material at 1s 2d per lb.[21]

High-Explosive Shell Manufacture

The other problem highlighted by Repington and Sir John French had been the lack of high-explosive shells. These were needed to demolish enemy emplacements and cut barbed-wire entanglements, but their production was contingent upon the availably of chemicals, which at the start of the war had become difficult to acquire. This shortage was about to change thanks to Dr Chaim Azriel Weizmann, Zionist and biochemist, who demonstrated in 1915 how, using bacterial fermentation, his new anaerobic fermentation process (the acetone-butanol-ethanol fermentation process) could convert 100 tons of grain into 12 tons of acetone. When first approached, Churchill asked him whether he could supply 30,000 tons of acetone; he answered that he could if he was given the necessary resources.[22] These resources were quickly provided by commandeering brewing and distillery equipment, and by building factories to utilize the new process in Dorset and Norfolk. These produced more than 90,000 gallons of acetone a year, though this figure was reduced due to the unrestricted submarine warfare in 1917, which diminished the supply of North American maize.[23]

Controlling the Workforce

Another major problem faced by the manufacturers, and therefore the ministry, was the control of the workforce. Lloyd George said:

> [It is] obviously better to get your men under the direct supervision and control of those who for years have been undertaking this kind of work, obviously better than going to those without experience. The failure (of the Board of Trade to get men through Labour Exchanges) drove us to other courses....[24]

The other course was the National Registration Bill, introduced in June, requiring all men and women aged between fifteen and sixty-five to register their details, and more importantly their employment skills, with those already involved in essential war work to be added to a separate list.[25]

Parties of munition factory workers visited the front with representatives of trade unions, giving the workers the opportunity to see with their own eyes what their work meant to the soldiers fighting for the country, inspiring them to greater levels of production. Ben Tillett, the leader of the dock strikes of 1889 and 1911 and founder of the Docker's Union, later the Transport & General Workers' Union, together with Monsieur Bruhl, the French socialist, were among those who visited the front.[26] Both men were well known for their views on civil liberties and favouring restrictive practices for their members, as well as their hostility to militarism in every form. Haig was given the job of managing their visit and he disarmed them by giving orders that they were to be shown everything that they wished to see; further he provided opportunities for them to have time with men of all ranks, officers becoming scarce at the appropriate time to allow a free exchange of views.

Women took up the factory work of men going to the front, despite not yet having the right to vote. They would underpin much of the expansion in industry, undertaking twelve-hour back-breaking shifts. In an interview for the *Radio Times*, Kate Adie, presenter of BBC2 programme *Women of World War One*, said, 'The war could not have been won without the immense contribution of women.'[27] Women had worked in the munitions factories before the war, mainly because of their small hands, but by mid-1915, the industry employed 200,000, and just a year later that number would rise to 500,000.[28] The twelve-hour days for poor pay dragged on, but for those who had lost family members, husbands, and sweethearts, the work was a chance to hit back at the Germans. Talking about her grief at losing a loved one, Gladys Hayhoe recalled: 'It made me very bitter towards the Germans, and it made me work that bit harder.'[29]

The suffragettes sought the vote for women, and the Government's reluctance to agree to this demand caused politicians and civil servants severe problems in their dealings with women's organisations. However, Lloyd George, desperate to staff the factories, saw that women's rights and winning the war could be one moulded into one and the same cause. Discussing the situation with Emile (Emily) Pankhurst, the two reached an agreement which resulted in 'The Women's Right to Serve March' on 17 July, where banners, paid for by the Government, stating 'We Demand the Right to Serve' announced the future expansion in role of women in the war effort.[30]

The Western Front

Despite the new ministry and the reorganisation of industry and workforce controls, the munitions shortage was not resolved quickly; by November, the production of shells had increased twenty-fold, but that was yet to come.[31] Understanding this and appreciating the effect that it would have on Britain's allies, Lloyd George met his opposite number in the French Government, Albert Thomas, in June 1915. He warned Thomas that the British did not possess sufficient guns and shells to mount a successful major offensive; the French and British prime ministers agreed at Chantilly on 7 July that, for the time being, resources would be concentrated on the Dardanelles theatre, and the Western Front would be held as a defensive position. Joffre disagreed and promptly prepared to mount an attack, and persuaded Kitchener to support him.[32] When Kitchener told Churchill that he had agreed with the French to launch an offensive on the Western Front, Churchill recorded his response:

> I said at once that there was no chance of success. He said that the scale would restore everything, including of course the Dardanelles. He had an air of suppressed excitement like a man who has taken a great decision of terrible uncertainty, and is about to put it into execution.[33]

While the French were producing 100,000 shells a day, and Germany and Austria combined were producing 250,000 a day, British factories were only producing 22,000 shells a day.[34] By careful rationing of shell expenditure, added to the increasing level of manufacture, it was hoped that by delaying the offensive until September 1915, there would be a chance that sufficient guns and ammunition would be available for an attack on the scale proposed by Joffre.[35] However, fielding some 900 guns, of which only 117 were of heavy calibre, the British shell expenditure would still be greatly outmatched by the French with 420 guns in the north and 850 guns in the south of the battlefield. Despite the assurances he received, Lloyd George was far from confident that there were enough shells to equal shell expenditure during the Battle of Neuve Chapelle, where the barrage over a period of thirty-five minutes delivered five shells onto each yard of trench, with a total weight of 288 lb. It was estimated that during the forthcoming British offensive, there would only be sufficient munitions to deliver 7/10 of a shell, weighing 62 pounds, on each yard of trench during the first forty-eight hours.[36] In an effort to ensure that the offensive would only proceed when there was a sufficient supply of munitions, Haig made it clear that ammunition requirements were not to be underestimated merely to please GHQ, saying: 'If we had not enough ammunition now, we must wait until it accumulated.'[37] To mitigate the problem of the required ammunition not arriving in time, artillery plans were adapted so that wire-cutting guns were reduced. The hurricane bombardment, which gave the enemy the opportunity to repair any damage before the infantry attack went in, was not to be repeated.[38]

Further Casualties in Battle and Politics

The Battle of Loos

The initiative of Joffre's offensive, which aimed to eradicate the enemy salient that was projecting towards Paris, lay very much with the French. In a pincer movement the French were to attack Champagne in the south, while a joint-venture between the French and British would form the northern arm of the pincer and attack Artois, with Loos as the specific target for the British.[1]

Loos was in a coal mining district, and the enemy defences were built among pit-heads, slag-heaps, and workers' villages. Haig described the battlefield as:

> ...bare and open and so swept by rifle and machine-gun fire from the German trenches and the numerous fortified villages immediately behind them that a rapid advance would be impossible.[2]

Haig discussed his concerns with Sir John French on the afternoon of 28 May:

> ...the Germans are very well posted there in an exceptionally strong position. That the advantage of artillery positions and observation lies entirely with them. That Loos is a veritable "shell trap" and that the French, after taking the town about the 11th or 13th, were driven back to their original trenches by artillery fire alone.[3]

Sir John French advised Haig that the attack was to be made chiefly with artillery and that a large force of infantry was not going to be used. Joffre, however, disagreed with this plan and insisted to Kitchener that the attack be made with the maximum force available. Haig recorded what Kitchener said to him and French: 'He had decided that we must act with all our energy, and do our utmost to help the French, even though by doing so we suffer very heavy losses indeed.'[4]

Haig felt that in the circumstances a strong reserve must be readily available to support the attack and ensure that any breakthrough was properly followed through. On 18 September, Haig requested that as the reserve troops would advance slowly through the congested rear areas, the two divisions of the General Reserve should be moved up to Noeux les Mines and Verquin respectively. In view of the great length of line for which the British were responsible, French felt that this was too close and could be detrimental to the defence of a counter-attack. Unhappy with the decision, Haig approached Kitchener, but found him insensitive to his cause. Haig moved on to Foch, who agreed with him. With the addition of Joffre's support, Haig again approached French who advised him, said Haig, that 'he would release XI Corps to support me on the earliest possible moment'. [5]

Haig appreciated the problems associated with the terrain and the reserves of munitions and troops, but he decided that the availability of 150 tons of chloride gas counter-balanced these unpropitious elements.[6] Gas had first been released by the Germans during the Second Battle of Ypres; Sir John French called it a 'cynical and barbarous disregard of the well-known usages of civilised war',[7] while Sir Michael Redgrave, in his narration of the documentary *The Great War*, stated that its use heralded the '…day when the last vestige of glory and glamour went out of war'.[8] A prophetic young German officer put its use into context when he wrote in his diary:

> The effects of the successful gas attack were horrible. I do not like the idea of poisoning men. Of course the entire world will rage about it at first and then imitate us.[9]

As the date of the battle approached, Haig became more 'bullish'. Rawlinson produced detailed plans for the battle that were limited and cautious, which Haig overturned and replaced with much more ambitious ones.

The battle commenced on 25 September 1915, with the gas being released from the British trenches; in many instances it hung a few yards away, before returning back from where it came.[10] In other sectors the wind took the gas into the German trenches, resulting in them scrambling for their gas masks. German artillery began bombarding the British trenches, damaging some of the gas cylinders that had not been opened and causing further problems among the waiting troops. The assault troops started their advance at 0630 hours, after a delay designed to coincide with the period of time that enemy gas masks provided protection and to provide the British artillery time in which to blast holes in the defences and entanglements.

The 15th Highland Division on the right of the British line stormed forward, overrunning the first German line and pushing on to Hill 70, one of Haig's prime targets. Having breached the summit and begun to advance down the far side, they were hit by murderous fire from an intact second line. The 47th Territorial Division crossed the first line of enemy trenches and captured Loos itself, before coming to a halt against sustained enemy fire, with 15 per cent casualties.[11] Meanwhile other units were able to breach the second line of defences around Hulluch, but the effort had exhausted them.

There were now two 'hand-holds' deep inside the German lines, and this prompted a report to headquarters stating that the enemy 'appeared to be retiring'.[12] Based on this report, the reserve battalions were pushed forward, but to the undamaged and secure defences at Lone Tree rather than the forward positions. The delay allowed the Germans to regroup;

having received reinforcements, they launched various counter-attacks, prompting Haig to request that the General Reserve divisions be released to allow the advance to continue. In his desire to be nearer to the battle, Sir John French was at the Château du Philomel, near Lillers, approximately 20 miles from his Chief of Staff and Headquarters at St Omer. He met Haig at 1100 hours:

> [I] decided to send him [Haig] the 21st and 24th Divisions of the Eleventh Corps to support his attack. He told me he was holding the 3rd Cavalry Division (2 brigades) in readiness to follow up any gap made between Hulluch and Loos. It was then arranged that the 21st and 24th divisions were to move forward at once under orders from Haig, and that the Guards Division was to be detached from Eleventh Corps in GHQ Reserve.[13]

By midday the order was received and put into action by the General Staff. The General Reserve consisted of the 21st and 24th Divisions of General Haking's XI Corps, comprised of new army recruits fresh from England with generally no battle experience. They immediately began moving through congested and badly controlled rear areas, marching overnight to arrive at the assault trenches at daybreak on 26 September, exhausted and soaked through from a rain storm.[14] The 10,000 men of the General Reserve lost no time in forming an extended line and began to advance across open ground. With no element of surprise, inadequate artillery support, un-cut barbed-wire entanglements, and undamaged emplacements, they were massacred. The Germans saw an entire front covered with the enemy's infantry; they stood up, some even stood on the parapets, firing into the approaching wave of infantrymen as they advanced over open ground. German reports confirmed the slaughter:

> Never had machine-guns had such straightforward work to do … with barrels becoming hot and swimming in oil, they traversed to and fro along the enemy's ranks. One machine-gun alone fired 12,500 rounds that afternoon.[15]

Four out of every five men were killed or wounded,[16] and the Germans were surprised at the efficiency of their MG8 machine guns. They named the battle 'Field of Corpses of Loos'.[17]

The battle continued until 4 November, when at a cost of about 60,000 casualties, the gains of a double line of enemy trenches on a 6,500-yard front were consolidated, with captured prisoners amounting to 57 officers and 3,000 other ranks, and material including 25 field guns and 40 machine guns.[18] French considered that despite the heavy losses, the British Army had, thanks to the magnificent efforts on the part of the troops involved, splendidly carried out the role assigned to it.[19] The British military historian John Terraine described the Battle of Loos as '…the true beginning of the martyrdom of the British Army'.[20] By the time the battle had finished, the destruction of the old, highly trained and professional Expeditionary Force was complete. Throughout the war the British Army was handicapped by a desperate shortage of properly trained staff officers, and after Loos it was calculated that almost a third of the Staff College graduates had been killed.[21] The average survival time for a British Army junior officer during the Western Front's bloodiest phases was six weeks.[22] In 1912, 9 per cent of newly commissioned officers came from titled families and 32 per cent from landowning families; nearly all the rest came from upper middle-class families, while only about 2 per cent of the officer corps were promoted rankers.[23] As the war progressed, the working classes began appearing in the officers' mess in greater numbers.

Sir John French Comes Under Attack

Disagreements, Machiavellian in nature, now began to take place between the senior military figures. Lord Bertie wrote in his diary: 'I am so grieved for [French]! Asquith's observation to me that there was a movement against him at home was ominous of evil'.[24] Haig did not wait for the battle to finish before criticising French to Kitchener on 29 October:

> You will doubtless recall how earnestly I pressed you to ensure an adequate Reserve being close in rear of my attacking division, and under my orders.... No Reserve was placed under me. My attack, as has been reported, was a complete success. The enemy had no troops in his second line, which some of my plucky fellows reached and entered without opposition.... The two Reserve divisions were directed to join me as soon as the success of First Army was known at GHQ. They came in as quick as they could, poor fellows, but only crossed our old trench line with their heads at 6pm. We captured Loos 12 hours previously, and Reserves should have been at hand then.... The final result is that the enemy has had been allowed time in which to bring up troops and strengthen the second line, and probably to construct a third line.[25]

The relationship between Kitchener, French, and Haig began to break down. Haldane was sent out by the Cabinet on 9 October to interview witnesses on the spot to see what had gone wrong. Haig spoke with unrestrained candour:

> C-in-C nor his staff realised the necessity of reserves being close up before action began;
> The two divisions of the reserve were billeted a long way from where they would be wanted;
> When reserves were required to exploit Victory, they were hurried forward without full consideration to sustenance and were worn out by the time they arrived, and;
> The divisions forming the reserve had only recently arrived in France and were untried.[26]

Haig had been given the 3rd Cavalry Division (less one brigade) as a reserve and the 28th Infantry Division was at Bailleul for use as required, but he felt that if the General Reserve had been released to him before the battle commenced he would have broken through. However, in view of the importance that he attaches to this requirement, he appears not to have protested to any great degree, instead complaining to Robertson and Haking and taking refuge in the vague belief that 'the three divisions will, I hope, be close up in the places where I have arranged to put them, and will go forward as soon as any opportunity offers'.[27] Haig also does not take into account that there were other parts of the British line besides that occupied by the First Army which might have needed support, and that consequently it was incumbent upon French to retain control of an adequate reserve force to enable him to deal with situations as they arose in any part of the extensive front for which he was responsible.[28]

In Sir John French's words, Haldane had obtained the 'correct version' of the course of the battle from Colonel Maurice, Director of Military Operations Imperial General Staff. Meanwhile, Kitchener wrote to French regarding the rumours, and French noted the letter in his diary entry of 10 October:

> There is an idea abroad that the Reserves were kept some way in rear—that they were too late into the fight—that they were sent to the attack of a string position in a state of exhaustion, and without food or water. These rumours are confirmed by a 'private and secret' letter I received from Kitchener on the 8th inst. He wrote very kindly and (as he expressed it) 'with great reluctance'. It was evident that his 'colleagues' forced him for an explanation. It is all, of course, absolutely false and stupid, and full explanations have been given. The situation as it existed, has been fully explained to Haldane.[29]

Haldane reported back to London that no blame for failure could be attached to Sir John French and that the relationship between him and Haig had simply become overheated, but this did not quieten the controversy that raged in London.[30]

Haig had been asked to keep Kitchener appraised of any important matters that took place at the front. Haig said, 'He would treat my letters as secret, and would not reply, but I would see my proposals given effect to and must profess ignorance when that happened!' [31] In asking the subordinate Haig to report in this way, Kitchener deliberately breached the authority of Haig's commanding officer, Sir John French. The controversy grew further when the same request was asked of Haig by Asquith, which now circumvented the authority of not only Sir John French, but also the Secretary of State for War, Lord Kitchener. It would not end there.

Sir John French issued his ninth despatch on the conduct of the war published in *The London Gazette* on 1 November. Repington reported on the despatch the next day in *The Times*, with the banner headline: 'The Battle of Loos—A Question of Reserves'. Repington wrote:

> …The dispatch does not enable us to ascertain why the first line of the attack remained unsupported throughout the day of September 25. Sir Douglas Haig had the 3rd Cavalry Division, less one brigade, under his hand. The 21st and 24th Divisions of the New Armies, posted at Beuvey and Noeux les Mines, were placed under his orders at 9.30am on September 25, and were at once ordered up by him in support, but do not figure at all in the report of the operations of this day.

The complete history of this battle, which appears to have cost us nearly 50,000 casualties, remains, it will be seen, to be written. It cannot be entirely understood until we have before us the orders....

The article, as well as the original despatch, seemed to lay some of the blame at Haig's door, putting further pressure on his relationship with French.[32] Haig complained vigorously in his diary:

It is full of misstatements of fact. My staff are comparing the Despatch with the orders and telegrams received from GHQ and will make a note on the subject. It is too disgraceful of a C-in-C to try and throw dust in the eyes of the British people by distorting the facts.[33]

French's relationship with Kitchener had been difficult since the early stages of the war when, in French's view, Kitchener had withheld troops and interfered with his operations, undermining his authority. French recorded how their relationship deteriorated further in early 1915:

[Kitchener said] that he considered Joffre and I [to be] "on trial"—that if we showed within the next month or 5 weeks that we really could make "substantial advances" and "break the German line" he would—so far as he was concerned—always back us up with all the troops he could send. But if we failed it would be essential that the government should look for some other theatre of operations.[34]

The relationship broke down beyond practical issues. Haig stated that French 'had an unreasoning and bitter hatred of the Secretary of State. Kitchener's sentiments towards the Commander-in-Chief was simply of contempt.'[35]

In July King George V had conferred on Haig the GCB (Knight Grand Cross of the Most Honourable Military Order of Bath). Haig recalled that afterwards the King

... referred to the friction between Sir John and Lord K and hoped that I would do all I could to make matters run smoothly.... He (the King) criticises French's dealings with the press, *The Times*, Repington and Lord Northcliffe, etc. All most unsoldier-like and he (the King) had lost confidence in Field Marshal French. And he had told Kitchener that he (K) could depend on his (the King's) support in whatever action he took in dealing with French.[36]

In the beginning of October, Robertson was contacted by Arthur Bigge (Lord Stamfordham), Private Secretary to the King, and asked on orders of the King if he did not think that it was time for French to go.[37] Robertson asked Haig for his view:

Now at last, in view of what had happened in the recent battle over the Reserves, and in view of what happened in the general military situation, I had come to the conclusion that it was not fair to the Empire to retain French in command on this main battle front.[38]

Robertson thanked Haig, saying that: 'He knew now how to act and would report to Stamfordham.'[39] A week later the King met with Haig and again asked him about French:

> I told him that I thought the time to have removed French was after the Retreat (1914), because he had so mismanaged matters, and shown in the handling of the small Expeditionary Force in the Field a great ignorance of the essential principles of war.... Since then ... I have therefore done my utmost to stop criticisms and make matters run smoothly.... French ought to be removed. I, personally, was ready to serve under anyone who was chosen for his military skill to be C-in-C.[40]

Generals Gough and Haking supported Haig's assessment. Following the publication of the edited version of Haig's diary in 1952, he was much criticised for his apparent disloyalty to French and for intriguing against him. Walter Reid writes:

> Haig's behaviour at this time has to be looked at in the context of his enthusiasm for confidential letters to his superiors throughout his military career.[41]

French was, by this time, feeling isolated and began to fear that his command of the BEF was about to be taken away.[42] He was not wrong. Asquith felt that French had tried to portray Loos as a victory; this had fooled the newspapers, but not the Cabinet. Asquith had never forgiven French for exposing the shell scandal to the public; using the pretext of the Battle of Loos, he now decided to replace him as Commander-in-Chief of the British Expeditionary Force.[43] Writing to French, Asquith said that his age and the great strain that he was under made it advisable that he should come home, but that as Prime Minister he would not insist or recall him.[44] Lord Esher was despatched to council French, telling him the King had agreed to make him a Viscount and that he would be appointed Field Marshal, Commander-in-Chief, Home Forces. Sir John took the news badly. Esher wrote to Asquith, 'I know you will make things as easy for him as possible, He is a poor man, and he has served his country well.'[45] Joffre lamented: 'If they do things like that, how can we hope to win the war?'[46]

On 10 December, Haig received a letter from Asquith marked 'Secret', and sealed in two envelopes. It read:

> Sir J French has placed in my hands his resignation of the Office of Commander in Chief of the Forces in France. Subject to the King's approval, I have the pleasure of proposing to you that you should be his successor. I am satisfied that this is the best choice that could be made in the interests of the Army and the Country.[47]

On 15 December, the following announcement was made by the War Office:

> General Sir Douglas has been appointed to succeed Field-Marshal Sir John French in command of the Army in France and Flanders.

Since the commencement of the War, during over sixteen months of severe and incessant strain, Field-Marshal Sir John French has most ably commanded our Armies in France and Flanders, and he has now at his own instance relinquished that command.

His Majesty's Government with full appreciation of and gratitude for the conspicuous services which Sir John French has rendered to the country at the front, have, with the King's approval, requested him to accept the appointment of Field-Marshal Commanding-in-Chief the troops stationed in the United Kingdom, and Sir John French has accepted that appointment.

His Majesty, the King has been pleased to confer upon Sir John French the dignity of a Viscount of the United Kingdom.[48]

Haig took command of the BEF on 19 December at noon. Now, stripped of French's support, the trickle of Territorial units, or 'Saturday Afternoon Soldiers' as Kitchener called them, coming to France virtually ceased.[49] Haig was charged by his political masters to achieve success whatever the cost.

The End of 1915

The year ended with the Western Front positions much as they were in January, but with a loss of almost half a million dead and wounded due to a catalogue of failures. The old professional army was no more and the new armies were struggling to take their place. Gas and flame throwers had been used for the first time, but the promised breakthrough by either side did not materialise. Many considered 1915 to be a learning curve; the main lesson learnt, however, was that the war was not going to be over anytime soon.

Kitchener's role as Secretary of State for War was diluted further by the appointment of Robertson as Chief of the Imperial Staff. His role encompassed 'issuing the orders of the Cabinet in regard to military operations',[50] circumventing Kitchener and leaving him with only a precarious hold over his position. In Lord Derby's opinion, the view of the General Staff had never been truly presented to the Cabinet or the War Office, and was constantly adulterated. As a soldier, Kitchener should have been appointed as Commander-in-Chief and not given a position within the Cabinet; both Derby and Repington considered that the Secretary of State for War should not have been a military man, supporting George Clemenceau's statement, 'War is too serious a matter to leave to soldiers!' [51,52]

For his part, Kitchener had never been happy in the political theatre. He felt separated from the other members of the Cabinet, a professional soldier standing apart from civilians. 'It is repugnant to me to have to reveal military secrets to 23 gentlemen with whom I am barely acquainted,' he said.[53] Moreover, if he were to impart secrets to the Cabinet, 'they would all tell their wives—except Lloyd George, who would tell other people's wives.'[54]

Meanwhile Lloyd George's career was ascending along with his Ministry of Munitions as state-managed capitalism, geared to the needs of war, ran rampant through the manufacturing industries. Lloyd George brought in managers who in the private sector had commanded huge salaries; men like James Stephenson, joint managing director of Walker's Whisky, exchanged a salary of £14,000 per annum to work at the Ministry of Munitions for nothing.[55] The management of Woolwich had been replaced with those previously employed at the North Eastern Railway, and Arthur Lee of the ministry extolled how easily the work progressed with the ex-businessmen in charge.[56] Churchill described Lloyd George's achievements:

> Production of every kind was already on a gigantic scale. The whole island was an arsenal. The keenest spirits in British industry were gathered as state servants in the range of palatial hotels which housed the Ministry of Munitions. The former trickles and streamlets of war now flowed in rivers rising continuously.[57]

Lloyd George's success made him all the more outspoken, especially when in December he caused a parliamentary sensation by commenting on the war in a manner of a back-bencher rather than a member of the Cabinet:

> [I have] summed up my considered opinion at the time on the muddled campaign of 1915. That is my judgement of history. Too late in moving here. Too late in arriving there. Too late in coming to this decision. Too late in starting with enterprises. Too late in preparing. In this War the footsteps of the Allied forces have been dogged by the mocking spectre of 'too late'; and unless we quicken our movements damnation will fall on the sacred cause for which so much gallant blood has flowed.[58]

The *Liberal Magazine* took up the argument, but managed to end their article on a positive note:

> We have made mistakes which would seem to be inseparable from the conduct of the war, we have not achieved in 1915 what we had too confidently reckoned on achieving before the year was out; but 1916 finds us undismayed.[59]

Conscription

The overriding problem faced by the Army was that of manpower; the war's requirement for men seemed to be insatiable. The professional armies of the BEF had been effectively consumed in battles to date, and the Territorial regiments were reduced as their casualty lists began to match those of the regulars. Meanwhile, the number of volunteers feeding the new armies was in decline. Why should some men fight at the front while others stayed at home? Some form of coercion was needed to recruit the 1½ million that Kitchener let it be known was needed.[60] Kitchener was wedded to voluntary recruitment, which matched the liberal ethos and had worked so well since the beginning of the war. Lord Derby, who had been appointed as Director General of Recruiting, began to formulate a new scheme to process registration of all men aged between eighteen and forty for call-up if required. After much argument, Kitchener had stated that he needed 30,000 recruits a week, although Derby felt that this figure should be revised to between 35,000 and 40,000.[61] The scheme was successful in producing well over 2 million actual and potential recruits, but many of these did not join up for many months.[62] However, this would do little more that bring the existing divisions back to full strength; the numbers were estimated to maintain that position until the autumn.[63] Accordingly, after operating for two months, the scheme closed in December 1915; although it had been successful, it was felt that it could not maintain sufficient recruits. The next step was conscription, another political casualty equating, in the eyes of many liberals, to '…the moral defeat of the British system and the victory of German methods'.[64]

Haldane had declared previously to the House of Lords that compulsory military service was not foreign to Britain: 'At a time of national necessity every other consideration must yield to national interest, and we should bar nothing in the way of principle if it should become necessary'.[65] The necessity had now arrived and the upshot was the Military Service Act, passed in January 1916, specifying that men between the ages of eighteen and forty-one years were liable to be called up for military service unless they were married, widowed with children, or working in a reserved occupation.[66] The Act came into effect on 2 March and was modified to remove the exclusion of married men in May 1916. Just as important was Lloyd George's success in exempting those involved in vital war-related work; the gap between the home front and the fighting front had further narrowed with the country was now firmly dedicated to total war.

By the end of the war, the BEF had expanded to a size which totally eclipsed the Army under Sir John French's command in 1914. This was the largest army that Britain had ever put into the field, and Haig was responsible for the command, training, feeding, and management of this vast operation. The 30-mile front of December 1915 had also expanded to 123 miles.

Kitchener

Further upheavals would take place during 1916 that would completely change the political landscape in which the country had gone to war. The first of these changes became apparent when the Secretary of the Admiralty received a telegram from the Commander-in-Chief of the Grand Fleet. *The Times* reproduced it:

> I have to report with deep regret that his majesty's ship *Hampshire* (Captain Herbert J. Savill RN), with Lord Kitchener and his staff on board, was sunk last night about 8 pm to the west of the Orkneys, either by a mine or torpedo.
>
> Four boats were seen by observers on shore to leave the ship. The wind was N.N.W. and heavy seas were running.
>
> Patrol vessels and destroyers at once proceeded to the spot, and a party was sent along the coast to search; but only some bodies and a capsized boat have been found up to the present.

As the whole shore has been searched from the seaward, I greatly fear that there is little hope of there being any survivors. No report has yet been received from the search party on shore. [67]

Kitchener had been *en route* to Russia when on the night of 5 June, in the icy waters off the Orkney Islands, HMS *Hampshire* hit a mine. Field Marshal Lord Horatio Kitchener and many of his staff died in the incident. The Berlin newspaper *Berlingske Tidende* spoke of Kitchener as being the '...veritable symbol of Great Britain's world power ... the stoutest heart, the most untiring energy, and the manliest will in England.'[68] This sentiment was unfortunately reversed on 10 June, when the views of the Imperial Chancellor Theobald von Bethmann-Hollweg were reported in the *Kreuz Zeitung*:

...we may, without hesitation express the feeling which the news of the death of Kitchener has caused in us. This is one of pleasure, as fierce as it is justified, that a man has met his death, and again through our navy, who was one of the most dangerous and most inexorable stirrers-up of the world war.

The King and Queen attended a memorial service at St Paul's Cathedral in Kitchener's memory on Tuesday 13 June 1916. Repington wrote:

A great figure gone! The services which he rendered in the early days of the war cannot be forgotten. They transcend those of all the lesser men who were his colleagues, some few of whom envied his popularity. His old manner of working alone did not consort with the needs of this huge syndicalism, modern war. The thing was too big. He made many mistakes. He was not a good Cabinet man. His methods did not suit a democracy. But there he was, towering above the others in character as in inches, by far the most popular man in the country to the end, and a firm rock which stood out amidst the raging tempest.[69]

As in the months directly before the war, Asquith temporarily took over the position of Secretary of State for War until a suitable candidate could be decided on. Eyes looked towards Bonar Law, but it was the success of Lloyd George in forming and managing the Ministry of Munitions that ensured that he took the over the position in July 1916, with his ministry being passed to the Liberal MP, the Honourable Edwin Samuel Montagu. In Lloyd George's first meeting with Haig, it became obvious that the relationship between the new Secretary of State for War and the Commander-in-Chief of the BEF would not be easy.

Asquith

The next upheaval reached its climax at the end of 1916, although it had been brewing since Asquith had completed his balancing act of May 1915. The Conservatives had been unhappy with the composition of the Coalition, which favoured the Liberals and kept Asquith at its head. Lord Curzon explained this unease in a direct fashion:

We know that with [Asquith] as Chairman, either of the Cabinet or War Committee, it is absolutely impossible to win the war.[70]

The new Government lacked strong support from either the country or the House of Commons, with many Liberals seeing their principles sacrificed not so much for military expediency and to win the war, but to ward off the political pressure threatening the Government and Asquith specifically. Conscription was the big battle, but once this had been put into law, the political arena seemed to quieten; no other issue had focused the aspirations of all the parties as this subject had. But with the Military Service Act the damage had been done—the prestige of the Government had been hit hard and the morale of those who believed in its liberal concepts was shattered. In *The Downfall of the Liberal Party*, Trevor Wilson writes:

> While the war was dissolving the allegiance of Liberal on both the left and right of the party, it was reducing the remainder to near-helplessness. Faithful to Liberalism, they yet could see no way to stave off the disaster threatening it, and often seemed to lack even the will-power to act on its behalf. Their impotence was in sharp contrast to the growing assertiveness not only of the leaders but even more the rank and file of the Conservative and Labour parties.[71]

There were many in the Liberal Party who felt that Lloyd George was actively seeking an alliance with the Conservatives, not for the good of the party or the Government but for his own personal advancement. It was suspected that he was intent on creating a coalition that had a Conservative majority, which in the eyes of many Liberals, would be used to attain objectives deeply contrary to their ethos. These included 'permanent curtailments on liberty, coercive measures against labour, the final alienation of Ireland, imperialistic war aims, and a punitive peace settlement.'[72] The *Manchester Guardian*, which supported Lloyd George, claimed that the war must take precedence over party or personal loyalties, and that the ill-equipped Asquith should be replaced by Lloyd George, who felt that a Tory administration had a better chance of winning the war. [73]

With the lead as Secretary of State for War, Lloyd George, with the support of the Conservatives, continued to demand changes, insisting that 'Total War' was the only way in which Britain could possibly win. The War Council, having met only twice under Kitchener, now met between two or three times a month, and when necessary, up to eleven times.[74] But there were still delays in reaching agreements on war-related matters. Lloyd George suggested that a small three-man committee, chaired by him, be formed to which decisions related to Britain's war effort could be delegated. The committee was to include the Irish Unionist Sir Edward Carson, and more to the point, exclude certain Liberals—colleagues of Asquith's, who were thought not to add a decisive element. Asquith would not be a regular member of the committee, but he agreed initially to its formation on the proviso that he could chair the committee if and when he felt it right to do so.

Repington wrote about the new committee in *The Times* on 4 December 1916, implying that the formation of the committee represented a personal political defeat for Asquith:

…we are at last within measurable distance of the small War Council, or super-Cabinet for war purposes, which has been steadily pressed in these columns for the last year and a half.

Of this Council Mr Asquith himself is not to be a member—the assumption being that the PRIME MINISTER has sufficient cares of a more general character without devoting himself wholly, as the new Council must be devoted if it is to be effective, to the daily task of organizing victory.

We imagine that all of them [politicians and soldiers] would privately express the view that great chances have been missed through weakness and vacillation in the supreme direction of the war…. But the conception of Mr LLOYD GEORGE as a Military Dictator is a little too grotesque even for the most imaginative mischief-maker. His whole past belies it. His real defect in our opinion, even in the last few months at the War Office has been too little, not too great, a power of sympathy with the military mind.

This is by no means the first time in the last two years that Mr LLOYD GEORGE has been on the verge of a rupture with his colleagues…. It was only a question of time before he found it impossible to work with the old digressive colleagues under the old wieldy system.[75]

Asquith withdrew his consent of the new committee and as a result Lloyd George, Bonar Law, and all the other Conservative ministers resigned. The Coalition had collapsed. Margot Asquith wrote:

Morally disgusted and shocked—the Government smashed to atoms in the greatest war and at the most dangerous moment … man after man on our side tumbled on top of each other into Lloyd George's simple trap of getting rid of Henry…. When a government falls in one week, you may be quite sure its overthrow has been planned long, long before.[76]

The fight was too one-sided for Asquith to form another government. With Lloyd George's success at the Ministry of Munitions and in promoting the culture of 'Total War', he was always going to be the people's favourite. Asquith therefore formally resigned, with Lloyd George accepting the King's request to form a government, with the co-operation of the Conservatives after a token gesture had been made to Bonar Law.[77] Asquith took to the opposition benches as the Liberal Party split—seeming to repeat Joseph Chamberlain's desertion of 1886. A new coalition was formed, headed by the man that had always had a tenuous association with the Liberal Party.[78] The new coalition, led by a Liberal, was formed of mostly Conservative members, and many Liberals saw this new Government as a further betrayal of liberal ideals; there was despair at whether liberalism and the Liberal Party would ever rise again.[79] The new Cabinet was as follows:

Position	Name	Parliamentary Party
Prime Minister	Lloyd George	Liberal
Lord Chancellor	Lord Finlay	Conservative
Chancellor of the Exchequer	Bonar Law	Conservative

Secretary of State for Home Affairs	Sir G. Cave	Conservative
First Lord of the Admiralty	Sir E. Carson	Conservative
Minister for Munitions	C. Addison	Liberal
Secretary of State for War	Earl of Derby	Conservative [80]

The cross-party War Cabinet was created, consisting of five members, although only the Conservative Lord Milner had experience in the civil direction of war:

Lloyd George (Liberal)
Lord Curzon (Conservative)
Bonar Law (Conservative)
Henderson (Labour)
Lord Milner (Conservative)

The British public, especially those women who had taken on the industrial strain, were rewarded when the Representation of the People Act 1918 was passed by the House of Lords, granting all males over the age of twenty-one years the vote in the constituency where they resided, and all women over the age of thirty years, if they were either married to a member on the Local Government Register or a member themselves, a property owner, or a graduate voting in a University constituency. The eligible age difference had been added to prevent women from becoming, overnight, an electoral majority in their own right.

The End of the War

As the war continued, the casualties mounted further and the thirst for shells and bullets seemed to be unquenchable, and yet still no breakthrough was made. Following Germany's resumption of submarine warfare and their approach to the Mexican Government to form a military alliance, the isolationist United States of America entered the war in April 1917, initially contributing maritime, financial, and diplomatic services, with soldiers supporting the French from May 1918.

Germany gambled everything on starving Britain into submission, which became impossible after America's entrance into the war. The Hindenburg Programme had forced the German economy into a downward spiral caused by rising prices, falling output, and monetary depreciation, but it had provided a huge stockpile of munitions, with neither shells or artillery weapons in short supply.[1] In Britain, the Ministry of Munitions had got to grips with the shell shortage; under Lloyd George's management it had expanded exponentially with deliveries between July and December 1915 amounting to 5,380,000 shells, rising to a staggering 35,407,000 between July and December 1916.[2] By the end of 1916 it took eleven days to produce the number of medium shells that in 1915 had been regarded as a reasonable annual output.[3]

In 1916, in a patriotic gesture, Crittall Manufacturing Company offered to produce 18-pdr shells at 12s 6d per shell, based on a cheaper material base and a greatly reduced profit margin. It led to a general reduction in the price for these shells across the country. The offer was accepted.[4]

The incredible increase in supply brought its own problems: in many cases quality suffered, with almost 60 per cent of shells not exploding during the Battle of Loos.[5] The problems also came from poor care taken in packing and transport. Storing shells on top of one another could damage them, while others had their drive bands damaged by being dropped into boxes carelessly. Inspections were increased, but the ministry took pains to ensure that the workers understood that the 'object of inspection is not to see how much work can be rejected, but to raise the standard of work ... and that they should take pride in their work.'[6] However, the message to management was more strict: occasional lapses may be tolerated, but continuous bad work will be returned wholesale. The problem continued and the ministry was forced on several occasions to take legal action.

Preparations for Peacetime

By early 1918 thoughts in Britain were turning to the possibility of a successful conclusion of the war, focusing the ministry's attention to the transformation of the country's wartime industries to peacetime capability. The ministry staff had increased from the initial 640 in July 1915, to 5,148 in July 1916, 11,219 in July 1917, and 18,342 in July 1918.[7] It was now evident that a peacetime establishment of even ten times that of pre-war levels would not require the number of staff employed by the ministry. The most extravagant estimates called for a reduction of between 1/10th or even 1/5th within eighteen months of the war ending. Based on Government returns for October 1917, it was estimated that some 3,106,000 people were employed in the chemical and metal trades, 90 per cent of whom were employed on Government work. Of these, 691,000 males and 524,000 females were employed in the manufacture of military equipment such as guns, shells, aeroplanes etc., while 1,537,000 men and 354,000 women were employed in manufacturing goods that could be used or adapted for use in peacetime.[8] However, most of these were still employed in fulfilling Government contracts. In order to protect their members, the trade unions had insisted that all 'dilutees' leave their occupations after the conclusion of hostilities. Dilutees were assumed to be all the males who have been drawn into various industries since July 1917, either to replace men conscripted or as a net addition to those previously employed. Female dilutees were those that had undertaken a job that was normally carried out by a man. It was therefore estimated that 1,025,000 men and 571,000 women would have to change their occupation at the end of the war.[9] These figures did not take into account those soldiers returning from the war who had previously worked in these industries and would no longer have a job to go to.

It was therefore decided that upon the cessation of hostilities, those workpeople not required should be given notice terminating their employment, with, where possible, one week's pay *in lieu* of notice, in the following order:

(1.) Those not dependent on their earnings;
(2.) Those living away from home, in which case travel costs would be given in addition;
(3.) Local people without dependents;
(4.) The remainder in such order that those most likely to obtain alternative work be discharged first.[10]

However, many would bear the scars of industrialisation, especially those involved in explosive manufacture. They became known as 'Canary-girls' on account of Lyddite poisoning which turned their skin and hair yellow. Many died or had long-lasting medical problems.[11] The Ministry of Labour recommended that a temporary universal scheme of insurance against unemployment should be instituted, providing a weekly benefit of 15 shillings for men and 12s 6d for women, together with a contribution of 6d for men and 5d for women.[12]

The Government also faced the demobilisation of the factories directly managed by the ministry and the breaking of the contracts with private firms and the co-operatives such as the East Anglia Munitions Committee. The first decision that needed to be made related to what the ministry should do in the event of an armistice. Should the manufacture of war material and munitions continue or should it be suspended in the hope that the Armistice would lead to an end of the war? The main problems were firstly that munitions manufacturing was a continuous process, which once stopped could only be started again after a considerable period of time. Secondly, any clause in the Armistice agreement which limited movement would be detrimental to Britain due to the carriage of stocks across the Channel, whereas the Germans could pile stocks at railway bases for immediate transfer to the front in the event of a breakdown in negotiations.

Once this was decided, the factories acquired under the terms of DORA could be sold and the break-clauses of the contracts to supply munitions and war equipment could be activated, limiting the cost to the Government and providing the private factories with reimbursement for munitions and equipment manufactured but not delivered. The contracting firms would be given 'first-refusal' in the purchase of machinery, but the ministry would only accept reasonable offers and not those based on scrap-value. This only applied to machinery that could be used for peacetime purposes; those that could only be used for the manufacture of things like shells etc. would have to be treated on a different basis. The Royal Ordnance Factories would return to their previous role in the supply of munitions to the peacetime military establishment.

The Armistice

The October Revolution in Russia resulted in the peace treaty of 3 March 1918 signed between the Bolshevik Government of Russia and Germany and her allies. This released twenty divisions of battle-hardened troops from the Eastern Front to be used in the west.[13] At last the Central Powers were able to fight a war on a single front, with the added opportunity of transferring the bulk of their Eastern Front troops to the west before the troops of the United States could arrive to bolster the Allied lines.[14]

Those troops previously fighting in the east would be used in the German Spring Offensives, the first of which, and most well-known, was code-named 'Michael'. On 21 March, 6,608 guns—more than a third of which were 5.9-inch heavies—laid down a barrage on the 50-mile British front between Arras and the River Oise.[15] Suddenly what had seemed impossible for the last four years became a reality: the Germans smashed through the static trench lines manned by the thinly spread British Fifth Army located north and south of St Quentin, aiming for Amiens. They advanced 40 miles in a day on a front used to losses and gains measured in yards. Haig commented that 'British backs were against the wall of the Channel'.[16] But weariness soon started to affect the assault troops, and the advance only continued as long as limited fresh troops were available. By 29 March, the momentum had ceased, and the British were able to establish a defensive line. Operation Michael was brought to an end on 5 April.

Ludendorff had intended 'Michael' to win him the war, but all it had gained was a salient held by fatigued troops. There were further German offensives, each weaker than the last, as the under-nourished, demoralised troops of the Second Reich were finally brought to a halt along the River Marne on 15 July.[17] The spring offensives had cost the Germans a million men and severely depleted their stockpile of munitions; they would soon lose another million men to Spanish Influenza, while the Allies were bolstered by almost 1.9 million Americans.[18]

August 8, the day that the British offensives began, was described by the architect of the German war effort, General Erich Friedrich Wilhelm Ludendorff, as 'A black day for the German Army'.[19] The Battle of Amiens resulted in the British Fourth Army advancing to just short of Chaulnes, with the Germans incurring losses of 75,000, of which 50,000 became prisoners of war.[20] It was the last attack on 29 September, undertaken by General Rawlinson's Fourth Army along the St Quentin Canal, that was the most successful. Major Deneys Reitz, second-in-command of the 1 Royal Scots Fusiliers noted '…practically every battery had moved up and along the lip of the Hindenburg Line the guns stood in an unbroken line firing as fast as they could load'.[21] After a massive preliminary bombardment that landed 126 shells per minute for eight hours on every 500 yards of the German defences, the advancing troops broke straight through the German lines, storming across the canal. It was a disaster for the Germans, who did not expect the Hindenburg Line to be breached so convincingly, or so quickly.[22] The *Manchester Guardian* reported:

> The German retreat west of Lille continued yesterday, and last night Sir Douglas Haig reported an advance of three miles since Thursday evening [October 3]. This gave us the whole of the Aubers Ridge and established our troops four miles from Lille…. The entrance of British troops into what was Armentières, other British troops inspecting at leisure the mazes of the German's wired battlements along the Aubers Ridge, from which they look down on Lille, La Bassée occupied one day and Lens the next—what events and places to see and chronicle.[23]

Aubers Ridge had fallen at last—Neuve Chapelle had been a front line since October 1914.

The hundred days between 21 August and 11 November 1918 were marked by a succession of advances that crumbled the German line, '…eroding it materially and morally, until it was stretched to bursting like the over-tensioned skin of a drum'.[24] Despite this, the drum-skin would not burst; ingresses were made, but there was still no major breakthrough followed by the rout that would force Germany to capitulate. The promise of peace became the desperate driving force of the German troops.

Foch's grand offensive of late September forced Ludendorff to realise that the end was in sight. He advised Hindenburg and Chancellor Count von Hertling that '…it was no longer possible to force the enemy to sue for peace by an offensive'.[25] The situation in the Balkans, where a ceasefire had been signed between the Franco-Serbian forces and those of Bulgaria, the high level of desertion in the German Army, and undertones of revolution in the Fatherland, convinced a demoralized Ludendorff that Germany should now seek an immediate ceasefire. He convinced Hindenburg, Foreign Secretary von Hintze, and Prince Max of Baden of the need for a ceasefire and they all approached the Kaiser, who agreed with his generals and appointed a new government that approached the United States on 4 October, with a request for an armistice.[26] The peace negotiations had begun, but unconditional surrender was not on the cards; Haig stated to the War Cabinet on 19 October that should it be demanded: '…there would be no armistice and the war world continue for at least another year!'[27] Such a scenario would leave the Allies with the only option of a negotiated settlement.

Imperial Germany was being undermined from the outside and within: revolution had broken out in parts of the Fatherland, Turkey signed an armistice on 30 October, and Austro-Hungary signed with the Italians four days later. To save Germany, the Kaiser was left with no option but to abdicate as Emperor of Germany and King of Prussia. On 9 November, the Kaiser and his Government transferred power to the Reichstag; the new Chancellor, Friedrich Ebert, leader of the Social Democrat Party, formed a workers' government, turning Germany into a republic. After 400 years on the throne of Prussia, the Hohenzollern dynasty was no more.[28]

Armistice terms for a ceasefire were agreed, with Lloyd George reading out the severe conditions to Parliament:

The Germans to evacuate all invaded territory and to be 10 kilometres east of the Rhine with 31 days;

The Allies to occupy all the left bank of the Rhine and the towns of Mayence, Coblenz, and Cologne, with a radius of 30 kilometres of the east bank;

They are to hand over 5,000 guns, 25,000 machine-guns, 3,000 *minenwerfer*, and 1,700 aeroplanes;

They are to pay for the occupation by Allied troops;

All prisoners are to be returned at once;

All specie, stock and paper money stole is to be returned;

All submarines, including mine-layers, to be surrendered;

Six battle-cruisers, ten battleships, eight light cruisers, and fifty destroyers are to be disarmed and interred in a neutral or Allied port;

All Russian warships to be handed over to the Allies;

5,000 locomotives, 150,000 wagons and 6,000 motor wagons, all in good working order, to be handed over to Allies to assist evacuation and;

Allies may occupy all the German forts and batteries at the entrance to the Kattegat and the Baltic.[29]

As the thirty-four clauses detailing the terms of the Armistice were too lengthy to be sent by cable, the Armistice was presented by hand to Chancellor Friedrich Ebert, now known as the People's Commissar. He replied, 'The German Government accepts the conditions of the Armistice communicated to it on 8 November'.[30] The delegation accordingly signed the document in Marshal Foch's dining carriage in the Compiègne Forest, north of Paris, at 5.12 a.m. on 11 November 1918.[31] The ceasefire came into effect at 11 a.m., at which time the guns became silent and everyone's thoughts turned to peace. First World War veteran Peter Hart wrote:

The Bloody war is over! It's over! And it was.

No more slaughter, no more maiming, no more mud and blood, no more killing and disembowelling of horses and mules. No more of those hopeless dawns, with the rain chilling the spirits, no more crouching in inadequate dugouts scooped out of trench walls, no more dodging snipers' bullets. No more of that terrible shell fire. No more shovelling up of bits of men's bodies and dumping them into sandbags.[32]

Big Ben, silent since the beginning of the war, rang out at 11 a.m., and Lloyd George addressed the House of Commons: 'I hope we may say that this fateful morning came an end to all wars.' The following celebrations lasted for three days.

The Armistice of 11 November effectively brought an end to hostilities, but the enemy had not been defeated in their own country, and it was not until 12 December that Haig watched the British Army pass into Germany. The terms gave the Ministry of Munitions breathing space to begin the demobilization of war industries without the threat that the Central Powers would renege on the ceasefire. Despite talk of a Ministry of Supply being created to handle future military establishment requirements, the Ministry of Munitions continued until 1921, when it was disbanded due to budget cuts.

The peace terms, based on President Woodrow Wilson's famous Fourteen Points, were hammered out by delegates from twenty-five states who met in Paris for the Peace Conference beginning on 21 January 1919.[33] Wilson still suspected Britain, France, and Italy of imperialism, and these suspicions were reinforced when the Bolsheviks published the secret treaties concluded between the European Allies and Tsar Nicholas II.[34] While avoiding a demand for unconditional surrender, Wilson steered the negotiations towards the payment of reparations to Allied countries and the degradation of German military power to prevent the chance of another war. At the time, the negotiations were considered to be a 'great diplomatic victory'.[35] The treaty also called for Germany to accept responsibility for the following:

> All the loss and damage to which the Allied and Associated Governments and their nationals had been subjected as a consequence of the war, imposed upon them by the aggression of Germany and her Allies.[36]

Initially the reparations were set at £4 billion to be paid in thirty annual instalments starting in 1923. After much wrangling, this figure was increased to £6.5 billion, with repayments due to begin immediately.[37] Germany lost 22 per cent of its territory and incurred debts of 135 per cent of Gross Domestic Product, most of which was owed to foreign powers.[38] According to the German Federal Budget, the remaining debt was repaid in October 2010 with a payment of £60 million, the core debt was repaid in 1983, but the interest was required to be paid to bond and debt holders in the event that Germany was reunited, with repayments beginning again in 1996.[39]

The Versailles Treaty was finally signed on 28 June 1919 in the Hall of Mirrors at the Palace of Versailles. It was no coincidence that it was also in this room that, in 1871, following the Franco-Prussian War, the King of Prussia was crowned Emperor of a united Germany, ending the Second French Empire of Napoleon III.

Repington had always considered that the exclusion of unconditional surrender in the Armistice and Treaty of Versailles was a mistake. The title of his book, *The First World*

War 1914–1918: Personal Experiences, published in 1920, demonstrated his belief that more trouble was on the horizon—it was the first time the phrase 'First World War' had been used in print. It was only nineteen years until Repington's prediction was validated.

The Rifle Brigade—The Human Cost

The younger generation of the upper classes and landed gentry, the majority of whom had been junior officers—those who were first over the top and last to retire—was severely reduced. The historian A. J. P. Taylor cited the 'lost generation' as the cause in the grave deficiency in men of political talent in the turbulent decade of the thirties.[40] Debrett's struggled to keep track of the haemorrhage of blue blood; their 1915 publication recorded 800 members of the peerage, baronage, and knights of the realm killed in action or having died of their wounds.[41] The Rifle Brigade as a regiment suffered 11,575 men killed in action, as shown on their memorial at Grosvenor Gardens in London; no doubt there were many more who later died of their wounds.[42] The 2nd Battalion, which had fought at both Neuve Chapelle and Aubers Ridge, had joined the BEF in 1914 with twenty-nine officers and 930 riflemen. By the end of the war there were only seventeen of the original members of the battalion remaining.[43]

It was decided that the dead would remain in the 'foreign field' where they fell; it was felt that if only the rich could afford to bring their dead back, then all should remain. However, as an alternative, many relatives purchased land in France and Belgium to erect their own memorials. On the Fromelles Road—the second objective of the Rifle Brigade at the Battle of Aubers Ridge—there is a memorial to Captain Paul Adrian Kennedy and his fellow officers and men who fell on 9 May 1915. Kennedy's mother had lost two other sons during the war, for whom graves were known, but Captain Kennedy's grave is sadly unknown. The memorial, on a small piece of land at the furthest point reached by the Rifle Brigade during the battle, commemorates his death as well the deaths of his fellow riflemen.[44] The cross has been replaced, and the original is held at Fromelles Church.

Following the Armistice, the battlefields were searched with metal rods for bodies and body parts. These were collected together and buried, resulting in some 187,853 unidentified burials.[45] The Menin Gate is one of four huge memorials to those who lost their lives in the Ypres salient, but do not have a grave. When it was unveiled on 24 July 1927, Field Marshal Lord Plumer gave a speech that ended with the following words:

> It was resolved that here at Ypres, where so many of the 'Missing' are known to have fallen, there should be erected a memorial worthy of them which should give expression to the nation's gratitude for their sacrifice and its sympathy with those who mourned them. A memorial has been erected which, in its simple grandeur, fulfils this object, and now it can be said of each one in whose honour we are assembled here today: 'He is not missing; he is here'.[46]

Between ten and fifty bodies are found every year, and each case has to be investigated by the local police to ensure that it is an historical death and not a recent one.[47]

The Excess of Shells

During the war approximately 187 million shells were manufactured and delivered.[48] What was to be done with those that remained at the end of the war? A sub-committee was formed to estimate the amount of ordnance required to fill the available storage facilities; after this was taken into account it was estimated that a surplus equal to an eight-week stock of breech-loading ammunition, plus 10,000,000 rounds of quick-firing ammunition and 10,000,000 brass fuzes would remain.[49] The East Anglia Munitions Committee had produced 4,653,927 fuzes with a total value of £1,596,290, and 5,397,192 shells of all classes to a value of approximately £6,000,000.[50] Out of the forty-two Boards of Management throughout the country, they came third for output, being surpassed only by London and Manchester.[51] At the end of the war they came up with a novel way of reducing their stock. Each worker involved in the war production was presented with a certificate and an 18-pdr shell (without explosive!) as a memento, which many used as a door stop. The certificate read:

1914   CRITTALL   1918

This is to certify that [name] was engaged on Munitions Work with the above Firm during the Great War 1914–1918, assisting in the production of upwards of 13,000 tons of projectiles, 13,000,000 fuse forgings innumerable parts of aeroplanes and equipment for War Factories.

As a memento, the firm have much pleasure in presenting him/her with an 18 PDR High Explosive Shell.

Signed
General Manager
November 1918 [52]

This however, was not sufficient to rid the ministry of the surplus. A value was assigned to each of the products in preparation for their sale. The shell bodies, including driving bands and nose bushes, would be sold as scrap at £5 a ton; ammonium nitrate would be sold as fertilizer at £20 a ton; TNT, being a drug currently on the market, could not be sold for more than £20 a ton.[53]

Therefore:

The breech loading ammunition would provide 240,000 tons of scrap metal achieving:	£850,000
plus 24,000 tons of explosives worth:	£255,000
Quick-firing ammunition would provide 5,000,000 high-explosive shell bodies; 2,000 tons of explosives; 5,000,000 shrapnel shell bodies; shrapnel bullets; and 10,000,000 brass cartridges with a total value of:	£1,150,000
The cost of breaking down the shells,	

their recovery and transport was estimated at:	(£700,000)
Brass fuzes would give a net value of:	£200,000
This would provide the exchequer with:	£1,755,000

However, in monetary terms, this would only scratch the surface of Britain's war cost, totalling some £9,593,000,000.[54] Based on the loss of life during the war, a quite distasteful calculation can be made: it cost the Central Powers approximately £2,300 to kill a soldier of the Triple Entente, whereas it cost the governments of the Triple Entente £7,500 to kill a soldier of the Central Powers.[55] The war left Britain on the verge of bankruptcy.

The Iron Harvest

Industry and invention had joined hands to produce ever more inventive ways to kill men; by the end of the war there were aeroplanes, tanks, flame-throwers, and gas-filled artillery shells, all designed to exact the maximum damage on the enemy. Seven thousand five hundred and seventy-eight British guns and howitzers remained in France and Belgium after the war, with nearly 16 million shells stored, not counting those that had been fired and did not detonate.[56] It is these shells, known to the French and Belgian authorities as 'The Iron Harvest' that are still causing problems a century later.

Soldiers trained in bomb disposal check drop-off sites on a weekly, sometimes daily basis to collect shells that have been disturbed by farmers ploughing their fields. In 2014 the Belgian authorities collected 105 tons of munitions, while the French, who operate out of Arras, collected 8 tons. The year before that, the combined total for what was the Western Front was 274 tons.[57] The consistently large volumes are not surprising when your think that between 1914 and 1918 the opposing armies fired an estimated 1.45 billion shells at each other along a front that changed very little in four years. The journalist Martin Fletcher writes:

> Every year or two a farmer detonates a shell while ploughing his fields and destroys if not himself, then at least his tractor. More would be killed or wounded were it not for the fact that they almost always plough in the same direction, giving the buried shells glancing blows that gradually nudge them into line so their noses are less likely to be hit.[58]

There have been 358 people killed and 535 injured by First World War munitions since 1918 in the Ypres area; they are recognised as official victims of war—'*mutilée dans la guerre*'— and those surviving receive a war pension.[59]

Those shells containing explosives only are put into a wooden crate in a storage shed, with each crate containing approximately 50 kg of explosives. Each morning, six crates are taken to a nearby wood and lowered into a freshly dug pit along with an M6 anti-tank mine and a lump of TNT. At 11.30 a.m. daily, the crates are detonated one by one, and the process is repeated at 4 p.m. Those containing toxic chemicals are analysed and dealt with in various ways.[60]

Conclusion

The lesson of 1915—that Britain must pay in shells or human lives—was definitely learnt. By the end of the war, the Ministry of Munitions, originally controlled by Lloyd George and now by Winston Churchill, had changed the nation's attitude to 'Total War'; the priority of every citizen was now to defeat the Central Powers. Women worked in the factories, having taken the place of men fighting at the front, and the Government was at last acting on a cross-party basis—although still top-heavy with Conservatives—to ensure that the country could defeat the 'Boche'. The lessons learnt would be put to good use in the next worldwide conflict.

Field Marshal French would remain the Commanding Officer of the Home Army until the war ended, when Douglas Haig took over the position. Repington would never again rise to the dizzy heights reached in 1915; despite earning the epitaph, 'The most brilliant military writer of the day', he would struggle financially for the rest of his life. Lloyd George earned the title of 'the man that won the war' and would continue as Prime Minister until 1922, when the Conservatives at last governed again in their own name. The Liberal Party was not so fortunate; they have never run the country in their own right since 1915, and a century on, the 2015 election has exposed their weakness in British politics like never before.

Despite the political nature of the shell scandal, we must not forgot the human element. The men of the Rifle Brigade were awarded twelve Victoria Crosses during the war, five of which were during the actions of 1915.[1] The 2nd Battalion, who had fought at Neuve Chapelle and Aubers Ridge, started the war with a compliment of 29 officers and 930 riflemen; they left 800 men buried in France.[2]

Epilogue
The Fall of the Liberal Party

The shell shortage was only one of the two scandals that erupted over the weekend of 15/16 May 1915. But what was really the cause for the downfall of the great Liberal Government?

Trevor Wilson, Emeritus Professor of the University of Adelaide and one of the world's leading military historians, views the events as follows:

> The Liberal Party can be compared to an individual who, after a period of robust health and great exertion, experienced symptoms of illness (Ireland, Labour unrest, the suffragettes). Before a thorough diagnosis could be made, he was involved in an encounter with a rampant omnibus (the First World War), which mounted the pavement and ran him over. After lingering painful, he expired. A controversy has persisted ever since as to what killed him. One medical school argues that even without the bus he would soon have died; the intimations of illness were symptoms of a grave disease which would shortly have ended his life. Another school goes further, and says that the encounter with the bus would not have proved fatal had not the victim's health already been seriously impaired. Neither of these views is accepted here. The evidence for them is insufficient, because the ailments had not reached a stage where their ultimate effect could be known. How long, apart from the accident, the victim would have survived, what future (if any) he possessed cannot be said. All that is known is that at one moment he was up and walking and at the next he was flat on his back, never to rise again; and in the interval he had been run over by the bus. If it is guess-work to say that the bus was mainly responsible for his demise, it is the most warrantable guess that can be made.[1]

Entering the country into a world war was against the solid liberal ethos. The party had a core of non-conformists, many of whom were pacifists, and their moderate politicians could not deal with the war-related decisions that needed to be made, let alone placate the suffragettes, trade unions, and Ireland. Churchill later wrote, 'A vast fog of information envelops the fatal steps to Armageddon.'[2] Lloyd George supported the declaration of war, but what had been the party's greatest strengths during peacetime became debilitating liabilities when it found itself fighting the largest war that the world had witnessed up to that point.

This does not mean that war itself made the party's destruction inevitable; it was the Liberal Party's failure to adapt a cohesive, unified response to the war that sealed their fate. Lloyd George:

> There was a sense of revolt against the attitude of the Government and was regarded as its leisurely and take-for-granted attitude in dealing with vitally serious matters. Matters of life and death to the whole of the Allies, to the British Empire, and to hundreds of thousands of gallant young men, who had offered their lives to their country.[3]

The opposing arguments for the specific scandal that caused Asquith to form the Coalition Government of 1915 were the resignation of Admiral Lord Fisher and the shell scandal. In *Politicians at War*, published in 1920, Max Aitken, Lord Beaverbrook, is quoted as identifying the resignation of Lord Fisher as the crisis that fell the Government, further arguing that the shell scandal was not important at this stage and did not become a public issue until after the Coalition was formed.[4] Lady Violet Bonham Carter, daughter of Asquith, endorses Roy Jenkins' statement in his biography of her father that the 'situation at the Admiralty and not the shell crisis … was the real cause of the fall of the Liberal Government'.[5] I leave the last statement in support of this argument to Roy Hattersley, author of *The Great Outsider—David Lloyd George*:

> When the war was over, the idea that the 'shell scandal' had brought down the government was invented by Churchill to protect him from the accusation that his breach with Fisher had destroyed the Liberal ministry.[6]

The public was unaware of the turbulent nature of Fisher's relationship with Churchill or of his seven attempts to resign during his final six and a half months as First Sea Lord. Fisher perceived Churchill as being high-handed in his attitude for pressing ahead with his own plans, often circumventing his authority by communicating directly with the naval commanders. Above all he hated Churchill's unbridled enthusiasm.[7] It was the loss of the battleship HMS *Goliath* on 13 May that made Fisher change his mind and, after 'anxious reflection', decide that he wanted to disassociate himself from the whole affair.[8] This prompted his final letter of resignation, written and sent on Saturday, 15 May, which was accepted by both Churchill and Asquith on the following Sunday.[9] By that afternoon, Churchill had not only made plans to replace Fisher but had ensured that all the other junior members of the Board remained in place.[10]

Fisher had many friends in the Conservative ranks, Bonar Law was unsure whether his fellow Tories would be docile if Fisher was allowed to go, especially as he had little confidence in the Dardanelles venture. Hazelhurst states, 'No Liberal government could continue successfully in the teeth of well-founded Conservative attacks.'[11] It may therefore be construed that Fisher, being aware of Repington's article in *The Times* of 14 May, used its release to further his own and Bonar Law's cause.

In his documented study, 'The Destruction of Britain's Last Liberal Government', Dr Stephen Koss, historian of British politics, Professor of History at Columbia University, and commentator for the BBC, undertook a detailed investigation 'to answer at least some of the riddles posed by the formation of the first wartime coalition, by dissecting several newly discovered pieces of "solid evidence"'.[12]

Hazelhurst considers Koss's conclusions to be startling, stating that if they are accepted a new appraisal of the motives and behaviour of most of the leading participants in the events of May 1915 is required.[13] He summarizes the thesis as follows:

> The fall of the Asquith government in May 1915 cannot be attributed to the crisis at the Admiralty created by Lord Fisher's refusal to serve any longer as First Sea Lord under Churchill. The most important of the causes contributing to the fall of the government was the so-called 'shell scandal'.
>
> The shell scandal did not, as is usually supposed, originate with a leak of information from a member of the British Expeditionary Force to Colonel Repington, the military correspondent of *The Times*. Nor, according to Dr Koss, did Sir John French act entirely on his own initiative when he sent emissaries to leading politicians in London with information which confirmed Repington's story. Behind, and enveloping, French and Repington was a wider conspiracy. Arthur Balfour, David Lloyd George, and Winston Churchill intrigued to achieve 'the disruption of the ancien regime'. Repington was probably briefed and 'unquestionably inspired' by Churchill who conferred with him in France on the week-end of May 8–9.
>
> The downfall of the Liberal ministry was precipitated by the publication of Repington's dispatch and the accompanying editorial, 'Shells and the Great Battle', in *The Times* on 14th May 1915. Asquith did not choose to create a coalition because of the fear of criticism. He acted not to forestall parliamentary opposition over munitions or the Admiralty but to 'to avert pressures from within the government that had taken him completely by surprise'.[14]

It is well documented that the shell crisis predated Fisher's resignation, which came the day after the publication of Repington's article in *The Times*. It was a threatening political issue before the news of Fisher's departure had spread outside official circles. If the shell shortage was not a live issue, why did Asquith feel obligated to make his statement in Manchester that there was no shortage? Why was he considering the creation for a new post in March, headed by Lloyd George as Director of War Contracts, or something of the kind?[15] Bonar Law, as well as many others, made a strong reference to it in April:

> It is common knowledge—I knew it was not guess work, but as knowledge—that we were short of ammunition months ago.[16]

It appears that Dr Koss considers the disruption within the Admiralty to have been of little consequence:

> It remained possible for Asquith either to retain Fisher's services or to replace him with reconstructing the ministry.[17]

Until the morning of 17 May, Asquith seemed intent on doing no more than consulting the Conservative leaders on the steps to be taken concerning the Admiralty and the disclosure of the shell shortage.[18] Churchill had already secured the assurance of the junior members of the Admiralty that they would remain *in situ*, and proposed a replacement for Fisher.

After discussions with Lloyd George and Bonar Law, Asquith acted to avert the parliamentary storm that would certainly have ensued had both the shell shortage and Fisher's resignation been raised simultaneously in the Commons. His solution was to create the Coalition, thereby removing the danger of the Liberals completely losing power at the General Election due later in the year. Following the discussion, Asquith wrote a memorandum stating that, due to two matters, a change in government was necessary to avoid an attack by the Conservative Party:

> Resignation of Lord Fisher, which I have done my best to avert, and the more than plausible parliamentary case in regard to the alleged deficiency of high-explosive shells.[19]

A. J. P. Taylor has labelled these crucial developments as '…one of the few political episodes in the first world war on which solid evidence is lacking'.[20] Conversely, Hazlehurst considers that 'the frank accounts of both Repington and French—though they do not settle every question—have long provided a satisfactory explanation'.[21] None of the principal players were diarists, therefore historians lack the sources with which to build strong hypotheses. Alfred M. Gollin, Professor Emeritus of History at the University of California, has marvelled at the 'many different interpretations' to which this episode has been subjected and has concluded that Asquith's motives must remain a matter for surmise.[22] Therefore, the question remains whether it was the debacle within the Admiralty, bringing with it the threat of a Conservative attack, or the shell scandal, turning the opinion of the British public against the Government, that finally brought down Asquith's Government.

Endnotes

Introduction and Chapter I—Guns, Shells, and Britain's Pre-War Munitions Industry

1. Buchan, *Nelson's History of the War* (1993)
2. 'Behind the Image' article *Military History Magazine* (March 2014)
3. Holmes, *The Western Front* (2001)
4. *My Family At War*, BBC Documentary
5. Bridger, *The Great War Handbook* (2001)
6. *Treatise on Ammunition* (1915)
7. Bridger, *The Great War Handbook (2001)*
8. *Ibid.*
9. Crittall Archive Reference BRNTM 2010.587
10. *Treatise on Ammunition* (1915)
11. Crittall Archive Reference BRNTM 2010.587
12. *Treatise on Ammunition* (1915)
13. Royal Powder Mills Exhibit
14. Youngson, *Collins Dictionary of Medicine* (1992)
15. *Treatise on Ammunition* (1915)
16. Bridger, *The Great War Handbook (2001)*
17. Hart-Davis, *The Big Bang: A History of Explosives* (1998)
18. Urbanski, *Chemistry and Technology of Explosives* (1963)
19. *Treatise on Ammunition* (1915)
20. *Ibid.*
21. *Ibid.*
22. *Ibid.*
23. Bridger, *The Great War Handbook (2001)*
24. *The Passchendaele Experience*
25. Macdonald, *1915 The Death of Innocence* (1993)
26. *Firepower*—Souvenir Guide
27. *Countdown to War—Germany, Empire of Blood and Iron*
28. *Ibid.*
29. *History of the British Army in 25 battles—Amiens*
30. *Countdown to War—Germany, Empire of Blood and Iron*
31. David, *100 Days to Victory* (2013)
32. Harris, *The Ammunition Scandal* (1973)
33. *Ibid.*

Chapter 2—The Liberal Government and the Declaration of War

1. *http://www.theguardian.com/politics/electionspast/page/0,,1451427,00.html*
2. Shelden, *Young Titan* (2013)
3. *Ibid.*
4. *Ibid.*
5. Repington, *Vestigia—Reminiscences of Peace and War* (1919)
6. *Ibid.*
7. Goodwin, *Lincoln* (2009)
8. Repington, *Vestigia—Reminiscences of Peace and War* (1919)
9. Brazier, *'All Sir Garnet!' Lord Wolseley and the British Army in the First World War* (2013)
10. Holmes, *The Western Front* (2001)
11. Repington, *Vestigia—Reminiscences of Peace and War* (1919)
12. Shelden, *Young Titan* (2013)
13. *http://www.election.demon.co.uk/geresults.html*
14. Faulkner, *Britain—Perfidious Albion* (2014)
15. Beatty, *The Lost History of 1914* (2012)
16. Repington, *Vestigia—Reminiscences of Peace and War* (1919)
17. Hoare, *What Caused the Great War*
18. Fergusson, *The Pity of War*, a televised debate (2014)
19. Hoare, *What Caused the Great War* (2013)
20. Corrigan, *Mud, Blood and Poppycock* (2004)
21. Hoare, *What Caused the Great War* (2013)
22. Faulkner, *Countdown to War* (2014)
23. Faulkner, *Austria-Hungary: Prison-house of Nations* (2014)
24. Beatty, *The Lost History of 1914* (2012)
25. Heffer, *Honour the Dead* (2014)
26. Faulkner, *Austria-Hungary: Prison-house of Nations* (2014)
27. Fergusson, *The Pity of War*, a televised debate (2014)
28. Wilson, *The Downfall of the Liberal Party 1914–1935* (1966)
29. *http://www.telegraph.co.uk/history/world-war-one/11002644/First-World-War-centenary-how-events-unfolded-on-August-1-1914.html*
30. Bridger, *The Great War Handbook* (2001)
31. *http://www.1914-1918.net/greys_speech.html*
32. French, *The Life of Field-Marshal Sir John French First Earl of Ypres* (1931)
33. *Ibid.*
34. *http://www.bbc.co.uk/history/worldwars/wwone/mirror01_01.shtml*
35. *Ibid.*
36. *Ibid.*
37. *http://www.telegraph.co.uk/history/world-war-one/11006820/WW1-centenary-how-the-events-of-August-4-1914-unfolded.html*
38. *Ibid.*
39. Hastings, *The Necessary War* (2014)
40. Faulkner, *Britain—Perfidious Albion* (2014)
41. Wilson, *The Downfall of the Liberal Party 1914–1935* (1966)
42. Ryan, *"Shells Scandel" to Bow Street: The Denigration of Lieutenant-Colonel Charles a' Court Repington* (1978)
43. *Ibid.*
44. Brock, *Margot Asquith's War Diary 1914–1918* (2014)
45. Wilson, *The Downfall of the Liberal Party 1914–1935* (1966)
46. An advisory committee to the Prime Minister that concentrated on defence planning for the whole British Empire and consisted of Cabinet Ministers, Heads of Military Services and key Civil Servants

47. Neiberg, *The Western Front 1914-1916* (2008)
48. Bridger, *The Great War Handbook (2001)*
49. Holmes, *The Western Front* (2001)
50. Sloggett, *Depicting the Great War* 2014)
51. Price, *If You're Reading This … Last Letters Home* (1913)
52. *The Rifle Brigade Journal* (2014)
53. Bridger, *The Great War Handbook (2001)*
54. *The Rifle Brigade Journal* (2014)
55. Bridger, *The Great War Handbook (2001)*
56. *Ibid.*
57. Senior, *Home before the Leaves Fall: A new history of the German invasion of 1914* (2014)
58. French, *The Life of Field-Marshal Sir John French First Earl of Ypres* (1931)
59. *http://www.firstworldwar.com/source/georgev_aug1914.htm*
60. Lewis-Stempel, *Six Weeks* (2010)
61. *Ibid.*

Chapter 3—The Opening Stages of the War

1. Snow, *General Snow remembering a First World War General* (2014)
2. Brewer, *The Chronicle of War* (2007)
3. Macdonald, *1915 The Death of Innocence* (1993)
4. Brewer, *The Chronicle of War* (2007)
6. Bridger, *The Great War Handbook* (2013)
7. Reid, *Douglas Haig Architect of Victory* (2009)
8. *Ibid.*
9. Neiberg, *The Western Front 1914–1916* (2008)
10. Repington, *The First World War 1914–1918 Personal Experiences of Lieut-Col. C. à Court Repington CMG* (1920)
11. Bridger, *The Great War Handbook* (2013)
12. *The Great War © BBC 1964 Parts Seven and Eight* (1964)
13. David, *100 Days to Victory* (2013)
14. *Briefing Room The Industrialisation of War by Andy Lawrence*
15. *The Great War © BBC 1964 Parts Seven and Eight* (1964)
16. Harris, *The Ammunition Scandal* (1973)
17. Repington, *The First World War 1914–1918 Personal Experiences of Lieut-Col. C. à Court Repington CMG* (1920)
18. Harris, *The Ammunition Scandal* (1973)
19. Macdonald, *1915 The Death of Innocence* (1993)
20. Harris, *The Ammunition Scandal* (1973)
21. *Ibid.*
22. *Ibid.*
23. *Ibid.*
24. *http://spartacus-educational.com/FWWfeather.htm*
25. *Ibid.*
26. Harris, *The Ammunition Scandal* (1973)
27. *Ibid.*
28. *East Anglian Munitions Committee Minutes of the 5 June 1915 Reference 2013–213*
29. Harris, *The Ammunition Scandal* (1973)
30. Repington, *The First World War 1914–1918 Personal Experiences of Lieut-Col. C. à Court Repington CMG* (1920)
31. *Ibid.*
32. *Ibid.*

33. Harris, *The Ammunition Scandal* (1973)
34. *Ibid.*
35. *The Great War © BBC 1964 Parts Seven and Eight* (1964)
36. Hazelhurst, *Politicians at War July 1914 to May 1915* (1971)
37. Repington, *The First World War 1914–1918 Personal Experiences of Lieut-Col. C. à Court Repington* (1920)
38. Harris, *The Ammunition Scandal* (1973)
39. *Ibid.*
40. Hazelhurst, *Politicians at War July 1914 to May 1915* (1971)
41. Harris, *The Ammunition Scandal* (1973)

Chapter 4—The Battle of Neuve Chapelle

1. *History of the British Army in 25 battles—Loos*
2. *The Great War © BBC 1964 Parts Seven and Eight* (1964)
3. Sir John French memorandum dated January 3, 1914 National Archive CAB/241/1
4. Hancock, *Aubers Ridge* (2005)
5. Neiberg, *The Western Front 1914–1916* (2008)
6. Macdonald, *1915 The Death of Innocence* (1993)
7. Wilson, *The Downfall of the Liberal Party 1914–1935* (1993)
8. French, *The Life of Field-Marshal Sir John French First Earl of Ypres* (1931)
9. *History of the British Army in 25 battles—Loos*
10. French, *The Life of Field-Marshal Sir John French First Earl of Ypres* (1931)
11. Sir John French memorandum dated January 3, 1914 National Archive CAB/241/1
12. French, *The Life of Field-Marshal Sir John French First Earl of Ypres* (1931)
13. *Ibid.*
14. Repington, *The First World War 1914–1918 Personal Experiences of Lieut-Col. C. à Court Repington* (1920)
15. Edmonds, *History of the Great War, 1915* Vol. IV, Military Operations (1947)
16. Hancock, *Aubers Ridge* (2005)
17. Macdonald, *1915 The Death of Innocence* (1993)
18. 'The Glorious Story of Neuve Chapelle', *Daily Mail,* April 19, 1915
19. The Passchendaele Experience—Memorial Museum Passchendaele
20. Berkley Seymour, *History of the Rifle Brigade in the war of 1914–1918* (1936)
21. *Ibid.*
22. *www.Cartesfrance.fr* and Bridger, *The Battle of Neuve Chapelle* (2005)
23. Sir John French's Seventh Despatch, 5th April 1915
24. Berkley Seymour, *History of the Rifle Brigade in the war of 1914–1918* (1936)
25. *Ibid.*
26. Bridger, *The Battle of Neuve Chapelle* (2005)
27. Reid, *Douglas Haig Architect of Victory* (2009)
28. *Ibid.*
29. Bridger, *The Battle of Neuve Chapelle* (2005)
30. *Ibid.*
31. *Ibid.*
32 Neiberg, *The Western Front 1914-1916* (2008)
33. Reid, *Douglas Haig Architect of Victory* (2009)
34. Bridger, *The Battle of Neuve Chapelle* (2005)
35. *Ibid.*
36. 'The Glorious Story of Neuve Chapelle', *Daily Mail,* April 19, 1915
37. Bridger, *The Battle of Neuve Chapelle* (2005)
38. *Ibid.*

39. Sheffield and Bourne, *Douglas Haig—War Diaries and Letters 1914–1918* (2005)
40. Neiberg, *The Western Front 1914–1916* (2008)
41. Macdonald, *1915 The Death of Innocence* (1993)
42. *Ibid.*
43. 'The Glorious Story of Neuve Chapelle', *Daily Mail,* April 19, 1915
44. Berkley Seymour, *History of the Rifle Brigade in the war of 1914–1918* (1936)
45. Long strips of serge material that was wrapped around the lower leg, ankle to knee, to prevent water and insects from getting into boots
46. German officer similar in rank to an army captain
47. Prisoners taken later had confirmed that this section of trench was well aware of the massed troops
48. Bridger, *The Battle of Neuve Chapelle* (2005)
49. Sheffield and Bourne, *Douglas Haig—War Diaries and Letters 1914–1918* (2005)
50. Bridger, *The Battle of Neuve Chapelle* (2005)
51. Neiberg, *The Western Front 1914–1916* (2008)
52. The 35-minute barrage saw more shells fired than the British Army had expended during the whole of the South African War—Neiberg, *The Western Front 1914–1916* (2008)
53. Bridger, *The Battle of Neuve Chapelle* (2005)
54. Letter to Lt Chan Hoskyns from Lt Charles Pennefather held at the National Army Museum
55. 'The Glorious Story of Neuve Chapelle', *Daily Mail,* April 19, 1915
56. Bridger, *The Battle of Neuve Chapelle* (2005)
57. *Ibid.*
58. The preparation process included siting the gun properly, having it restrained on a firm platform that would absorb the recoil, bringing the gun back to its correct position, before firing again
59. Bridger, *The Battle of Neuve Chapelle* (2005)
60. *Ibid.*
61. *Ibid.*
62. *Ibid.*
63. *Rifle Brigade War Diary* National Archive WO95—1731-1
64. Thanks to the members of the Gurkha Museum in Winchester for the translations
65. 'The Glorious Story of Neuve Chapelle', *Daily Mail,* April 19, 1915
66. Bridger, *The Battle of Neuve Chapelle* (2005)
67. Letter to Lt Chan Hoskyns from Lt Charles Pennefather held at the National Army Museum
68. Macdonald, *1915 The Death of Innocence* (1993)
69. *Ibid.*
70. Sheffield and Bourne, *Douglas Haig—War Diaries and Letters 1914–1918* (2005)
71. Berkley Seymour, *History of the Rifle Brigade in the war of 1914–1918* (1936)
72. *Ibid.*
73. Letter to Lt Chan Hoskyns from Lt Charles Pennefather held at the National Army Museum
74. *The Rifle Brigade Chronicle*
75. Bridger, *The Battle of Neuve Chapelle* (2005)
76. *Ibid.*
77. *Ibid.*
78. *2nd Battalion Rifle Brigade War Diary*
79. *2nd Battalion Rifle Brigade War Diary*
80. *Ibid.*
81. Berkley Seymour, *History of the Rifle Brigade in the war of 1914–1918* (1936)
82. Bridger, *The Battle of Neuve Chapelle* (2005)

83. Letter to Lt Chan Hoskyns from Lt Charles Pennefather held at the National Army Museum
84. Bridger, *The Battle of Neuve Chapelle* (2005)
85. Macdonald, *1915 The Death of Innocence* (1993)
86. Letter to Lt Chan Hoskyns from Lt Charles Pennefather held at the National Army Museum
87. Bridger, *The Battle of Neuve Chapelle* (2005)
88. *Ibid.*
89. *Ibid.*
90. *Ibid.*
91. *The Rifle Brigade Journal 2014*
92. Berkley Seymour, *History of the Rifle Brigade in the war of 1914-1918* (1936)
93. Letter to Lt Chan Hoskyns from Lt Charles Pennefather held at the National Army Museum
94. *Ibid.*
95. *Ibid.*
96. Harvey, *The Rifle Brigade* (1975)
97. Berkley Seymour, *History of the Rifle Brigade in the war of 1914–1918* (1936)
98. Bridger, *The Battle of Neuve Chapelle* (2005)
99. Confirmed by interrogated prisoners
100. Bridger, *The Battle of Neuve Chapelle* (2005)
101. *Ibid.*
102. Macdonald, *1915 The Death of Innocence* (1993)
103. Wallace, Lt-Gen. Sir Christopher and Major Ron Cassidy MBE *Focus on Courage*
104. Bridger, *The Battle of Neuve Chapelle* (2005)
105. Wallace, Lt-Gen. Sir Christopher and Major Ron Cassidy MBE *Focus on Courage*
106. *Ibid.*
107. Daniels returned to the regiment and in later actions was awarded a Military Cross, retiring in 1934 as a Lieutenant-Colonel
108. Letter to Lt Chan Hoskyns from Lt Charles Pennefather held at the National Army Museum
109. Bridger, *The Battle of Neuve Chapelle* (2005)
110. Letter to Lt Chan Hoskyns from Lt Charles Pennefather held at the National Army Museum
111. Sir John French's Seventh Despatch, 5 April 1915
112. *Ibid.*
113. Letter to Lt Chan Hoskyns from Lt Charles Pennefather held at the National Army Museum
114. Wallace, Lt-Gen. Sir Christopher and Major Ron Cassidy MBE *Focus on Courage*
115. Reid, *Douglas Haig Architect of Victory* (2009)
116. Bridger, *The Battle of Neuve Chapelle* (2005)
117. Reid, *Douglas Haig Architect of Victory* (2009)
118. Macdonald, *1915 The Death of Innocence* (1993)
119. *Ibid.*
120. Bridger, *The Battle of Neuve Chapelle* (2005)
121. Reid, *Douglas Haig Architect of Victory* (2009)
122. Repington, *The First World War 1914–1918 Personal Experiences of Lieut-Col. C. à Court Repington (1920)*
123. Macdonald, *1915 The Death of Innocence* (1993)
124. *Ibid.*
125. *Ibid.*
126. *Ibid.*

Chapter 5—The Shell Shortage Reaches Home

1. Hazelhurst, *Politicians at War July 1914 to May 1915* (1971)
2. Macdonald, *1915 The Death of Innocence* (1993)
3. Wilson, *The Downfall of the Liberal Party 1914–1935* (1966)
4. *Ibid.*
5. *Ibid.*
6. French, *The Life of Field-Marshal Sir John French First Earl of Ypres (1936)*
7. Harris, *The Ammunition Scandal* (1973)
8. *Ibid.*
9. *Ibid.*
10. Hancock, *Aubers Ridge* (2005)
11. Hazelhurst, *Politicians at War July 1914 to May 1915* (1971)
12. Harris, *The Ammunition Scandal* (1973)
13. Hazelhurst, *Politicians at War July 1914 to May 1915* (1971)
14. Hancock, *Aubers Ridge* (2005)
15. French, *The Life of Field-Marshal Sir John French First Earl of Ypres* (1936)
16. *Ibid.*
17. *Ibid.*
18. *Ibid.*
19. *Ibid.*

Chapter 6—The Battle of Aubers Ridge

1. Edmonds, *History of the Great War, 1915 Vol IV, Military Operations* (1947)
2. Hancock, *Aubers Ridge* (2005)
3. Holmes, *The Western Front* (2001)
4. Hancock, *Aubers Ridge* (2005)
5. Edmonds, *History of the Great War, 1915 Vol IV, Military Operations* (1947)
6. Hancock, *Aubers Ridge* (2005)
7. *Ibid.*
8. Neiberg, *The Western Front 1914–1916* (2008)
9. Hancock, *Aubers Ridge* (2005)
10. Neiberg, *The Western Front 1914–1916* (2008)
11. *Ibid.*
12. Hancock, *Aubers Ridge* (2005)
13. *Ibid.*
14. *Ibid.*
15. French, *The Life of Field-Marshal Sir John French First Earl of Ypres* (1931)
16. Hancock, *Aubers Ridge* (2005)
17. Reid, *Douglas Haig Architect of Victory* (2009)
18. Hancock, *Aubers Ridge* (2005)
19. *Ibid.*
20. Repington, *The First World War 1914–1918 Personal Experiences of Lieut-Col. C. à Court Repington* (1920)
21. Lewis-Stempel, *Six Weeks* (2010)
22. *Ibid.*
23. Bull, *War in the Trenches*
24. *Treatise on Ammunition* 10th Edition War Office 1915
25. Bull, *History of War July 2014 War in the Trenches* (2014)
26. Hancock, *Aubers Ridge* (2005)
27. *Ibid.*

28. Tobin, Richard H., *'I was there'—Great War Interviews*
29. Hancock, *Aubers Ridge* (2005)
30. Macdonald, *1915 The Death of Innocence* (1993)
31. Hancock, *Aubers Ridge* (2005)
32. Berkley and Seymour, *History of the Rifle Brigade in the war of 1914–1918* (1936)
33. Hancock, *Aubers Ridge* (2005)
34. *Ibid.*
35. *Ibid.*
36. *Ibid.*
37. *Ibid.*
38. *War Diary* reproduced in Hancock, *Aubers Ridge* (2005)
39. Hancock, *Aubers Ridge* (2005)
40. *Ibid.*
41. *Ibid.*
42. *Ibid.*
43. Edmonds, *History of the Great War, 1915 Vol IV, Military Operations* (1947)
44. Hancock, *Aubers Ridge* (2005)
45. *Ibid.*
46. *Ibid.*
47. *Ibid.*
48. *Ibid.*
49. *Ibid.*
50. Berkley and Seymour, *History of the Rifle Brigade in the war of 1914–1918* (1936)
51. Hancock, *Aubers Ridge* (2005)
52. Berkley and Seymour, *History of the Rifle Brigade in the war of 1914–1918* (1936)
53. *Ibid.*
54. Edmonds, *History of the Great War, 1915 Vol IV, Military Operations* (1947)
55. Hancock, *Aubers Ridge* (2005)
56. *Ibid.*
57. Some commercial firms produced good-luck charms that the men held, such as 'Tommy Touchwud', a fashioned piece of wood
58. Berkley and Seymour, *History of the Rifle Brigade in the war of 1914–1918* (1936)
59. Lewis-Stempel, *Six Weeks* (2010)
60. Bull, *History of War July 2014 War in the Trenches* (2014)
61. Berkley and Seymour, *History of the Rifle Brigade in the war of 1914–1918* (1936)
62. Hancock, *Aubers Ridge* (2005)
63. *Ibid.*
64. *Ibid.*
65. *Ibid.*
66. *Ibid.*
67. Edmonds, *History of the Great War, 1915 Vol IV, Military Operations* (1947)
68. Hancock, *Aubers Ridge* (2005)
69. Extensive enquires after the battle into the retreat incident failed to determine a reason for the unauthorised and mysterious withdrawal. It was not established whether Captain Dee had shouted the order or not
70. A service was held in 2009 at the old German lines taken by the RB and where Stephens was notified that he was in command of the brigade. Victoria Burbidge, Great War Forum, 26 April 2009
71. Hancock, *Aubers Ridge* (2005)
72. Reid, *Douglas Haig Architect of Victory* (2009)
73. Edmonds, *History of the Great War, 1915 Vol IV, Military Operations* (1947)
74. Reference 2nd Rifle Brigade, Aubers Ridge—Great War Forum, 6 July 2008
75. Hancock, *Aubers Ridge* (2005)

76. Edmonds, *History of the Great War, 1915 Vol IV, Military Operations* (1947)
77. Hancock, *Aubers Ridge* (2005)
78. *Ibid.*
79. Berkley and Seymour, *History of the Rifle Brigade in the war of 1914–1918* (1936)
80. Hancock, *Aubers Ridge* (2005)
81. 2nd Rifle Brigade, Aubers Ridge—Great War Forum, 6 July 2008
82. Berkley and Seymour, *History of the Rifle Brigade in the war of 1914–1918* (1936)
83. The priest was killed in action subsequently, and the letter was found on his body and forwarded to Intelligence by whom it was given to a British War Correspondent, Mr Valentine Williams. Berkley and Seymour, *History of the Rifle Brigade in the war of 1914–1918* (1936)
84. 2nd Rifle Brigade, Aubers Ridge—Great War Forum, 6 July 2008
85. Berkley and Seymour, *History of the Rifle Brigade in the war of 1914–1918* (1936)
86. Macdonald, *1915 The Death of Innocence* (1993)
87. *Ibid.*
88. *Webmatter: Battle of Aubers Ridge*
89. Edmunds, *History of the Great War, 1915 Vol IV, Military Operations* (1947)
90. Hancock, *Aubers Ridge* (2005)
91. Neiberg, *The Western Front 1914–1916* (2008)
92. Sheffeild and Bourne, *Douglas Haig—War Diaries and Letters 1914–1918* (2005)
93. Sir John French's Eighth Despatch
94. Neiberg, *The Western Front 1914–1916* (2008)
95. French, *The Life of Field-Marshal Sir John French First Earl of Ypres* (1931)
96. Neiberg, *The Western Front 1914–1916* (2008)
97. Repington, *The First World War 1914–1918 Personal Experiences of Lieut-Col. C. à Court Repington* (1920)
98. French, *The Life of Field-Marshal Sir John French First Earl of Ypres* (1931)
99. Hancock, *Aubers Ridge* (2005)
100. Davidson, *A Doctor in the Trenches*
101. *The Guardian*, 15 September 1993
102. Macdonald, *1915 The Death of Innocence* (1993)
103. Davidson, *Doctor in the Trenches*
104. *Ibid.*
105. Hancock, *Aubers Ridge* (2005)
106. *Ibid.*
107. *Ibid.*
108. Beaverbrook, *Politicans and the War 1914–1916* (1928)
109. Hancock, *Aubers Ridge* (2005)
110. Repington, *The First World War 1914–1918 Personal Experiences of Lieut-Col. C. à Court Repington* (1920)
111. French, *The Life of Field-Marshal Sir John French First Earl of Ypres* (1931)
112. *Ibid.*
113. Repington, *The First World War 1914–1918 Personal Experiences of Lieut-Col. C. à Court Repington* (1920)
114. French, *The Life of Field-Marshal Sir John French First Earl of Ypres* (1931)
115. *Ibid.*
116. Repington, *The First World War 1914–1918 Personal Experiences of Lieut-Col. C. à Court Repington* (1920)
117. The days following such a battle are often confused and therefore the numbers of casualties often take some time to become definitive. The officer numbered relates only to Gray; another officer, Captain Chichester-Constable, had been wounded earlier in the day and returned to the battalion later
118. Repington, *The First World War 1914–1918 Personal Experiences of Lieut-Col. C. à Court Repington* (1920)

Chapter 7—The Fallout from *The Times* Article

1. Supplement to *The London Gazette*, 1 September 1914
2. Hazelhurst, *Politicians At War, July 1914 to May 1915* (1971)
3. *http://spartacus-educational.com/FWWdora.htm*
4. Hazelhurst, *Politicians At War, July 1914 to May 1915* (1971)
5. Lewis-Stempel, *Six Weeks* (2010)
6. *Ibid.*
7. *Ibid.*
8. *BBC Magazine*—The Post Office
9. MUN5/19/221/8 (NOV 1914)
10. *Ibid.*
11. Evans, *From the Front Line*
12. Hattersley, *The Great Outsider—David Lloyd George* (2010)
13. Macdonald, *1915 The Death of Innocence* (1993)
14. *Ibid.*
15. Paxman, *Great Britain's Great War* (2013)
16. *Daily Mail*, 3 January 2014, letters submitted by Phil O'Brien and *http://izquotes.com/quote/243252*
17. Repington, *Vestigia—Reminiscences of Peace and War*
18. *Ibid.*
19. Spencer-Wilkinson, *Twenty-five years, 1874–1909 by* (1933)
20. Repington, *The First World War 1914–1918 Personal Experiences of Lieut-Col. C. à Court Repington* (1920)
21. Rippington Family—Registered with the Guild of One-Name Studies
22. Ryan, *Shells Scandal to Bow Street: The Denigration of Lieutenant-Colonel Charles à Court Repington* (1978)
23. 'Playboy of the Western Front' article in *The Spectator*, 12 February 2000
24. Repington, *The First World War 1914–1918 Personal Experiences of Lieut-Col. C. à Court Repington* (1920)
25. Ryan, *Shells Scandal to Bow Street: The Denigration of Lieutenant-Colonel Charles à Court Repington* (1978)
26. Repington, *The First World War 1914–1918 Personal Experiences of Lieut-Col. C. à Court Repington* (1920)
27. *Ibid.*
28. *Ibid.*
29. Marcossan, *Adventures in Interviewing*
30. *The Great War* © BBC 1964 Parts Seven and Eight (1964)
31. David, *100 Days to Victory* (2013)
32. French, *The Life of Field-Marshal Sir John French First Earl of Ypres* (1931)
33. Repington, *The First World War 1914–1918 Personal Experiences of Lieut-Col. C. à Court Repington* (1920)
34. *Ibid.*
35. Wilson, *The Downfall of the Liberal Party 1914–1935* (1966)
36. Repington, *The First World War 1914–1918 Personal Experiences of Lieut-Col. C. à Court Repington* (1920)
37. *Ibid.*
38. *Ibid.*
39. Shelden, *Young Titan, The Making of Winston Churchill* (2013)
40. *Ibid.*
41. *Ibid.*
42. *Ibid.*

43. *Ibid.*
44. *Ibid.*
45. *Ibid*
46. *Ibid.*
47. *Ibid.*
48. Hazelhurst, *Politicians At War July 1914 to May 1915* (1971)
49. *Ibid.*
50. Jenkins, *Churchill* (2001)
51. *Ibid.*
52. *Ibid.*
53. *Ibid.*
54. Hazelhurst, *Politicians At War July 1914 to May 1915* (1971)
55. *Ibid.*
56. *Ibid.*
57. *Hattersley, The Great Outsider—David Lloyd George* (2010)
58. Hazelhurst, *Politicians At War July 1914 to May 1915* (1971)
59. Koss, *The Destruction of Britain's Last Liberal Government* (1968)
60. *Ibid.*
61. Hazelhurst, *Politicians At War July 1914 to May 1915* (1971)
62. *Ibid.*
63. Wilson, *The Downfall of the Liberal Party 1914–1935* (1966)
64. *Ibid.*
65. Hazelhurst, *Politicians At War July 1914 to May 1915* (1971)
66. Repington, *The First World War 1914–1918 Personal Experiences of Lieut-Col. C. à Court Repington* (1920)
67. Wilson, *The Downfall of the Liberal Party 1914–1935* (1966)
68. Shelden, *Young Titan, The Making of Winston Churchill* (2013)
69. Wilson, *The Downfall of the Liberal Party 1914–1935* (1966)
70. *Ibid.*
71. Hazelhurst, *Politicians At War July 1914 to May 1915* (1971)
72. *Ibid.*
73. Wilson, *The Downfall of the Liberal Party 1914–1935* (1966)
74. Brock, *Margot Asquith's War Diary 1914–1918* (2014)
75. Hazelhurst, *Politicians At War July 1914 to May 1915* (1971)
76. *Ibid.*
77. *Ibid.*
78. *Ibid.*
79. Wilson, *The Downfall of the Liberal Party 1914–1935* (1966)
80. Hazelhurst, *Politicians At War July 1914 to May 1915* (1971)
81. Wilson, *The Downfall of the Liberal Party 1914–1935* (1966)
82. Jenkins, *Churchill* (2001)
83. *Ibid.*
84. Shelden, *Young Titan, The Making of Winston Churchill* (2013)
85. Brock, *Margot Asquith's War Diary 1914–1918* (2014)
86. *Hattersley, The Great Outsider—David Lloyd George* (2010)
87. Harris, *The Ammunition Scandal* (1973)
88. *Ibid.*
89. Sheffield and Bourne, *Douglas Haig—War Diaries and Letters 1914-1918* (2005)
90. *The Great War* © BBC 1964 Parts Seven and Eight (1964)
91. Harris, *The Ammunition Scandal* (1973)
92. *Ibid.*
93. *http://www.royal.gov.uk/monarchUK/honours/Orderofthegarter/orderofthegarter.aspx*

94. *Kitchener Papers National Archive*
95. Repington, *The First World War 1914–1918 Personal Experiences of Lieut-Col. C. à Court Repington* (1920)
96. Ryan, *Shells Scandal to Bow Street: The Denigration of Lieutenant-Colonel Charles a' Court Repington* (1978)
97. *Ibid.*
98. Wilson, *The Downfall of the Liberal Party 1914–1935* (1966)
99. *Ibid.*
100. Brock, *Margot Asquith's War Diary 1914-1918* (2014)

Chapter 8—The Ministry of Munitions

1. *The Guardian,* 16 May 1915
2. Wilson, *The Downfall of the Liberal Party 1914–1935* (1966)
3. *History of the British Army in 25 battles—Ameins*
4. French, *The Life of Field-Marshal Sir John French First Earl of Ypres* (1931)
5. *Ibid.*
6. David, *100 Days to Victory* (2013)
7. *The Guardian,* 16 May 1915
8. *The Great War* © BBC 1964 Parts Seven and Eight (1964)
9. Hattersley, *The Great Outsider—David Lloyd George* (2010)
10. *The Great War* © BBC 1964 Parts Seven and Eight (1964)
11. *WWI Tunnels,* Channel Four documentary
12. *History of the British Army in 25 battles—Loos*
13. Harris, *The Ammunition Scandal* (1973)
14. *Ibid.*
15. Crittall Archive Braintree Distinct Museum Reference BRNTM 1989–53
16. *Ibid.*
17. East Anglian Munitions Committee Minutes of the 5 June 1915 held at Braintree District Museum under reference 2013–213
18. Crittall Archive Braintree Distinct Museum Reference BRNTM 1989–53
19. *Ibid.*
20. *Ibid.*
21. East Anglian Munitions Committee Minutes of the 5 June 1915 held at Braintree District Museum under reference 2013–213
22. David, *100 Days to Victory* (2013)
23. *Ibid.*
24. Harris, *The Ammunition Scandal* (1973)
25. Lynch, *To The Trenches!—Conscription and the First World War*
26. Reid, *Douglas Haig Architect of Victory* (2009)
27. Adie, *Radio Times* interview, 25–31 January 2014
28. *History of the British Army in 25 battles—Loos*
29. David, *100 Days to Victory* (2013)
30. *WWI Tunnels,* Channel Four documentary
31. *Ibid.*
32. Hattersley, *The Great Outsider—David Lloyd George* (2010)
33. Reid, *Douglas Haig Architect of Victory* (2009)
34. *History of the British Army in 25 battles—Loos*
35. Hattersley, *The Great Outsider—David Lloyd George* (2010)
36. Reid, *Douglas Haig Architect of Victory* (2009)
37. *Ibid.*
38. *Ibid.*

Chapter 9—Further Casualties in Battle and Politics

1. Sheffield, *War on the Western Front* (2014)
2. *History of the British Army in 25 battles—Loos*
3. French, *The Life of Field-Marshal Sir John French First Earl of Ypres* (1931)
4. Reid, *Douglas Haig Architect of Victory* (2009)
5. *Ibid.*
6. *History of the British Army in 25 battles—Loos*
7. Neiberg, *The Western Front 1914–1916* (2008)
8. *The Great War* © BBC 1964 Parts Seven and Eight (1964)
9. *Ibid.*
10. *History of the British Army in 25 Battles—Loos*
11. *Ibid.*
12. *Ibid.*
13. French, *The Life of Field-Marshal Sir John French First Earl of Ypres* (1931)
14. *History of the British Army in 25 Battles—Loos*
15. Reid, *Douglas Haig Architect of Victory* (2009)
16. *History of the British Army in 25 Battles—Loos*
17. Reid, *Douglas Haig Architect of Victory* (2009)
18. French, *The Life of Field-Marshal Sir John French First Earl of Ypres* (1931)
19. *Ibid.*
20. Reid, *Douglas Haig Architect of Victory* (2009)
21. *Ibid.*
22. Lewis-Stempel, *Six Weeks* (2010)
23. *Ibid.*
24. French, *The Life of Field-Marshal Sir John French First Earl of Ypres* (1931)
25. Reid, *Douglas Haig Architect of Victory* (2009)
26. *Ibid.*
27. *Ibid.*
28. French, *The Life of Field-Marshal Sir John French First Earl of Ypres* (1931)
29. *Ibid.*
30. Reid, *Douglas Haig Architect of Victory* (2009)
31. *Ibid.*
32. Sheffield and Bourne, *Douglas Haig—War Diaries and Letters 1914–1918* (2005)
33. *Ibid.*
34. David, *100 Days to Victory* (2013)
35. Sheffield and Bourne, *Douglas Haig—War Diaries and Letters 1914–1918* (2005)
36. Reid, *Douglas Haig Architect of Victory* (2009)
37. *Ibid.*
38. *Ibid.*
39. *Ibid.*
40. *Ibid.*
41. *Ibid.*
42. Sheffield and Bourne, *Douglas Haig—War Diaries and Letters 1914–1918* (2005)
43. Hattersley, *The Great Outsider—David Lloyd George* (2010)
44. Repington, *The First World War 1914–1918 Personal Experiences of Lieut-Col. C. à Court Repington* (1920)
45. Reid, *Douglas Haig Architect of Victory* (2009)
46. Holmes, *The Western Front* (2001)
47. Sheffield and Bourne, *Douglas Haig—War Diaries and Letters 1914–1918* (2005)
48. French, *The Life of Field-Marshal Sir John French First Earl of Ypres* (1931)
49. Brazier, *'All Sir Garnet!' Lord Wolseley and the British Army in the First World War* (2013)

50. Hattersley, *The Great Outsider—David Lloyd George* (2010)
51. Clemenceau owned the newspaper *L'Homme Enchaîné* (*The Chained Man*). An outspoken critic of the French Government, he became Prime Minister of France in November 1917
52. Hampden, *Clemenceau and the Third Republic* (1948)
53. Reid, *Douglas Haig Architect of Victory* (2009)
54. *Ibid.*
55. Repington, *The First World War 1914–1918 Personal Experiences of Lieut-Col. C. à Court Repington* (1920)
56. *Ibid.*
57. Churchill, *The World Crisis* (2007)
58. Wilson, *The Downfall of the Liberal Party 1914–1935* (1966)
59. *Hattersley, The Great Outsider—David Lloyd George* (2010)
60. Macdonald, *1915 The Death of Innocence* (1993)
61. Repington, *The First World War 1914–1918 Personal Experiences of Lieut-Col. C. à Court Repington* (1920)
62. Bridger, *The Great War Handbook* (2013)
63. David, *100 Days to Victory* (2013)
64. Wilson, *The Downfall of the Liberal Party 1914–1935* (1966)
65. Hazelhurst, *Politicians At War July 1914 to May 1915* (1971)
66. *http://www.firstworldwar.com/atoz/ukconscription.htm*
67. *The Times*, Wednesday 7 June 1916
68. *Ibid.*
69. Repington, *The First World War 1914–1918 Personal Experiences of Lieut-Col. C. à Court Repington* (1920)
70. Wilson, *The Downfall of the Liberal Party 1914–1935* (1966)
71. *Ibid.*
72. *Ibid.*
73. *Ibid.*
74. Gooch and Beckett, *Politicians and Defence* (1981)
75. *The Times*, 4 December 1916
76. Brock, *Margot Asquith's War Diary 1914–1918* (2014)
77. Wilson, *The Downfall of the Liberal Party 1914–1935* (1966)
78. *Ibid.*
79. Wilson, *The Downfall of the Liberal Party 1914–1935* (1966)
80. *http://www.nationalarchives.gov.uk/cabinetpapers/cabinet-gov/david-lloyd-george-1916.htm*

Chapter 10—The End of the War

1. David, *100 Days to Victory* (2013)
2. *History of the British Army in 25 battles—Ameins*
3. Churchill, *The World Crisis* (2007) and Hattersley, *The Great Outsider—David Lloyd George* (2010)
4. Crittall Archive Braintree Distinct Museum Reference BRNTM 1989–53
5. *History of the British Army in 25 battles—Loos*
6. Crittall Archive Braintree Distinct Museum Reference BRNTM 1989–53
7. Memorandum on Demobilisation of Munitions Industries, 18 October 1918 National Archive CAB/24/67
8. *Ibid.*
9. *Ibid.*
10. *Ibid.*
11. David, *100 Days to Victory* (2013)
12. Ministry of Labour Note National Archive CAB/24/67

13. Stevenson, *With Our Backs to the Wall, Victory and Defeat in 1918*
14. David, *100 Days to Victory* (2013)
15. *Ibid.*
16. Stevenson, *With Our Backs to the Wall, Victory and Defeat in 1918*
17. Brewer, *The Chronicle of War* (2007)
18. David, *100 Days to Victory* (2013)
19. Brewer, *The Chronicle of War* (2007)
20. David, *100 Days to Victory* (2013)
21. *Ibid.*
22. Brewer, *The Chronicle of War* (2007)
23. *Manchester Guardian*, 5 October 1918
24. *History of the British Army in 25 battles—Ameins*
25. David, *100 Days to Victory* (2013)
26. Brewer, *The Chronicle of War* (2007)
27. Reid, *Douglas Haig Architect of Victory* (2009)
28. David, *100 Days to Victory* (2013)
29. Repington, *The First World War 1914–1918 Personal Experiences of Lieut-Col. C. à Court Repington* (1920)
30. David, *100 Days to Victory* (2013)
31. *Ibid.*
32. Hart, *No More War*
33. Repington, *The First World War 1914–1918 Personal Experiences of Lieut-Col. C. à Court Repington* (1920)
34. Stevenson, *Why didn't the Allies march on Berlin in 1918*
35. *Ibid.*
36. 'Doomsday', *Battle of Nations* documentary
37. Fergusson, *The War of the World* (2007)
38. Fergusson, *The Pity of War*—a televised debate (2014)
39. *Daily Mail*, 29 September 2010
40. Lewis-Stempel, *Six Weeks* (2010)
41. *Ibid.*
42. *The Rifle Brigade Journal* (2014)
43. 'All That is Left of Them' Photo Media Storehouse
44. *Ibid.*
45. Bridger, Geoff, *The Great War Handbook*
46. The Menin Gate Inaugural Ceremony at www.greatwar.co.uk
47. Hadley, Kathryn, *Remains of German Soldiers from WW1 found in France*
48. National Archives—Britain at War Exhibition
49. Memorandum on Demobilisation of Munitions Industries, 18 October 1918, National Archive CAB/24/67
50. Crittall Archive Braintree Distinct Museum Reference BRNTM 1989–53
51. *Ibid.*
52. *Ibid.*
53. Memorandum on Demobilisation of Munitions Industries, 18 October 1918, National Archive CAB/24/67
54. Tressel, *Contemporary Accounts of the First World War*
55. Fergusson, *The Pity of War*—a televised debate (2014)
56. Holmes, *Tommy: The British Soldier on the Western Front* (2005)
57. Fletcher, Martin, 'Lethal relics from WW! Are still emerging', *Daily Telegraph*
58. *Ibid.*
59. *Ibid.*
60. *Ibid.*

Conclusion

1. *The Rifle Brigade Journal*
2. 'All That is Left of Them', Photo Media Storehouse

Epilogue—The Fall of the Liberal Party

1. Wilson, *The Downfall of the Liberal Party 1914–1935* (1966)
2. Hazelhurst, *Politicians At War July 1914 to May 1915* (1971)
3. *The Great War* © BBC 1964 Parts Seven and Eight (1964)
4. Hazelhurst, *Politicians At War July 1914 to May 1915* (1971)
5. Wilson, *The Downfall of the Liberal Party 1914–1935* (1966)
6. Hattersley, *The Great Outsider—David Lloyd George* (2010)
7. Macdonald, *1915 The Death of Innocence* (1993)
8. Shelden, *Young Titan, The Making of Winston Churchill* (2013)
9. Hazelhurst, *Politicians At War July 1914 to May 1915* (1971)
10. Jenkins, *Churchill* (2001)
11. Hazelhurst, *Politicians At War July 1914 to May 1915* (1971)
12. *Ibid.*
13. *Ibid.*
14. *Ibid.*
15. *Ibid.*
16. Wilson, *The Downfall of the Liberal Party 1914–1935* (1966)
17. Hazelhurst, *Politicians At War July 1914 to May 1915* (1971)
18. *Ibid.*
19. Wilson, *The Downfall of the Liberal Party 1914–1935* (1966)
20. Koss, *The Destruction of Britain's Last Liberal Government* (1968)
21. Hazelhurst, *Politicians At War July 1914 to May 1915* (1971)
22. Koss, *The Destruction of Britain's Last Liberal Government* (1968)

Bibliography

Books and Journals

Beatty, J., *The Lost History of 1914: how the Great War was not inevitable* (London: Bloomsbury Publishing, 2012)

Beckett, I. F. W., *The Making of the First World War* (New Haven: Yale University Press, 2013)

Beckett, I. F. W. and Gooch, J., *Politicians and Defence* (Manchester: Manchester University Press, 1981)

Beaverbrook, Lord, *Politicians and the War 1914–1916* (London: Thornton Butterworth, 1928)

Berkley, R., and Seymour, W., *History of the Rifle Brigade in the war of 1914–1918* (Winchester: The Rifle Brigade Club, 1936)

Bridger, G., *The Great War Handbook* (Barnsley: Pen & Sword Military, 2013)

Bridger, G., *The Battle of Neuve Chapelle* (Barnsley: Pen & Sword Books Ltd, 2005)

Brewer, P., *The Chronicle of War,* (London: Carlton Books, 2007)

Brock, M. & E., *Margot Asquith's War Diary 1914–1918* (Oxford: OUP, 2014)

Bruce, R., *Machine Guns of World War I* (Marlborough: Crowood Press, 1998)

Churchill, W., *The World Crisis* (London: Penguin Classics, 2007)

Corrigan, G., *Mud, Blood and Poppycock* (London: Pheonix Paperbacks, 2004)

David, S., *100 Days to Victory* (London: Hodder & Stoughton, 2013)

Dixon, John, *Magnificent But Not War* (Barnsley: Pen & Sword Military, 2009)

Edmonds, Brigadier-General Sir J., *History of the Great War, 1915 Vol IV, Military Operations* (London: Her Majesty's Stationery Office, 1947)

van Emden, R., *The Trench* (London: Corgi Books, 2003)

Evans, R., *From the Front Line: The Extraordinary Life of Sir Basil Clarke* (Stroud: The History Press, 2013)

Ferguson, N., *The War of the World,* (London: Penguin Books, 2007)

French, Major Gerald, *The Life of Field-Marshal Sir John French First Earl of Ypres* (London: Cassell and Company, 1931)

Goodwin, D. K., *Lincoln* (London: Penguin Books, 2009)

Hancock, E., *Aubers Ridge* (Barnsley: Pen & Sword Books Ltd, 2005)

Harris, Major H., 'The Ammunition Scandal', *Purnells' History of the World Wars Special The Big Guns Artillery 1914–1918* (London: Phoebus, 1973)

Hart-Davis, A., *The Big Bang! History of Explosives* (Stroud: Sutton Publishing, 1998)

Hattersley, R., *The Great Outsider—David Lloyd George* (Little Brown, 2010)

Harvey, B., *The Rifle Brigade* (London: Leo Cooper Ltd, 1975)

Hazlehurst, C., *Politicians at War July 1914 to May 1915* (London: Jonathan Cape Ltd, 1971)

Holmes, R., *The Western Front* (London: BBC Books, 2001)

Holmes, R., *Tommy: The British Soldier on the Western Front* (London: Harper Perennial, 2005)

Jenkins, R., *Churchill* (London: Macmillan, 2001)

Knight, W. S. M., *The History of The Great European War* (London: Caxton Publishing, 1918)

Koss, S. E., 'The Destruction of Britain's Last Liberal Government', *JSTOR* (Columbia, 1968)

Laffin, J., *British Butchers and Bunglers* (Stroud: Sutton Publishing, 2003)

Lattin, J., *On the Western Front* (London: Osprey Publishing)

Lewis, J. E., *True World War I Stories—Frank L. Watson MC* (London: Constable, 2009)

Lewis-Stempel, J. *Six Weeks—The Short and Gallant Life of the British Officer in the First World War* (George Weldenfeld & Nicholson, 2010)

Macdonald , L., *1915 The Death of Innocence* (London: Headline Book Publishing, 1993)

Macksey, K., *Technology in War* (London: Arms & Armour, 1986)

Men at War—The German Army in World War I (London: Osprey Publsihing, 2003)

Neiberg, M., *The Western Front 1914–1916* (London: Amber Books Ltd, 2008)

Paxman, J., *Great Britain's Great War* (London: Viking, 2013)

Reid, W., *Douglas Haig Architect of Victory* (Edinburgh: Birlinn Ltd, 2009)

Repington, Lt-Col. C. à Court, *The First World War 1914–1918 Personal Experiences* (Great Britain, Houghton Mifflin, 1920)

Repington, Lt-Col. C à Court, *Vestigia—Reminiscences of Peace and War* (Houghton Mifflin, 1919)

Ryan, W. M., 'Shells Scandal to Bow Street: The Denigration of Lieutenant-Colonel Charles à Court Repington' *JSTOR* (Chicago, 1978)

Senior, I., *Home Before the Leaves Fall: A new history of the German invasion of 1914* (London: Osprey Publishing, 2012)

Sheffield, G. and Bourne, J., *Douglas Haig—War Diaries and Letters 1914–1918* (London: Weidenfeld & Nicholson, 2005)

Shelden, M., *Young Titan, The Making of Winston Churchill* (London: Simon & Schuster, 2013)

Silbey, D., *The British Working Class and Enthusiasm for war 1914–1918* (London: Routledge, 2004)

Spencer-Wilkinson, H., *Twenty-five years, 1874–1909* (London: 1933)

Stevenson, D., *With Our Backs to the Wall, Victory and Defeat in 1918* (London: Penguin Books, 2011)

Streitweiser and Heathcock, *Introduction to Organic Chemistry* (New York: Macmillan, 1992)

Taylor, A.J. P., *English History 1914–1945* (Oxford: OUP, 1965)

'The Victoria Crosses of the Royal Green Jackets', Calendar 2014

Treatise on Ammunition, 10th Edition, War Office 1915

Urbanski, T, *Chemistry and Technology of Explosives* (London: Penguin Pergamon, 1963)

Wallace, Lt Gen. Sir C. and Cassidy, Major R., *Focus on Courage* (Winchester: The Royal Green Jackets Museum Trust, 2006)

Wilson, T., *The Downfall of the Liberal Party 1914–1935*, (London: Collins, 1966)

Youngson, R. M., *Collins Dictionary of Medicine* (Glasgow: Harper Collins, 1992)

Articles in Magazines and Newspapers

'Austria-Hungary Prison-House of Nations' by Neil Faulkner, *Military, History Magazine*, March 2014

'Behind the Image', *Military History Magazine*, March 2014

'Britain—Perfidious Albion' by Neil Faulkner, *Military History Monthly*, July 2014

'Countdown to War—Germany Empire of Blood and Iron', *Military History Magazine*, May 2014

'Depicting the Great War' by Dave Sloggett, *Military Times Magazine*, June 2011

'Desperate Defence' by Patrick Mercer, *Military History Monthly*, September 2014

'Doctor in the Trenches' by Andrew Davidson, *Military History Magazine*, December 2013

'First Blood' by John Grehan, *Britain at War Magazine*, October 2007

'General Snow—Remembering a First World War General' by Dan Snow, *Military Times Magazine*, May 2011

'Haig's Mistakes' by Julian Brazier, *Military History Magazine*, June 2013
'History of the British Army in 25 battles—Amiens', *Military History Magazine,* March 2013
'History of the British Army in 25 battles—Loos', *Military History Magazine*, January 2013
'History of the British Army in 25 battles—The Somme', *Military History Magazine*, February 2013
'Honour the Dead' by Simon Heffer, *Daily Mail*, 4 August 2013
'If You're Reading This…Last Letters Home' by Siận Price, *Military History Magazine*, April 2012
'In Flanders Fields' by Ian Hislop, *BBC History Magazine*
'In Flanders Fields Museum' by Keith Robinson, *Military Times Magazine*, November 2011
'Lethal relics from WW1 Are still emerging' by Martin Fletcher, *Daily Telegraph*
'Lions and Donkeys? Not at the Somme', *Military History Magazine*, April 2013
'No More War' by Peter Hart, *BBC History Magazine*
'Planning Armageddon' by David Porter, *Military History Magazine*, August 2014
'Playboy of the Western Front' in *The Spectator*, 12 February 2000
'Remains of German Soldiers from WW1 found in France' by Kathryn Hadley, *History Today*, 7 November 2011
'The Glorious Story of Neuve Chapelle', Daily Mail, April 19, 1915
The London Gazette, Supplement dated 1 September 1914
The Rifle Brigade Association Journal 2014
'To The Trenches! Conscription and the First World War', *Military Times*, July 2011
'V Beach Madness' by Peter Hart, *Military Times Magazine*, June 2011
'War in the Trenches' by Dr Stephen Bull, *History of War*, July 2014
'Wills of the First World War fallen go on line', *Daily Mail*, 29 August 2013
'What caused the Great War' by James Hoare, *All about History*, September 2013
'Who Started the First World War' by Nigel Jones, *Military Times Magazine*, May 2011
'Why didn't the Allies march on Berlin in 1918' by David Stevenson, *BBC History Magazine*

Documents and Papers

Cabinet Papers
Crittall Archive held at Braintree District Museum, Reference BRNTM 2010.587
Crittall Archive held at Braintree District Museum, Reference BRNTM 1989 - 53
Kitchener Papers, National Archives, Reference PRO 30/57/50 and PRO 30/57/53
Letter to Lieutenant Chan Hoskyns from Lieutenant Charles Pennefather held at the National Army Museum
National Archives, Reference MUN5/19/221/8 (November 1914)
National Army Museum, Reference BR75
2nd Battalion Rifle Brigade War Diary, National Archives, Reference WO95-1731-1
Rippington Family—Registered with the Guild of One-Name Studies
Sir John French's Seventh Despatch 5th April 1915
Sir John French's Eighth Despatch

Documentaries

'37 Days' by *Hard Pictures* for the BBC
'Doomsday', *Battle of Nations* documentary produced by AZDF & ZDF Enterprise Productions
The Great War, Parts Seven and Eight, BBC
My Family at War, BBC
The Necessary War, Max Hastings, by Blakeway Productions for the BBC
The Pity of War, a televised debate chaired by Niall Fergusson
'WWI Tunnels', *Big Dig* documentary, Channel Four

Websites

http://www.1914-1918.net

http://www.army.mod.uk/armoured/regiments/33784.aspx

http://www.bbc.co.uk/history/worldwars/wwone/mirror01_01.shtml

http://www.Cartesfrance.fr

https://dianaoverbey.wordpress.com/2012/01/13/trench-construction-in-world-war-i/

http://www.election.demon.co.uk/geresults.html

http://www.firstworldwar.com/source/georgev_aug1914.htm

http:// www.greatwar.co.uk)

Great War Forum - http://1914-1918.invisionzone.com/forums/index.php

http://www.iwm.org.uk/history-tags/censorship

http://izquotes.com/quote/243252

http://www.labour.org.uk/history_of_the_labour_party

http://www.liberalhistory.org.uk/

http://www.royal.gov.uk/monarchUK/honours/Orderofthegarter/orderofthegarter.aspx

http://spartacus-educational.com.htm

http://www.telegraph.co.uk/history/world-war-one/11002644/First-World-War-centenary-how-
    events-unfolded-on-August-1-1914.html

http://www.theguardian.com/politics/electionspast/page/0,,1451427,00.html

http://www.webmatters.net/

Index